THE EXPANDING STATE

THE EXPANDING STATE

**Class and Economy in
Europe since 1945**

Doug McEachern

**St. Martin's Press
New York**

© Doug McEachern 1990

All rights reserved. For information write:
Scholarly and Reference Division,
St. Martin's Press, Inc., 175 Fifth Avenue, New York, NY 10010

First published in the United States of America in 1990

Printed in Great Britain

ISBN 0-312-04652-9

Library of Congress Cataloging-in-Publication Data

McEachern, Doug.
   The expanding state : class and economy in Europe since 1945/
Doug McEachern.
     p. cm.
   Includes bibliographical references.
   ISBN 0-312-04652-9
   1. Europe—Economic conditions—1945- 2. Europe—Economic policy,
   Europe—Politics and government—1945- 4. Social conflict—
Europe—History—20th century. I. Title.
0240.M38 1990   90-31758
388.94′009′045—dc20   CIP

CONTENTS

Acknowledgements vii
Abbreviations ix

Introduction 1

Chapter 1 **State and Political Regime** 13
    Introduction 13
    Capitalism and Class 13
    Class and State 17
    From State to Political Regime 31
    Corporatism, Representation and
      Intervention 34
    Conclusion 40
    Notes 41

Chapter 2 **The Passing of the Liberal Order** 45
    Introduction 45
    The Liberal Order as a Political Regime 45
    Issues in the Liberal Era 52
    The Passing of the Liberal Order 55
    Conclusion 65
    Notes 70

Chapter 3 **The Post-War Reconstruction of the Regime** 73
    Nationalisation 74
    Economic Planning 78
    Welfare Policy 82
    Classes in the Construction of the New Order 84

vi *Contents*

	Character and Logic of the New Political Regime	88
	Notes	91
Chapter 4	**Between Boom and Recession**	**94**
	Responses to the New Regime	94
	Problems in the Pursuit of Growth	100
	Conclusion	111
	Notes	112
Chapter 5	**With the State – Into the Recession**	**115**
	Introduction	115
	Class and State Responses to the Onset of Recession	119
	Investment, Planning and Growth	122
	Wages, Prices and Profits	131
	The Neo-Corporatist Phase	139
	The Recession Goes On	141
	Notes	142
Chapter 6	**With the Recession – Against the State**	**145**
	The Popular Political Explanation	146
	The Problems of Prolonged Recession	150
	The Strategy in Practice	154
	National Variations	169
	Conclusion	179
	Notes	179
Conclusion	**Class Struggles in a Cyclical Economy**	**183**
	Alternative Explanations for the Changing Relations of Classes and the State	185
	The Changing Relationship Between Politics and Economics	197
	Class Struggles in a Cyclical Economy	201
	Notes	212
Bibliography		214
Index		229

ACKNOWLEDGEMENTS

I would like to thank Charmaine Collett, Robyn Williams, Alan Warde, Chris Hill, Ruth Ellickson and Greg O'Leary for their assistance. I would also like to thank the Politics Department, University of Adelaide, the Sociology Department of the University of Lancaster and the Politics Department of the University of Leeds for their facilities and their support. Part of the research on which this is based was funded by the University of Adelaide's Study Leave Scheme.

ABBREVIATIONS

BDA	Bundesvereinigung der Deutschen Arbeitgeberverbände
BDI	Bundesverband der Deutschen Industrie
CBI	Confederation of British Industry
CFDT	Confédération Française Démocratique du Travail
CGT	Confédération Générale du Travail
CNPF	Confédération Nationale du Patronat Français
FDP	Freie Demokratische Partei
NEB	National Enterprise Board
NEDO	National Economic Development Organisation
OECD	Organisation for Economic Cooperation and Development
PCF	Parti Communiste Français
PS	Parti Socialiste
RPR	Rassemblement du Peuple pour la République
SPD	Sozialdemokratische Partei Deutschlands
TUC	Trades Union Congress
UDF	Union pour la Démocratie Française

INTRODUCTION

During the long boom of the 1950s and early 1960s a consensus emerged on the positive contribution the state could make to economic and social developments. A prolonged economic recession and the revival of liberal free-market economic doctrines challenged this post-war consensus. Recession was thought to have been banished by the expansion of the state during the years of post-war reconstruction, and the Keynesian revolution was believed to have given governments the techniques for managing a mixed economy so that full employment was combined with increasing economic benefits for all. Free-market rhetoric was treated as an ideological gloss on the activities of private business, made irrelevant by the modernised capitalist economy where the fate of many sections of business was dependent on the actions of the state. At the very least, the return of recession and the rise of neo-liberalism makes it necessary to reconsider the economic and social forces embedded in the period of post-war reconstruction and growth.

If the 'mixed economy' was a necessary and functional response to the inter-war depression, the attempt to reduce the role of the state would be difficult and could plunge the economy back into recession. The neo-liberal argument was explicit on this point. Increased state action was not a response to some undefined accumulation imperative, nor was it necessary or functional. Increased state provision of welfare, nationalisation or economic planning, were examples of wrong-headed interference with the workings of the market. The prolonged recession of the 1970s and 1980s was proof that state intervention did not work and that the market had to be set free. Not only neo-liberal critics of the mixed economy argued in this way. Some of the more orthodox

Marxist economists also asserted the supremacy of the market and the law of value and rebuked reformers for believing that a mixed economy and expanded state could end the possibility of recession. Neither neo-liberals nor orthodox Marxists could foretell the date of the economic downturn but they could both assert that there would come a day of reckoning to confirm the accuracy and adequacy of their analyses.

This book examines the steady expansion of the state since the end of the Second World War. The analysis is directly focused on the relationship between increased state action and the claims and concerns of the two main classes of industrialised capitalist society. In doing this, the argument of the book is an assessment of the extent to which the expansion of the state was either a necessary response to economic problems or simply a consequence of party-political competition and a contingent balance of class forces. Identifying the factors which made for the unrelenting and systematic expansion of the state in the post-war period makes it possible to see if those very same factors will undermine recent neo-liberal experiments and set the scene for a new period of growth in the size and role of the state.

Several things stand in the way of making such an assessment. The very way in which state action has been treated in the extensive debate over state theory is a problem. Despite the many different positions taken, most participants have sought a general theory which can explain why the state does what it does and its economic and social significance. They have sought an all-embracing theory to explain why state action, even when opposed by significant sections of business, secured the long-term health and well-being of capitalism as a system. They have looked for guarantees and imperatives that turn the state in a capitalist society into, inevitably and invariably, a capitalist state. Yet, if the expansion of the state protects the interests of capital in that way, it is difficult, but not impossible, to see why sections of business have embraced a neo-liberal campaign to reduce the size of the state and to get it out of the economy.

The problem with a general theory of the capitalist state is greater than that. This search for imperatives compelling the state to conform to the logic of capital accumulation stands in the way of a thoroughgoing analysis of what happens in specific instances; in the making of particular state policies and the struggles over their economic and social consequences. Such a general theory can conceal or devalue the significance of times when state action may not advance the class interests of capital and where it may, in fact, harm capital accumulation.

Chapter 1 deals with the state debate to identify those factors necessary for the examination of the developing relationship between classes and the state. One object of this discussion is to reduce the scope for using the term 'capitalist state' to imply that the actions of the state almost automatically conform to the class or accumulation requirements of capitalist society. Instead I have argued for the greater efficacy of the more open-ended conception of political regime, which sets out different aspects of state-class relationships that can change over time, and which does not make assumptions about how those relations work to protect, further or hinder capital accumulation and class rule. There is, however, one underlying assumption: combining class rule and capital accumulation is difficult and continuous effort is required to ensure harmony between the two objectives.

After assessing the analytical and theoretical problems associated with the attempt to construct general theories of the capitalist state, it is possible to consider various accounts of the changing relations between classes and the state in the years since the inter-war depression. Recently, the most common approach has been through the revival of the concept of 'corporatism', which is used to produce an 'institutional' history of the patterning of class-state relations. To the extent that it displaces the previous use of 'pluralism' this should be welcomed, although, it still distorts what has happened, especially in its assessment of the role of organised labour and the significance of political control of the economy. Accounts of the growth of tripartite bodies linking capital, labour and the state are frequently unable to explain why these bodies come into being, the significance of their actions or existence, or why they should pass away at the times that they do. Even the most rigorous usage fails to reveal the dynamics behind the growth of these institutional arrangements in terms that go much beyond simple notions of incorporation, co-option and social pacification.

The greater analytical utility of the conception of 'political regime' lies in three areas. Firstly, it leaves open the assessment of the workings of the relations between class organisations and the state, the discussion of which is often short-circuited by the basic assumptions embodied in general theories of the capitalist state. Secondly, the very ingredients denoted by the concept 'political regime' mean that the analysis must be concerned with questions of dynamics, how a particular situation changes and why. Thirdly, given the emphasis on change, there must be a concern with the question of agency. This is a problem treated in the state debate but it has not been given sufficient attention in the subsequent reevaluation of the initial exchanges.

From the start the question of agency was at the centre of the dispute between Miliband and Poulantzas.[1] Poulantzas characterised 'English' Marxism as deformed by its concern with 'the subject' and the question of human agency. Thus, when Poulantzas wrote about *The State in Capitalist Society*, he characterised Miliband's approach in these terms.[2] Miliband, it was claimed, remained trapped in a paradigm of the subject, of human agency, and thus the consequences of state action were reducible to the motivations of state actors; whom they knew and what they thought explained why the state acted to support capital and to protect the capitalist system. Poulantzas' version of structuralist Marxism broke with the subject completely. Structures were central and constructed people as individuals and as 'bearers' of the structures. The emphasis was on objective rather than subjective factors. When he explained the congruence of state action and the protection of capitalism he stressed the objective function of the state, as given by the structure, as the prime determinant.

There is a sharp contrast between the two approaches but the question of agency was not resolved at this or subsequent stages of the debate. The whole question became confused with the discussion of the significance of various kinds of connections between state officials and members of the capitalist class in explaining the consequences of state action. The relevant details of the Miliband-Poulantzas exchange are considered in Chapter 1, but at this stage it is necessary to pursue the question of agency a little further.

In its own way the Miliband-Poulantzas exchange restated part of a classical sociological debate about the relationship between structure and action and the most appropriate set of methodological assumptions for the study of a dynamic social order. If the crude characterisations of the participants were to be believed, Poulantzas stood with structure and Miliband with action and agency. This is not correct. Poulantzas starts from the primacy of structure and assigns a quite minimal importance to action and agency. Miliband also starts from a conception of structure (less determining and determinate than Poulantzas it is true) but he also operates with a conception of the importance of agency and of action. Even when the terms of the argument may be flawed (and sharpened and corrected in later pieces), the emphasis is correct. Questions of action, agency, motivation and of mechanism cannot be ignored.

Poulantzas and Althusser take their stand against action and agency on the ground that such an emphasis represents a sociological and/or Weberian contamination of Marxism. In Miliband's words, they make way for a form of structural superdeterminism as part of their attempt to destroy the appeal of instrumentalist and economistic forms of Marxism. To the extent that Poulantzas and Althusser were opposed to forms of sociological reductionism, where society was simply the construct of individuals motivated and active, then their naive structuralism may be the first approximation of a reply. But it stands in the way of a better assessment of the workings of class-state relations in capitalist societies. It is perfectly possible to construct accounts of agency, of action, motivation and intention that do not simply recreate the position opposed by Poulantzas and Althusser. It is not necessary to assume that society is simply reducible to the meanings, motives and actions of individuals to make arguments about the role of agency within structured contexts of class relations and to argue forcefully about the ways in which classes act and, by their actions, shape the histories of the structures and societies in which they exist. What is necessary is an approach that gives appropriate weight to structure and agency, an approach that is able to identify the possible outcomes which emerge from struggles within a given structured context without being committed to the claim that it is the structure which determines either the outcome or its social significance.

To assess the significance and contributions of agency requires a willingness to see the ways in which classes are historically organised and constituted as social actors. Then it is a matter of considering the tactical and strategic purposes pursued by these organisations, and the ways in which these interact with the changing organisations and purposes of the state. Built into this treatment there needs to be a recognition that there is a learning process involved, that class organisations reflect on the successes and failures of their actions, explain them and, in response, the forms of organisation and the methods and goals pursued may be changed. Certainly it is easy to show the kinds of changes that have been a common part of the history of class organisations, their struggles with other classes and the state. Indeed, much of the discussion of this book is just such an illustration.

As an example of the way in which such changes occur, and the effects that these struggles can have, consider the success of the struggle by reformers to displace the revolutionary perspective from labour organisations. It would be pointless to assert that the triumph of reformism was an expression or product of the structure, though it has played its part in the continued survival of industrialised capitalism as a class system. The defeat of a revolutionary perspective and the success of social democracy has had important consequences for the class histories of particular societies. The durability of the reformist perspective and the changes in tactics and policy packages that go with it must be considered further.

Marx's account of reformism, and his assumption that its effects would be limited, is an important one. Much of his assessment was based on the naive assumption that the reality of capitalist society would tend to generate, in the workers' movement, the consciousness necessary for its historical mission of radical social transformation.[3] It was this emphasis that was picked up by Rosa Luxemburg in her critique of Bernstein's *Evolutionary Socialism*.[4] Experience has taught that this explanation and expectation is unlikely to be correct. The reality of capitalist society has taught the workers' movement many things but it has not as yet taught, in any industrialised capitalist society, that its best interests are served by the revolutionary destruction of capitalist class society. Some of those lessons learned within the perspective of reformism are very important and are discussed in subsequent chapters which examine the response of social democracy to affluence and the onset of renewed and sustained recession.

The reason for introducing these comments relates to the attempts to interpret the consequences of state action without the presumption that some aspect in the very nature of the capitalist state ensures compatibility between state policy and capital's class interest. Those who reject or minimise the importance of structure or structured context most often explain the consistency of state outcomes in terms of either class struggles won by capital or the power of a dominant ideology. To explain state outcomes by reference to capital's victories in class struggles over state policy must confront a number of difficulties as when, for example, the state acts against the wishes of capital, or those parts of capital most vocal in the struggle, and the tautology of identifying victories through the consequences of state action. Reference to shared ideologies or the effects of dominant ideology or hegemony explain the congruence of state action with capital's class interest by reference to the character and quality of the thought of those that staff the state, either as officials or as members of an elected government. These people either understand and accept and, hence, act to preserve the existing social order (a unity of intention and outcome); or they fail to understand the system and their purposes are confounded by the disjuncture between their beliefs and reality. Undoubtedly these propositions do characterise much of what goes on in the political process, and yet there is also much that such formulations fail to catch in their account of why the system is safe from radical assault. To the extent that the explanation stresses the confining role of ideology, then, there are the problems of functionalism and instrumentalism. Ideology is known by its effect (the failure to transcend the existing mode of production) which is functional for the protection of the existing social order. There is little scope for contradictions within the ideology or between ideologies and no sense in which the attitudes of the oppressed groups can be seen as a response to the material situation of that oppression. If the account is not constructed in functionalist terms (ideology arises to preserve the social order) then there is the problem that the usage will turn into a form of class instrumentalism. Dominant groups manipulate ideologies to conceal the reality of the system and to protect the advantages that they gain from it. In both accounts the origins of ideology are confused and the dominated are treated as very passive recipients of messages, perspectives and commands from others.

If these ways of analysing ideology are rejected, it is necessary to find another way of approaching the question without recourse to functionalist, instrumentalist and passivist terms. Here ideology would need to be conceived as an active response by people, as individuals or as parts of classes and groups, to the circumstances in which they live, circumstances marked by the class realities of the social order. It may be true that the most common forms of ideological response do not challenge the basic features of the class environment but this does not end what needs to be said about ideology. It is useful to leave open the possibility that ideologies change over time, in quite significant ways, and that there may be a sense in which what is thought by class organisations comes closer to a recognition that society is structured along class lines.

In the account here of the changing relationship between class organisations and the political process, the consideration of ideology will be largely confined to the tactical and strategic conceptions of the various contending class and social organisations and the state. It is these aspects of class organisation which are the most important crystallisations of the ideological perspectives of their members, not in the sense that they represent what most of their members think, but rather it is this version of their thought which enters the political and social arena and has a most obvious effect. Hence, it is important to analyse the changes in these perspectives in the terms suggested above. The tactical and strategic perspectives of these subordinate class organisations can not be treated as either static or passive. It is necessary to explore the way in which these perspectives have changed as a result of the experience of success and failure in the political arena and as a response to other changes in their class and material circumstances. There is a dynamic in the tactical and strategic thinking of class organisations, one which perhaps parallels the changes in the working of the relationship between classes and the state and between the political and economic processes, that is, parallels the development of the political regime.

The suggestions about the treatment of ideology leave no analytical space for a conception of 'false consciousness'. This is deliberate. The beliefs of individuals, class organisations or of classes may contain elements that are false, that is a belief that can be contradicted by reference to available evidence. For example, survey techniques may reveal that a voting population believes taxes in a particular country are far higher than elsewhere when this is not the case. Such discrepancies do not justify the characterisation of the whole 'consciousness' of those individuals as false. What is normally designated as false consciousness is the failure of members of the subordinate class to recognise that they are members of an exploited class which would be best served by the total transformation of the social order that assigns them such a subordinate role. False consciousness is conceptually opposed to a conception of class consciousness. As far as this goes, I prefer to treat class consciousness as the actual consciousness of the class as expressed through organisation and tactical or strategic initiatives, thus not making a prior judgement as to the adequacy of that consciousness. In considering the actual class consciousness, I would also ignore the supposed distinction between a class 'in itself' and a class 'for itself', one of Marx's less revealing throw-away lines. It is useful to have some conception of the growth of a class from only an aggregate of people with a shared market situation (though I suspect that historically such a state of affairs has never existed) through the developments of organisations and strategies. It is also important to chart the extent to which class organisations recognise the class character of society and chart their actions to maintain or destroy that situation accordingly. This does not require assumptions about either the 'quality' of the consciousness or some pre-defined end-process. Indeed, one aspect of this book is the argument over the kind of class consciousness implicit in the persistence of 'reformism' within the social democratic organisation of the working class.

In joining with people like Jessop and Urry in rejecting the usefulness of efforts to construct a general theory of the capitalist state, it is still necessary to use some of the conclusions of the state debate to frame the area in which the enquiry proceeds. It is necessary, for example, to remain sensitive to the conclusions drawn about the generality of the outcomes of state policy. Though individual state actions may confer advantages on the working class (and the assessment of these advantages is often a finely judged matter), the long-term consequence of state action, so far, has not been to disadvantage the class of capital, nor to weaken its position of social dominance. It remains as described in the debate on the general theory of the capitalist state that, in a capitalist society, over time, the state tends to act in ways that reinforce the dominant class relations and initiatives that would tend to weaken these are (after various periods of time) transformed, modified, thrown out or whatever, so that they no longer threaten the basic class relations of the capitalist social order. The purpose of the discussion in Chapter 1 is not to reject this conclusion but to broaden and deepen the understanding of what is involved in the continuing struggles amongst the classes and between the classes and the state. It is on such a basis that the assessment of the long-term historical potential of the present conflicts between classes and the state is to be made.

Having made the argument over the efficacy of the conception of political regime in the first two chapters, it is possible to take the most important relationships identified and to use these to examine the ways in which classes and the state are linked, and the workings of the relationship between the political and economic processes. Most importantly, it is possible to construct an account that shows the broad ways in which these aspects have changed in the years since the inter-war depression. To make such an account help the assessment of the character, consequences, social significance and sources of state action, it is useful to construct this schematic history against the pattern of the almost cyclical phases of capital accumulation in those years. Hence the account starts with the inter-war depression (Chapter 2) and proceeds with the period of post-war reconstruction and the long boom (Chapter 3), the ending of the long boom and the years of uncertain growth before the onset of the recession (Chapter 4), and concludes with the sustained recession of the 1970s and 1980s (Chapters 5 and 6). Such an account is ordered by the chronological sequence of a cycle of capital accumulation, from depression through recovery and growth and then back into recession. Significantly, the same chronological periodisation can be established on a quite different basis: the changing relations between classes and the state. In this version, the argument starts with a liberal political and economic order and the first, inconclusive attempts to escape from the political and economic problems created in it (Chapter 2), and proceeds with an account of the post-war settlement between classes and the state which reordered the relationship between the political and economic processes and provided the social context for the long boom (Chapter 3). The period between the end of the long boom and the onset of the recession was one of experimentation in which various attempts were made to extend the role of the state and to explore different ways of linking class organisations and the state. In effect this was a time in which some of the avenues opened up by the post-war settlement were further explored (Chapter 4). The account of the recession has been divided between two different phases in the relations between class and the state. In the first, the emphasis was on the attempt to manage the recession by extending the role of the state and by promoting more institutionalised negotiations between class organisations and the state (Chapter 5). The neo-liberal experiment that sought to reverse the tendency expressed by the steady post-war expansion of the state is then considered in the light of the persistence of the recession (Chapter 6).

The presentation of the history of changing class–state relations in this way is deliberate since it highlights the key element of the analytical problem under consideration: the relationship between changes in the political and social spheres and the changing problems of capital accumulation summed up in the concept of a political regime. It might be assumed by presenting the account in this way, with a chronological sequence emphasising the coincidence of changes in the cycle of capital accumulation and changes in class–state relations, that the parallels suggest a resolution of the problem. This is not the case. Much more argument is needed to answer the question that is provided by noting that certain economic changes happen at roughly the same time as other political changes, suggestive though the coincidence might be. But the degree of coincidence needs to be probed and then the significance or meaning of the connection between phases in the cycle of capital accumulation and political or social change must be assessed. The problem to be solved is just that one which is exposed by the chronological division of the schematic history: is there a systematic connection between the problems of capital accumulation and political and social change? If it is established that such a connection exists, then it is necessary to show, by argument and illustration, just what kind of mechanisms are involved and the various ways in which these two processes are linked.

Clearly the account has to have an historical dimension. The problem cannot be considered without it. A further comparative dimension is also needed to guard against any too easy resolution. I have taken Britain as the main source of examples, since the events here most clearly illustrate the arguments about accumulation and politics that I want to make. To offset that, I have also drawn illustrations from the contrasting histories of France, which has had a long history of extensive state involvement in the economy, and of the Federal Republic of Germany, which abandoned its statist past in favour of an institutionalised version of neo-liberalism in the social market economy. The events in these two countries provide correctives to any generalisations made on the basis of the peculiarities of the development of class politics and state action in Britain. The extent to which the sequence of developments in accumulation and politics in France and Germany can be subsumed under the same periodisation as that used for Britain is an important test of the extent to which factors common to industrialised capitalist societies, rather than those of historical accident or special class histories, explain the steady expansion of the state in the years since the inter-war depression.

NOTES

1. The exchange was initially published in *New Left Review*, **58** and **59**, 1969 and 1970.
2. Miliband (1973a).
3. For an important discussion of this question see Johnson (1980).
4. See Luxemburg (1970).

1 · STATE AND POLITICAL REGIME

INTRODUCTION

The state debate sought to clarify the relations between classes and the state and it serves as a useful introduction to the terms of the analysis that are needed here. When looking at the different stages in the debate it is necessary to consider the broad terms of the arguments and to ask how these can be reconstructed to make a more dynamic analysis possible, one that focuses on both the changed ways classes are organised into politics and the changed patterns of state action towards the economy and society.

CAPITALISM AND CLASS

Capitalism is a distinct form of class society. It has special forms for the organisation of production, the payment of labour, the extraction and accumulation of surplus. The basic, defining relationship is between labour and capital. These classes are not income groups nor are they defined by some general distribution of personal or social attributes. Rather they have their distinctive characters as a consequence of their places in the process of social production, understood broadly to include both social reproduction and circulation; they are defined on the basis of the relationships to each other and to the means of social production. As the result of a lengthy, uneven process, one class, capital, has come to own, control and dominate the means of social production. These exist as the property of that class and, as the possessors, the members of the class have the ability to control the production process and its more immediate consequences. The same historical process that generated capital, a class that dominates production, also generates a class, labour, separated from the means of production. As a result, labour has no means of existence except by entering into a relationship with the means of production through a relationship with capital. The major division in capitalist society between labour and capital, based on the separation of labour from the means of production, implies that the major products of that society will take the form of commodities, goods or services produced for sale. The very ability to work assumes the form of a commodity, labour-power, which is sold by units of time and is then available to be set to work by capital.

This definition of class generates a two-class model of society. There is, however, a third class position implied by the logic of definition. The third class is made up of those who combine the basic attributes of the classes already identified. This is a class made up of those who own their own means of production which they work with their own labour, a self-owning, self-exploiting class. The units involved may be individuals, families or forms of cooperatives. It is these relations that are at the heart of what is frequently identified as the petty-bourgeoisie, a confusing term since it suggests that it is the size of the concern which determines the class character of those involved. Although there are many differences between large and small enterprises, it is not appropriate to define a new class on that basis.

It is necessary to make some comment on the scope of the working class identified here. True to its assumption that it is a relationship to the means of social production that determines class, the definition is a broad one. The observable differences between, say, those that work on production lines and those that work in offices does not change class definition. These 'empirical' differences are very significant when examining the behaviour of class members and the formation of class organisations but that is at a different level from the basic definition of classes. The class of labour is defined by its relationship to the means of social production and to capital. It does not matter whether capital is involved in production, circulation or exchange of commodities, the defining relationship remains the same. As such, this account rejects the attempt to use the categories of productive and unproductive labour to distinguish between a 'real' working class (understood to mean those involved in the direct physical production of commodities or in performing manual labour), and a variety of other groups who are not part of capital even though they may be employed by it.[1]

The classes identified here are the basic classes of a capitalist society, those at its centre and without which it could not exist, and the struggles between them constitute the key elements in the history and dynamic of that form of society. There are other bases on which politically active and significant groups can be formed: gender, race, religion and nationality are examples.[2] There are other sets of people in developed capitalist societies sharing 'market' situations that are not part of these basic categories.[3] Professionals such as lawyers, doctors, architects and accountants are examples, and they can and do organise on the basis of their shared positions and problems. The use of this way of identifying classes is not to close off the discussion of the forms of organisation and mobilisation that have greatest significance in any given situation but to identify those relations that are basic to capitalism as a distinctive historical social form. It is these relations that would have to be transformed to create a distinctly new social order.

Given the defining nature of the class divisions between them, labour and capital are invariably linked. They depend for their existence, under capitalism, on the working of the relationship between them. For labour to live, it needs to be able to sell its commodity to capital, enter into a relationship with the means of production, and hence gain the income it needs to buy the commodities upon which its physical and social survival depends. Capital, on the other hand, needs to hire labour to have the means of production activated to produce the commodities, on the sale of which the profitability of the capitalist enterprise depends. The interconnections between the two then present a pattern of co-operation and antagonism.[4] For capitalism to continue that co-operation is essential. So is the antagonism. Its expression may be blunted by a variety of different circumstances, strategies or techniques but the basic antagonism remains. The two classes are defined by antagonism; the attributes that one class has, the other lacks. More significantly, in the process of production, the very form in which labour-power is bought, the wage form, and the manner in which the surplus is extracted, in the form of surplus-value, implies an antagonism between the two classes over the sizes of their incomes and the division of the social product between the two classes. Regardless of the size of any given quantity of social production, and leaving aside the funds needed to renew production, the greater the share of wages the less the share of profits. This is certainly a matter known by all who run capitalist enterprises and explains their urgent and minute concern with changes in the wage bill. In no circumstances is this more pressing than in hard times.

If the relationship between the two classes is considered in an abstract manner, then the relationship involves two different processes. On the one side, there is the problem of class society and class rule. For this form of class society to reproduce itself and to expand it is necesary for the basic class relationship to be reproduced, for the social subordination of labour to be maintained, for the domination of capital to be assured. This implies an area of socio-political activity concerned with questions of class rule. On the other side, there are the economic activities of the two classes, the production and sale of commodities and the activities necessary to ensure capital accumulation, which is just the special form that expanded reproduction or growth assumes in a capitalist society. Though these two spheres of activity are everywhere inter-related, and often achieved on the same basis (the act of expanded reproduction, understood in an economic sense, is also a process by which the renewed subordination of labour is achieved), it is possible to treat these processes as analytically distinct, at least in the initial phase of the presentation. One of the main themes in this book is to consider the relationships between these two processes and especially the tensions that exist in seeking to fulfil them through common policies or actions. As such it raises the whole question of the place of the capitalist state in this network of class relations and class processes.

Before dealing with that question directly, it is necessary to make some observations on the nature of the relationship proposed here, between economics and the social-political sphere. It is not assumed that classes are defined in the economic sphere and that class rule is a later problem of a political sphere or instance, though some of the following discussion will take that form to make explication easier. It is assumed that social production involves more than economic production and economic matters. Classes are defined by their social relations in social production. Their basic aspects and attributes are derived from those social relations. Under capitalism, as indeed in most class societies, there are clearly defined aspects of the social relations which are economic in character and others which, in dealing with the maintenance of class rule, are social and political in character. In much of what follows I have assumed that the experience of the process of production and the consequences that stem from its class organisation give classes perceptions of the distinctive problems that confront them and that solutions are pursued in both the economic sphere and the political sphere. This is not to accord a primacy to the economic sphere. The real primacy lies in class relations and in the struggles to maintain or change the patterns of class domination and subordination.

CLASS AND STATE

It is not my intention in this deliberately brief discussion to present yet another summary of the developing debate on the nature of the capitalist state. Too many such summaries and divisions of the field into competing schools already exist.[5] Instead, I want to comment on those arguments and fragments of arguments that reveal the need to phrase analysis in more complex and dynamic terms than has hitherto been common.

In the first phase of the state debate the capitalist state was seen as, necessarily, relatively autonomous from class forces. The point of departure was opposition to those treating the state as an instrument of a class, or fraction of class, with its actions determined in an immediate, direct and uncomplicated manner. The concept of relative autonomy was designed to distance contemporary Marxist analysis from the crudity and limited analytical power of economism, the characteristic form of state analysis in the period of Comintern conformity. It was not intended to deny that often, capital as a class, or separate parts of capital, gained immediate and long-term benefits from state action. Rather it was to suggest that the relations between classes and the state were complicated. The emphasis on the 'relative' quality of the autonomy was to mark the account off from those who suggested an almost complete autonomy or independence for the state. Views that saw government as dominating the development of the economy, regulating the activities of business, imposing democratic authority on the operations of the market, tended to exaggerate the neutrality of the state and the classless character of its actions.[6]

With these two dimensions implied by the term 'relative autonomy' it is not surprising that different ways were found to explain how capital's interests were served by the actions of the state. The celebrated Miliband–Poulantzas exchange in *New Left Review* was just one example.[7] In later works Miliband and Poulantzas both significantly modified their initial positions. Poulantzas came to reject the emphasis on structural determinism and concentrated on the importance of class struggle within the state itself.[8] This is not a position that overcomes the flaws in his initial approach, but it does reduce the distance between his arguments and those of Miliband. Miliband's subsequent writings on the state reveal the distance that he also travelled. In *Marxism and Politics*, the conclusion on the approach to the state emphasises the combination of the 'subjective' and 'objective' factors in the notion of structural constraint and the imperatives built into the circumstances of state action and capital accumulation.[9]

Miliband does not specifically address the question of how classes are organised into politics, though he does note the importance of trade unions and the Labour Party and the politics of labourism for its impact upon the articulation of working class demands.[10] In *State in Capitalist Society*, he comments on the important 'connections' between business and state policy makers and on the role of the Conservative Party as a vehicle for promoting business's political goals. These are, of course, examples of how capital is organised into politics – though it is not treated in a systematic manner. Certainly, it does not form part of a discussion of changes in the way capital is organised and participates in politics, and the impact such variations have on the ability of capital to achieve its class goals. In his later comments on the state the matter is not pursued.

It is important to note that Miliband responds to the changed pattern of class–state interaction. In *State in Capitalist Society* the economy and economic growth are treated as 'taken-for-granted' assumptions. It is assumed that the state will seek to promote economic growth and that politicians will need to direct their policies towards economic growth to make them electable. The assumption of 'relative autonomy' fitted the situation at the peak of the long boom, when it was easy to harmonise the expansion of the state with the well-being of private capital. The recession of the 1970s and the rapid increase in the size of the state and its range of actions, saw a change in Miliband's stance. For this reason, his response to Skocpol's *States and Social Revolutions* did not simply criticise her overemphasis on the study of politics as a self-contained process but concedes the need to deal with the possible tensions between capital and the state as something more than epiphenomena.[11] It was not part of Miliband's brief to extend the discussion to probe changes in the workings of the relationship between politics and the economy.

For Poulantzas the problem was not so much how classes were organised into politics but rather how labour was 'disorganised' by the state so that its political actions were ineffective. For capital, its degree of organisation and its presence in politics was secondary to the objective role of the state, which both secured capital's class interests and protected the social relations of the capitalist mode of production. In his later work, as he abandoned structural determination, the way capital was present within the state became a way of discussing this question. On the changed patterns of class–state relations, Poulantzas remained quite orthodox and worked with the distinction between competitive, monopoly and state-monopoly capitalism.

Such a solution to the debate has a pleasing symmetry, but it is no more adequate for that. Both Miliband and Poulantzas fail to deal with one very important problem. It may be true that the picture given by Miliband and Poulantzas is correct, that in the long run, the capitalist state generates policies that are for the best interest of capital as a class, or at a lower level, on balance, the policies of the capitalist state bring more benefit to capital than to labour. This is the general conclusion of all Marxist writings on the state (and of some non-Marxist writing as well)[12] but it does not explain how this happens, nor why it should be so. Poulantzas can provide no assistance in analysing why particular policies implemented by the state could or should have such a consequence. Although Miliband can give a general answer, it is only by extension that his approach can deal with particular instances. How is it that, in a given set of circumstances, state policies can have such a precise class relevance? Indeed, does state action invariably have such precise relevance and is it always so functional?

Claus Offe translated questions about the character and role of the state into propositions about the guarantors of state action's class effectivity. Thus, in his assessment of the Miliband–Poulantzas exchange Offe rejects their emphasis on external factors compelling the state to act in class-pertinent ways.[13] As an alternative, he suggests that if the state is a *capitalist* state (as something other than a state in a capitalist society) there must be processes of internal policy generation and selectivity that provide just such guarantees of the class sensitivity and relevance of state action. His search is true to the assumption that the state is most functional for capital when the ties between capital and the state are least. Offe suggests that there are a number of different ways in which these generation and selection mechanisms could work to produce the broadly observable coincidence of state action and general benefits for capital as a class. His work derives its power from his concern with the factors or processes that provide the guarantees of class relevance and effectivity of state action. Unfortunately his conclusions are rather indeterminate.

From the Miliband–Poulantzas exchanges, through Offe and beyond, ran an attempt to find a general theory of the capitalist state.[14] If it were invented, such a general theory would have explained both why and how it was that the capitalist state invariably acted to secure the long-term, class interests of capital. As such it could be used to decode the particular actions of the state and to explain its expected consequences. Here Offe's failure to find the sources of that 'guarantee' is most significant and signals the end of the search for a general theory. For it is only Offe who follows through the logic of the claims about the special character of the capitalist state to generate a total explanation for the consequences of state action. If there are no guarantees, if there are no mechanisms internal to the state to provide that guarantee, then the whole argument about the analysis of the capitalist state needs to be recast so that it does not imply some automatic adjustment of state action to system and class-serving consequences. In the pursuit of just such an interpretative schema, Bob Jessop, Fred Block, John Urry and Theda Skocpol have made important contributions. Although they have all sought, in different ways, to go beyond general theory, they do not provide a clear set of propositions that escape from the limitations of general propositions about the state.

As an example of the development of this second stage in the state debate consider Fred Block's arguments as they developed from his 1977 piece 'The ruling class does not rule' to his 1980 piece 'Beyond relative autonomy'.[15] Block constructs the elements of Miliband's account into two 'structural mechanisms' that ensure the proper fit between state action and class usefulness.[16] Miliband's portrait of the social 'connections' and his account of the processes of political socialisation appear as subsidiary mechanisms; his argument about the effects of political management of the state within a capitalist economic context becomes a major structural mechanism.[17] The constraint of 'business confidence' is still of central importance.[18] The main emphasis in Block's explanation turns on the attitudes and actions of the state managers who act in the context of working class initiatives and who are important for securing the coincidence of state action and class consequences. Block sees no role for a politically conscious ruling class and substitutes the partial consciousness of state managers in an environment shaped by class struggle:

> ... capitalist rationality emerges out of the three-sided relationship among capitalists, workers, and state managers. The structural position of the state managers forces them to achieve some consciousness of what is necessary to maintain the viability of the social order. It is this *consciousness* [my emphasis] that explains both the reluctance of state managers to offend business confidence, and their capacity to rationalize a capitalist society. However, the fact of consciousness does not imply control over the historical process. State managers are able to act only in the terrain that is marked out by the intersection of two factors – the intensity of class struggle and the level of economic activity.[19]

This shifting emphasis is consolidated in a later piece 'Beyond relative autonomy: state managers as historical subjects'. Here Block addresses the problem directly by his claim that state power is not reducible to class power (rejecting the central thrust of Poulantzas's work that previously influenced him). He draws on Weber to identify the separate source of the state's power derived from:

> ... the monopoly over the means of violence, which is the basis on which the managers of the state apparatus are able to force compliance with their wishes. ... But the exercise of state power occurs within particular class contexts which shape and limit the exercise of that power.[20]

For Block, 'state managers collectively are self interested maximisers, interested in maximising their power, prestige, and wealth.[21]

Constrained only by the class contexts in which they operate, they act in their own interests and are perfectly able to act against the interests of the bourgeoisie, if it is in their interests to do so and if they can get away with it. Block recognises a problem, since, for much of the time, his state managers have not acted in this way but have acted to fulfil their own interests in the context of *protecting* the class interests of capital. Once again we are returned to the relationship between capitalist control of the economy and the state's need for revenue as the mechanism which keeps the state in line. As Block expresses it:

> If state managers pursue policies that large sections of the capitalist class see as posing serious challenges to their property rights, the results are likely to be a collapse of domestic and international business confidence, leading to high levels of unemployment and an international payment crisis. Even when motivated by a desire to break with a capitalist mode of production, state managers are likely to respond to such a collapse of business confidence by retreating from their proposals for reform.[22]

Block's interest in how classes are organised into politics is limited. He comments on working-class political initiatives as creating the circumstances within which his state-managers can act to expand the state and advance their interests. Capital needs no organisation (it may have organisation but it needs no organisation) since 'business confidence' acts as an effective barrier to a fully independent state. On the question of changes in the size of the state, the scope of its actions and the relations between state action and classes, Block is interesting since he starts asking about a 'tipping point' – where the expansion of the state threatens the class interests of private capital. Although he exaggerates the extent and significance of the expansion of the state under Carter, the question is important and an answer is explored in Chapters 5, 6 and the Conclusion. Block did not go back to consider what such changes did to his basic argument about the relationship between classes and the state.

The contemporary debate on the state has been dominated by those working within a very broadly defined Marxist tradition.

With Fred Block the scope of that tradition needed to be interpreted very broadly indeed, since the basis for his conceptualisation of the interests and power base of his 'state managers' was explicitly derived from Max Weber. One who works outside of and against the Marxist tradition but who has made a considerable impact on the debate has been Theda Skocpol. Skocpol explicitly rejects the Marxist approach and draws inspiration from the works of Weber, Hinze and Tilly.[23] She describes her own position as 'organisational' and 'realist'.[24] Her reiterated emphasis is on the state and the political process as the central explanatory variable and her arguments and examples show the extent to which all forms of Marxist interpretation have downplayed the significance of the state as a positive, 'autonomous' source of political initiative. She makes the case explicitly for the capitalist state in an article evaluating 'Neo-Marxist' interpretations of the New Deal. Her overall alternative is well summarised in her conclusion:

> I have argued that many of the limitations on effective state intervention and on liberal reforms in the New Deal can be traced to the existing U.S. national administrative arrangements, governmental institutions, and political parties. These same structures, moreover, shaped the piecemeal reforms and the partially successful efforts to proffer relief and to promote recovery in response to the Depression. Capitalists, industrial workers, and farmers certainly helped to shape and limit the New Deal, as did the contours of the massive economic crisis itself. But economic and class effects were all mediated through the distinctive structures of U.S. national politics. The immediate changes were not fully intended by anyone, were not consistently in conformance with the interests of any one class, and were not smoothly functional for the system as a whole. But the changes did make sense as the product of intensified political struggle and undertakings within given, historically, evolved structures of political representation and domination. Such structures are the key to any satisfactory explanation of the New Deal – and to other episodes, past, present and future, of political response to economic crises within capitalism.[25]

On this basis it is easy to establish the style of analysis she opposes and the style she supports. She is against accounts that do not see economic and class effects mediated through the political process, that stress the intentional character of outcomes, that imply a smooth conformity between class interests and 'immediate changes', and which imply a smooth functionality between state actions and the requirements of the system.

Skocpol's work is important because she has demonstrated by the considerable power of her interpretations of social revolution that a much greater emphasis on the state as an independent variable and a social actor in its own right can yield valuable insights into the significance of political actions and outcomes. Her own analytical presentation fails to do more than to assert that this is the case as she does not provide a systematic set of concepts that go beyond interpreting political events in their own terms. The relationship between state power, class power and class interests remains inadequately theorised and appears as little more than 'social context' when she comes to consider, not revolutionary transformations but the normal operations of the capitalist state. Nonetheless, the point that she makes is very significant and cannot be ignored. The character of the state and the specifics of the political process need to be treated much more seriously than has hitherto been the case in the analysis of the politics of industrialised capitalism.

Skocpol, with her concern to 'bring the state back in', necessarily devalues the significance of classes and class organisations. The emphasis on the state as a central determinant, and in politics as a fairly self-contained process means that forms of class organisation are present in her analysis but they are shorn of their class relevance. Similarly, her focus identifies changes in the size of the state and the scope of state action, or at the very least increasing 'state capacities' but again devalues the class significance of these actions. Given her argument these are a matter of greatly reduced interest.

Whereas Fred Block and Theda Skocpol derive the special character of the state from the arguments of Max Weber, John Urry and Bob Jessop consistently seek to set their account within a Marxist tradition. Like all representatives of this second phase of the state debate they move a considerable distance away from the attempt to generate a general theory of the capitalist state. Nonetheless, they share some of the key assumptions of the previous stage, as in Urry's concern to accept the broad compatibility of state action with the class interests of capital,[26] and with both their efforts to define what would be theoretically essential for an adequate analysis of the capitalist state.[27] This attempt to set out *a priori* theoretically derived criteria for assessing the analytical adequacy of an account of the capitalist state seems to be quite at variance with their emphasis on treating much of what the state is and does as the result of certain structured but largely contingent events.[28] The tensions between these two elements in their accounts reflects the unfinished character of the present attempt to retheorise both the character of the capitalist state and the best methods by which this character is to be understood.

John Urry bases his account of the capitalist state on a distinctive reading of Marx which displaces the state itself as the object of study and focuses attention on civil society instead. Urry emphasises the sphere of circulation as the centre of a fairly extensive arena of 'civil society', which in turn becomes the basis for his examination of the role and character of the capitalist state. The state is not derived nor defined from the economic sphere or the mode of productions(s), instead it is based in and on the separate existence of civil society.[29]

The strength and importance of Urry's account lies in the emphasis which he places on the struggles that take place in society/civil society and the important consequences that they have had on the construction of that society and its political institutions. Hence, his analysis of liberal, representational democracy as the product of working class struggles which did not overthrow capitalism but certainly changed the way in which it worked. The same analytical point is made in his account of the debate over the interpretation of the welfare state and other issues of social reform; although they may be functional to capitalism they are also positive achievements of working class political struggle. These points are important and need to be considered in any full account of the relationship between classes and the state and the evaluation of the outcomes of the conflicts between them. For Urry, the state is only a capitalist state to the extent that it secures the interests of capital and this is not a pregiven but a contingent matter. This represents a return to Miliband's concern with the balance of power resources between capital and labour but with an added emphasis on the circumstances within which these two struggle. It still does not constitute an explanation for why, over time, the actions of the state should protect the class interests of capital, nor why the reforms pushed through by popular-democratic struggles so frequently turn into measures that are advantageous to the interests of capital.

Urry is concerned with the way groups are organised into

politics. The focus is on groups formed in 'civil society' and that means, with either non-class based groups or class based groups, pursuing what he sees as 'popular–democratic' struggles. As such he has little to say about how capital is present in politics. Like most of those involved in the state debate he is not seriously concerned with the changes in the patterns in the relations between classes and the state or in the pattern of state action in the society, except to open it up to the evaluation of its functionality (for capitalism) and an improvement in the position of labour, as a class within capitalism.

Over a number of years now, Bob Jessop has made a very substantial contribution to the analysis of the capitalist state with analytical summaries of the literature and keen assessments of key issues in the relationship between classes and the state and between the political and economic processes of capitalist society.[30] His most important arguments have concerned the different 'forms' of the capitalist state and the periodisation of its development.[31] From an account of the different approaches to the capitalist state to the discussion of the relationship between capitalism and representative democracy, Jessop has shown a healthy scepticism about the adequacy of these arguments and the possibility of making broad, general assumptions about the nature of the capitalist state.[32] This culminated in his recent book on the subject with a measured rejection of the attempt to construct any general theory of the capitalist state akin to the account given by Marx of the capitalist economy.[33] Unlike Urry, who bases his rejection of a general theory of the capitalist state on the specific character of capitalist society, Jessop derives his objection from methodological precepts and, as a result, places his emphasis on the 'contingent necessity' that needs to be discovered in each particular set of circumstances for why the state has come to act in a manner that is compatible with the broad class interests of capital.[34] It is this assumption which underlies his edicts on what would constitute an adequate account of the capitalist state.

His rejection of a general theory has important practical consequences for his account of the capitalist state, since the emphasis moves from a general level to the particular instance and from a single, all embracing example of the capitalist state locked in either a specified or unspecified time to a consideration of the differing ways in which class and state have interacted over time and in changed economic, political and social circumstances.[35] If we leave aside his attempts to link these to developments in the capitalist economy/mode of production (this will be discussed in the next section) and the precise ways in which he sees these as having happened, these two terms designate changing ways in which the relationships between classes and the state (representation) and between politics and economics (intervention) operate and change over time. Jessop moves to this position for many of the same reasons for which I have developed the notion of political regime.

If the problems of generality are to be avoided, it is necessary to set out the framework of important interactions so that how classes and the state are linked and how the state's actions have consequences for the classes is the ever present setting for the discussion of the particular circumstances, struggles and outcomes which then become the centre of analytical attention. This similarity extends further to Jessop's (brief) discussion of the analysis of interests which he also moves away from a rigid identification of what is and is not in the interests of classes. Interests are treated as circumstances that bring advantage in securing 'conditions of existence' and are to be understood as involving judgements about 'comparative advantage'.[36] Jessop weakens this argument by failing to distinguish adequately between interests and policy preferences, by retaining a notion of subjective and objective interests and by reducing the concept of structural constraint to a relative assessment of an unchangeable social context within which class and other struggles occur.[37] Nonetheless Jessop's work is important for introducing the terms in which a more adequate analysis can proceed and by setting out the appropriate framework of analytical scepticism.

Of the authors considered here, Jessop is the first who takes seriously the two dimensions of class relations with the state and the patterns of state action in the economy. He is concerned with 'modes of representation' and 'modes of intervention', terms which parallel those used here. In the context of 'intervention' he introduces a distinction between 'strategies of accumulation' and 'hegemonic projects', a distinction which parallels the one used here between capital's concern with accumulation and rule. In his work this is, quite properly, an integral part of a discussion of periodisation, of the changing patterns of class state relations, and it will be discussed in that context.

On the basis of the preceding discussion of the two broad phases of the debate on the state it is possible to summarise the problems faced in the attempt to construct an effective approach to the changing actions of the capitalist state. The most enduring problems surround the degree of congruence between state actions and the class interests of capital in a political system which gives working-class people a degree of influence through their use of the right to vote. So far this has not been translated into a strategy to destroy the class power of private capital although it has had important effects on the way in which the social order works. In the absence of such a class conscious strategy by the working population, capital's class interests have been protected by the actions of the state. And yet, in considering the actions of the capitalist state, and the consequences of those actions, it is only possible to detect the congruence of these with the long-term, class-wide interests of capital in the broadest terms. Such general observations have a degree of truth and are useful to refute those who wish to interpret the state as a set of neutral institutions and with any class character in their actions as either accidental, balanced by other actions, or in the eye of the beholder. When it comes to particulars, to the details of a given policy, conflict or course of action, it makes no sense to search for the guarantees of class relevance or class effectiveness. Such guarantees do not exist. Consciousness, shared ideology, structural determination or structural constraint are all equally ineffective to explain the particularities of the class role of the capitalist state. Nobody under capitalism can know, with any certainty, what the best policy is to solve the class problems of capital (or within capitalism, the class problems of labour). Policies are more or less adequate to the task, and circumstances are frequently most important. It is not a simple matter in which there is one appropriate policy for each problem that confronts capital as a class or one of the constituent parts of the class. Instead the situation is complicated both by the divisions that exist within capital and the potential for a number of different strategies to more or less fit the problems that are generated in the processes of social reproduction and capital accumulation. Further, there is the additional complication of the consequence of action, which may often not conform with intentions. Though it is possible to argue that the very fact of class relations under capitalism may be such that they are able to twist or transform policies so that they are more or less adjusted to meet the problems confronted by capitalism. Nonetheless, this is only the first approximation of an adequate response to the analytical problem. Instead, to approach the whole question of the congruence between state action and class interests it is necessary to recast the framework within which the subject is approached. The limited ability of classes and the state to generate such secure futures for themselves needs to be left to one side and the possibility considered that the way in which the state 'serves' the class interests of capital is far more problematic than would appear from retrospective consideration of the generality of the consequences of state action.

In retrospect, it is possible to recognise the enduring qualities of Miliband's initial account of the capitalist state. Although it lacked the analytical precision of Poulantzas's approach and lacked the elegance of later attempts to find the guarantees of the class effectivity of state action, it more than compensated for these deficiencies by its clear statement of what was involved in assessing the actions of the capitalist state and in exploring different arguments about why the state, constituted as it was in the political system, still generated solutions that were, on the whole, more favourable to capital than to labour. Poulantzas's alternative account, despite the great influence that it had in the state debate was less influential in generating detailed accounts of the actions of the capitalist state. Now it can be seen that the line of enquiry opened up by his emphasis on theoretically deducing the character of the political instance and the state from a reading of Marx's texts was ultimately unproductive. In assessing the first phase of the state debate it is necessary to remember that it has as its point of reference the actions and character of the state at the end of the years of post-war economic expansion, largely before the onset of the period of renewed class and social struggles that followed the events of May 1968 and which influenced (but did not cause) a substantial expansion of the state both before and in the first phase of the present period of prolonged recession.

The second phase of the debate, although this point is not explicitly recognised, has been shaped by that expansion of the state and the various strategies to respond to prolonged recession. Hence, it is unsurprising that it is in this second phase that the possibilities of the state acting against the interests of capital should be written into the analytical framework for the assessment of the character of the capitalist state. It is here that the question of the extent to which the state can be treated as the central explanatory variable is raised. It should be noted that Poulantzas's original contribution raised the prospects of self-contained political analysis, that is an account of political events that did not need an external point of reference to classes outside of their political manifestation, nor a reference to capital accumulation as anything other than a broad social or economic context. Miliband, in a much less explicit manner, also raised this question through the way in which his account of the state was presented.

The problem raised in the second phase of the debate then is the extent to which the actions and consequences of action of the state are to be interpreted on the basis of the relationships that exist with social classes, class organisations and other groups in society or on the basis of the intrinsic character of the state itself. In the past, those working on the state have been too willing to reduce the significance of the power resources of the state itself, and since the state frequently acted to advance the interests of capital, in part or on the whole, to interpret state power as simply a variety of class power. It is possible now to assert the immense difference between the two, because of the perceived conflict between capital and the state over the strategies for managing the present recession. Yet, this overstates the case. As yet the state has not exerted the kind of independence that this approach suggests: the state has not acted decisively to displace capital in either the economic or social sphere, regardless of the assertions about the special character of its own power and its interests and social character. That remains the problem to be solved: why, with the political system constructed in the way that it is and with the state organised in the way that it is, does the state *not* make such a bid to realise its potential for full autonomy and social dominance? The antagonism between private capital and the state has frequently been asserted by representatives of private capital, even over expansions of state action that eventually come to be accepted and recognised as beneficial. In the absence of that claim being made by private capital, how is the point at which the state actions *do* threaten the economic and social dominance of private capital to be recognised? If the point has been reached, what does it signify? These are some of the questions that are considered in this book and which have been given a more extensive treatment than has been possible in the brief articles that have raised the possibilities so far.

FROM STATE TO POLITICAL REGIME

This brief consideration of the development of the argument over the relations between classes and the state reveals a need to think about the problem in different terms. The level of generality is now inappropriate as is the sense of 'timelessness' in the general observation. The specific details of how classes are organised into the political process and the ways in which the state 'intervenes' in the economy need to be established as does the changed relationship of state action to classes. It can not be assumed that an analysis of one particular period will reveal the full range of historical options, nor that it can identify, generally correct, elements of the interpretation. It is now necessary to consider moving the focus from the state to a consideration of political regime.

If it is accepted that classes are, under capitalism, both unified and divided, then a number of things follow of relevance to the link between class interest, policies, state actions and their consequences. Firstly, class interests and policies are not the same thing. Policy claims are constructed on the basis of interests but there is a distance between them. There are no guarantees, and in the abstract or particular, no ways of knowing which policy more effectively embodies the interest of the class. Such matters are settled by experience, conflict and consequences. The policy that most effectively expresses the class interest is not a constant, but varies with circumstances. Secondly, interests do not come into the world automatically clothed with policies. Forms of organisation are necessary to unify the particular parts of the class or classes and to respond to the problems that they face. In doing so they generate policies that seek to embody that particular interest, though there is no guarantee that the most appropriate policy has been found. Nor is it only the immediate organisations of class that generate policies and act to secure class interests. The classes do not have class-wide organisations at either the economic or political level and many bodies can seek to propose policies and generate class-wide perspectives for both labour and capital. A particular section of the class (banks or trade unions), political parties, the state or parts of the state can all act in this way, equally without guarantees about the relevance or usefulness of their policy suggestions. Though it is possible for some to implement their proposals (banks, for example, can use their lending procedures to influence commercial and industrial policy), it is largely the state which is in a position to take decisive action and implement policies. The fact of state action may bear the marks of the influence or initiative of one section of a class, its organisation or political party but this does not indicate the consequences of the policy, understood in terms of its impact on classes and class interests. This must be assessed separately. It is only on the basis of an analysis of this whole process, the linked sequence of interests, policy suggestions, state action and the pattern of class consequence that it is possible to understand how it is that, and the extent to which, state action tends (or has tended) to advance and protect the class interests of capital as a whole. Further, why, in a system that operates without certainty and implicit guarantees, should this be so?

On the basis of this account of the complexities of the links between interests, policies, actions and consequences, it is possible to propose a broad model of the relationship between classes and the state and between economics and politics. This model is heuristic in character and intention. For the purposes of clear exposition, this model presupposes a separation between economics and politics as two spheres of class society and class relations and that there are links between the two in the form of organisation, interest representation and policy formation, and through action and consequence. Classes interact with each other in the economy, they experience the problems of the process of capital accumulation in this sphere and they have a certain framework of interest as a result of their place and interactions in this process of production, circulation, exchange and accumulation. As a result of these interactions and experience, organisations are formed that seek to represent members drawn from parts of this process. On the side of capital there are trade associations, on the side of labour, trade unions. Over time these bodies develop more inclusive and comprehensive forms of organisation. All these bodies seek to respond to the problems of their members, propose policies that would solve the problems, mitigate against their worst consequences or postpone their impact. Political parties extend the degree of competition as they try to devise programmes and images to ensure election or re-election. As such they also propose solutions to the problems faced by classes, though, given the assumptions of the formal political system, they will try to give the solutions a national and trans-class appearance. Political parties forming government become part of the state system and further process policies as solutions to the interests of classes and sections of classes. As the state, some such solutions are enacted and consequences flow that have implications for the interests of the class. In this way there is a process of interest articulation, interest representation[38] and policy formation and action that links the economic and the political areas of class interaction. The essential ingredients are interests, organisation, representation, action and consequence. It is this sequence that needs to be considered in an attempt to comprehend the complex realities of class struggles and interactions in developing capitalist societies.

The focus here is on those aspects that change and these occur in at least three different areas. Firstly, there can be changes in the ways that classes are organised, the way that institutions are created that respond to problems and seek to generate solutions that can be enacted by the state. Secondly, there are the changes that occur in the state itself. The internal organisation of the state, the balance that exists between different branches of the state apparatus, can alter in quite decisive ways. The rise of more obviously bureaucratic modes of organisation, the changing relationship between the executive and the assembly are examples of such changes. Of equal importance are changes in the range and character of state actions. At a suitably high level of generalisation, the defined functions of the state may remain unchanged, but in their particular details the way in which such functions are embodied or discharged does change. For the analysis to encompass more dynamic elements, it is necessary to remove this incipient functionalism. The range of state actions has changed, and it is the significance and consequences of such changes that is at the heart of present disputes. Thirdly, the way in which the relationship between class and state is actually organised has also changed. There is a development in the ways in which class organisations are linked to the state as a complex of institutions and to state action. It is also important to note at what times and in what circumstances the more obvious and formal relationships between class organisations and the state are reorganised. The construction of state provided welfare, and the institution of forms of state economic planning alter the institutional relations between class and state just as the negotiation of the 'social contract' in Britain in the 1970s did. What the conception of a changing political regime seeks to capture is the dynamic character of the relationship between class and state in industrialised capitalism and largely within one generally recognised form of the capitalist state, the liberal or representational political system.

The state debate has been very important for clarifying what is at stake in the discussion of the relationship between classes and the state on the basis of the degree of autonomy which the state has from class. This issue will be considered later in this book when it is necessary to evaluate the major changes caused by the significant expansion in the size and scope of state action. For the broad argument here it is necessary to move the focus away from the state debate because the issues that are central to this discussion were not central to the debate. It is only in broad terms that the state debate looked at either the changing ways of organising classes into politics or the changing pattern of state actions towards classes and the economy. It is useful to pursue this question further, into the literature on 'corporatism' which specifically focuses on the organisation of classes into politics.

CORPORATISM, REPRESENTATION AND INTERVENTION

Although the classic 'state debate' ignores changes in the way in which classes are organised into politics and changing patterns in class state relations, there is one body of literature that deals directly with this question, that of the 'corporatist' revival. On the whole, this literature developed as a response to the increased frequency with which governments set up direct and formal negotiations with the organised representatives of capital and labour, and of the tendency to proliferate 'tripartite bodies' involving representatives of capital, labour and the state, to investigate or manage developing problems. These events undermined some of the defining features of pluralist analysis which was then modernised to characterise and interpret these new events. As with pluralism the emphasis is on decision making and who is 'represented' in the political process, whose grievances are 'addressed' by state action and as a style of analysis, it shares many of the problems that weakened the power of the pluralist interpretation.

The body of work on 'corporatism' has grown enormously and the term is used in increasingly diverse ways. There is an extensive debate about the utility of the concept as well. It is not my purpose here to go through all that is available, but to consider a few central examples to illustrate how such a 'corporatist' approach deals with the relations between class organisations and the state and the limitations of this approach to these recent developments.

Many of the problems in the corporatist revival can be found in Schmitter's seminal essay 'Still the century of corporatism?'[39] In this piece Schmitter locates the definition and analysis of corporatism at the same level as that of pluralism, and necessarily embraces the same range of problems faced by pluralists in their attempts to interpret class organisations and the significance of the relationship between economic and political processes. This weakness is evident in the notion that the changes which have occurred are best approached through a discussion of the 'representation' and 'intermediation' and in the definitions of pluralism and corporatism proposed.

> Pluralism can be defined as a system of interest representation in which the constituent units are organized into an unspecified number of multiple, voluntary, competitive, nonhierarchically ordered and self-determined (as to type or scope of interest) categories which are not specially licensed, recognized, subsidized, created or otherwise controlled in leadership selection or interest articulation by the state and which do not exercise a monopoly of representational activity within their respective categories.[40]

> Corporatism can be defined as a system of interest representation in which the constituent units are organized into a limited number of singular, compulsory, noncompetitive, hierarchically ordered and functionally differentiated categories, recognised or licensed (if not created) by the state and granted a deliberate representational monopoly within their respective categories in exchange for observing certain controls on their selection of leaders and articulation of demands and supports.[41]

The use of the concept 'interest representation' (or 'intermediation') contains only a self-evident notion of interest in which interest only means what some organisation wants, and 'representation' or 'intermediation' refers only to the relations between the state and those 'interests' expressed by organisations. So much of the corporatist literature, even when it recognises the significance of the organisations of labour and capital, is unable to deal with the class character of these organisations. For most of the time they are treated as little more than obviously acting, important pressure groups and the links between politics and economics remain unexplored.

The limitation inherent in Schmitter's conception is further revealed in his distinction between societal and state corporatism.[42] It is only in state corporatism that the relations between organisations and the state are as defined. For societal corporatism, the relations are different, and the differences are more than just a matter of emphasis: they summarise not just a different history that brought a similar situation into being but a different situation with different relations between the class organisations and the state. For example, take the 'compulsory, hierarchically ordered, recognition by the state' aspects of the definition.[43] If compulsion is *'de facto'* through 'social pressure' it is quite different from the compulsion imposed by the state. Indeed it may not be compulsion at all. If the hierarchical order comes out of 'bureaucratic extension' it will be different in appearance and effect from a situation where the hierarchy is imposed by the state. The same is true in his use of state recognition (note he takes here the weakest of the formulations – ignoring 'licensed by or even created by' the state). Recognition based on political necessity describes a quite different relationship between class organisations and the state from that designated by a state defined legitimacy. It is not surprising, given Schmitter's own analytical concerns, that the basis for his definition should be state corporatism, nor that the extension to other situations should be on the basis of analogy. It is analogy that inspires all accounts that discern corporatism in recent developments in the institutional history of industrialised capitalism.

In a later article, 'Interest intermediation and regime governability in contemporary Western Europe and North America', Schmitter provides a more extensive account of the rise of societal corporatism both out of the decay of pluralism and as the easy outgrowth of developments in societies where pluralism has been less developed.[44] Schmitter works from a concept of the 'politicalogical' features of pluralism which place barriers in the way of an extension of organisation and increased formal association of organisations with the policy making of the state.[45] That logic is broken by the economic and social expansion of the state.

Only the coercive intervention of the modern bureaucratic state to subsidize organizational existence; to license respective jurisdictions; to grant monopolistic access; to delegate tasks; to ensure selective privileges; to render membership obligatory *de facto* or *de jure*; to define issues, and hence affected interests; to insist on the provision of associated information; to encourage the formation of functionally organized 'partners' for the implementation of public policy; and so forth is likely to bring forth such an organized response from civil society.[46]

These factors concern the way in which state action encouraged the transformation of the organisation of interest groups, from the perspective of the state. The groups respond to the demands of the modern bureaucratic state. To what is the state responding? Schmitter does not provide an answer. What is revealing about this comment and Schmitter's subsequent discussion is the way in which the changes identified are neither explained nor theorised. The increased range of state action referred to, all represent some reduction in the autonomy of market relations. The policies behind the expansion of the role of the state could have been encouraged or supported by any number of 'privileged interest groups'. Consequently the transformation of 'intermediation' could have been the product of struggle between these groups over the conditions of their existence and of struggles between them and the state. Such a possibility reveals the limits in Schmitter's conception of the process of intermediation. With the analysis set out in his way, it is impossible to trace the developing responses of class organisations to their social, economic and political environments and the changing interactions with the state within the context of efforts to secure class rule and capital accumulation.[47]

Leo Panitch avoids the analytical problems associated with Schmitter's work and most of those who have sought to reintroduce the concept of corporatism to the analysis of industrialised capitalism. Panitch does not treat corporatism as a modified version of pluralism as he writes from within a Marxist perspective and on the basis of an extensive consideration of the role of trade unions in the British political system. Significantly, Panitch finds a definition of corporatism that moves the debate forward by reconsidering the status of such institutions and provides a mechanism for explaining why these should appear at the time and in the way they do.

Panitch introduces his approach in the following way:

> The corporatist paradigm understood to connote *a political structure within advanced capitalism which integrates organized socioeconomic producer groups through a system of representation and cooperative mutual interaction at the leadership level and of mobilization and social control at the mass level* can be a heuristic tool for appropriating the social reality of many western liberal democracies.[48]

From the text it is clear that 'socioeconomic producer groups' is meant to designate classes and forms of class organisation; and that these groups are not thought to be equally powerful in the context of the corporatist structures or in the wider society; and that the influence of the state on these bodies is as significant as the representations made by these groups to the state. In other words, Panitch wants to make clear the class character of the most significant groups, the class character of the state and the importance of locating the analysis of political forces in a broader understanding of the relations between classes in their economic and social areas.

For Panitch, the rise of corporatist arrangements and their significance is a product of those factors in the post-war world that increase the bargaining power of trade unions.[49] He takes seriously Kalecki's speculations about the consequences of post-war governments using fiscal policy to promote full employment and the impact that this would have on the bargaining power of labour and capital. Kalecki saw the development of a political business cycle; Panitch saw the increasing attraction of corporatist structures to integrate trade unions and offset the weakening of the labour market mechanism. This explains why incomes policy is the most common form of the corporatist initiative.

Nonetheless, it is here that Panitch's conversion to the use of corporatism had its greatest analytical cost. Corporatism implies a structure that links business, labour and the state. Instead, incomes policy is most usually, as in the examples cited by Panitch, established on the basis of bilateral agreements between governments and trade unions. It is important to recognise this in any assessment of the dynamics and instability of incomes policies which are frequently treated as evidence about the character of the supposed corporatist structures. In this regard it should be noted that when Panitch speaks of the durability of corporatist structures he does not refer to those for incomes policy but to the less dramatic, less significant ones of economic policy making, NEDO and the sectoral working parties.[50] Even the social contract in both its incomes and planning aspects was more bilateral than tripartite and neo-corporatist, and its instability is as much related to this fact as to its failure to contain rank and file union pressures.

Indeed, Panitch's emphasis on trade union dissent and the contradiction between participation and remaining an 'autonomous' working-class institution picks up another problem in adopting even as rigorous a conception of corporatism as this.[51] The emphasis is on the relationship between trade unions and the state, largely in terms of the state seeking corporatist structures to contain the economic power of trade unions. The account then becomes a consideration of the weakness and problems in these attempts at incorporations where the rank and file become the bearers of opposition on the basis of their commitment to protecting their levels of real income. This misses the fact that it is not just the state which seeks to create these structures but that some parts of the trade union movement support these structures as avenues through which trade unions can increase their influence outside the realms of the wage bargain, in other areas that affect the fate of their members, areas in which they have less direct leverage.[52] Panitch notes these arguments but minimises their importance by distancing their advocates from the trade unions and by stressing the need for a revolutionary party to make the transition to socialism feasible. Not to note the significance of the debate within trade unions over the possible link between wage restraint and planning initiatives is to miss much of what made sense of these developments as part of a strategy for labour within a capitalist society. Secondly, this emphasis misses the importance of business organisations and business's response to the growth of corporatist structures. Panitch correctly notes that political organisation is of a different significance for trade unions and business.[53] This does not make business responses to corporatist developments irrelevant and the role of business hostility to the bilateral relations between trade unions and the state ought to play some part in an understanding of the instability of these arrangements.

In summary then, Panitch does as much as is possible to make the concept of corporatism useful and yet, even in this case, the term misnames and distorts the significance of the developments it emphasises.[54] The dynamic consequence of the state's commitment to economic growth and full employment is a significant factor in explaining a subsequent effort by the state to promote schemes to constrain the bargaining power of labour. To recognise and use the fact does not depend on a willingness to imagine the social development of capitalism in terms of corporatist political structures. Rather than structures, these attempts are parts of political strategies and there are other explanations for why tripartite structures should be continually created and recreated in the institutional development of capitalist class relations within the existing social order.

Although the corporatist literature does focus on the question of how classes are organised into the political process and how the patterns of class-state relations change, it does not do this effectively. The emphasis is too much on the political process as a process of 'representation' with only a limited concern with consequent changes in the pattern of state action. Most usually it is to note what the critics of pluralism had noted before, that the system of influence is skewed, that those who are not organised or who are poorly organised or who are not parts of the major business and labour organisations tend to get ignored or marginalised by the 'corporatist' political process. These observations are as true in this context as they were before but they need to be supplemented by an account of why these major forces are the ones organised into politics in this way. The conditions under which corporatist institutions are constructed and dismantled means that broader areas of state action and the political struggles between business and labour and the role of the state need to be probed. Further attention needs to be paid to the ways in which the state acts, changes in the characteristic forms of state action, and to the impact of change on the pattern of relations between political and economic processes in a capitalist society.

CONCLUSION

The problems revealed in this discussion of the literature on class, on the state debate and on corporatism reveal a fundamental set of problems only lightly touched on by most of the authors. Even when Jessop recognises the need to link systems of representations to forms of state action,[55] the argument is mechanical and schematic, pointing to the need, at the very least, to clothe the presentation in an account of the passage from one of these regimes to another. The conceptualisation of the history of political and economic evolution of capitalist society through the use of political regime is significant in that it breaks with these incomplete formulations. The concept of 'political regime' maps out a research agenda and a form of argument. The concept identifies a need to deal with what changes in the history of capitalist social relations, especially in the relations between classes and the state.

What I have done is to take this basic proposition and apply it to the history of class state relations in three capitalist countries starting with the inter-war period of Britain, France and Germany. The greatest emphasis is placed on Britain but the events in France and Germany are used to limit the scope of the claims made on the basis of one example and to shade in an important range of social and historical variation.

There is an underlying theme. The history of class–state relations is shaped by the political regimes that exist, the problems and characteristic forms of action that flow from them and the way in which intended and unintended consequences combine to change these political regimes. Further, that there is a tendency built into developments of political regime, thus far, for the relations to be reorganised as the state expands and increases its reach into the economy and society to solve the problems thrown up. For this reason, the chapters that follow chart the forces that make for, or secure, the continued, though not steady, expansion of the state, even during the most recent period when governments have been determined to reduce the size of the state.

NOTES

1. See Poulantzas (1975; 1977). For a survey of Marx's arguments see Gough (1972), esp. p. 69.
2. For an account which seeks to incorporate these elements into a broadly Marxist framework, see Urry (1981) esp. chaps. 1–5.
3. For a consideration of ways of characterising the positions of these people see the works of Poulantzas cited in note 1 and Wright (1976).
4. Marx comments on the interconnection between the two in the following way:

> Capital can only increase by exchanging itself for labour power, by calling wage labour to life. The labour power of the wage-worker can only be exchanged for capital by increasing capital, by strengthening the power whose slave it is. *Hence, increase of capital is increase of the proletariat, that is, of the working class.*
>
> The interests of the capitalist and those of the worker are, therefore, *one and the same*, asserts the bourgeois and their economists. Indeed! The worker perishes if capital does not employ him. Capital perishes if it does not exploit labour power, and in order to exploit it, it must buy it. The faster capital intended for production, productive capital, increases, the more, therefore, industry prospers, the more the bourgeoisie enriches itself and the better business is, the more workers does the capitalist need, the more dearly does the worker sell himself.
>
> The indispensable condition for a tolerable situation of the worker is, therefore, the fastest possible growth of productive capital . . .
>
> *To say that the interests of capital and those of the workers are one and the same is only to say that capital and wage labour are two sides of one and the same relation. The one conditions the other, just as usurer and squanderer condition each other.* Marx (1970)

Despite Marx's observations, many and varied are the schemes that have been put forward to harmonise the concerns of labour with the requirements of capital.

5. See, for example, Gold, Lo and Wright (1975). For a longer, better but by no means unflawed account, see Jessop (1982). For an account that concentrates on the weakness of the Marxist orthodoxy in the field, see Crouch (1979).
6. It was to counter this view that Miliband stressed the critique of pluralism in the presentation of the argument. See Miliband (1973a).
7. Poulantzas (1969); Miliband (1970). Poulantzas's initial position is to be found in Poulantzas (1973). For a careful and detailed explication and critique of Poulantzas's position see Jessop (1982), chap. 4.
8. Poulantzas (1978).
9. Miliband (1979, chap. IV; 1983).
10. For his account of the politics of social democracy, see Miliband (1973).
11. Theda Skocpol (1979); for his review see Miliband (1983).
12. See Lindblom (1977), chap. 13.
13. Offe (1974).
14. See, for example, Laclau (1975), and for the manner in which the German state-derivation debate was presented in English, Holloway and Picciotto (1978).

15. Block (1977; 1980, pp. 227–42).
16. It should be noted that Block makes no reference to Miliband's work. Instead, in footnote 3 he sees his arguments as 'influenced' by Poulantzas's review of *State in Capitalist Society* (1969). He also states that his position is closer to that of Offe's (1974) and Offe and Ronge (1975), an article which considers the constraints on politicians in the context of representational institutions and a capitalist economy. Despite this lack of reference to Miliband, the elements he identifies as his structural mechanisms are the broad contours of Miliband's account. What he owes to Poulantzas is his characterisation of these as 'structural' mechanisms. Since he also wishes to describe class struggle as a structural mechanism, there is some reason to be sceptical about the adequacy of this designation.
17. Block (1977), pp. 12–15.
18. *Ibid.*, pp. 16–19.
19. *Ibid.*, p. 27.
20. Block (1980), p. 229.
21. *Ibid.*, p. 232.
22. *Ibid.*, p. 232.
23. Skocpol (1979), fn 77, p. 301.
24. *Ibid.*, p. 31.
25. Skocpol (1980), p. 201.
26. Urry (1981), p. 106.
27. *Ibid.*, pp. 80–3; Jessop (1982), pp. 221–8.
28. Urry (1981), chaps. 7 and 8; Jessop (1982), pp. 211–13.
29. *Ibid.*, pp. 100, 121.
30. Jessop (1977; 1978).
31. Jessop (1979; 1980).
32. See especially his comments in Jessop (1978).
33. Jessop (1982), chap. 5.
34. *Ibid.*, pp. 212ff.
35. *Ibid.*, p. 228–52.
36. *Ibid.*, pp. 256–8.
37. For a more extensive comment on these problems see McEachern, (1980), chap. 2 and Conclusions.
38. See Urry (1981), pp. 65–6 for a critique of some forms of the argument about interest representation. As Urry argues, the case made in Antony Cutler, Barry Hindness, Paul Hirst and Athar Hussain, *Marx's 'Capital' and Capitalism Today*, volume 1 (1977, London; Routledge and Kegan Paul) chap. 9, is based on treating Marx's account of class in terms of the economic base-political superstructure metaphor and only holds so long as classes are treated as economic categories. Class is not treated in that way in this chapter. The problem of 'representation' remains. There is no sense in which the argument here is based on some concept of 'direct representation of [class] interests' in the political process (pp. 232–3). Indeed, the case made here turns around the distance between interests as the framework and policies and preferences as responses to problems on the basis of that

framework. Hence, due attention is given to the active role of organisations in political and other kinds of struggles. The use of the term 'representation' does not conflate the two levels of the argument, but expresses the necessary complexity and ambiguity of the process being analysed.
39. Schmitter (1979), pp. 7–52.
40. *Ibid.*, p. 15.
41. *Ibid.*, p. 13.
42. *Ibid.*, pp. 20ff.
43. *Ibid.*, p. 21.
44. Schmitter (1981), pp. 287–330.
45. *Ibid.*, p. 290.
46. *Ibid.*, p. 291.
47. *Ibid.*, p. 327 fn 25 for the influence of Leo Panitch.
48. Panitch (1979), p. 123.
49. *Ibid.*, pp. 132ff.
50. Panitch (1981), p. 40.
51. *Ibid.*, pp. 40–3.
52. Crouch (1980).
53. Panitch (1981), p. 26.
54. It should be noted that Panitch's commitment to the term was short lived and he subsequently criticised the varied uses of the term: Leo Panitch (1980).
55. Jessop (1978), pp. 10–51; (1979), pp. 185–213; (1980), pp. 23–93; (1982), pp. 228–41.

2 · THE PASSING OF THE LIBERAL ORDER

INTRODUCTION

The popular presentation of the liberal era as one that combined economic growth, prosperity, rising standards of life and culture and a maximum amount of personal freedom has had sustained ideological resonance down to the present day. It is assumed that this was the golden age of capitalism, one in which entrepreneurs were dynamic, the state was responsive to the dictates of liberal philosophy and did nothing apart from keeping public order, and that society was composed of individuals striving for greater freedoms and personal benefits. The nostalgia for this lost liberal order is intensified by the fact that it passed so easily from the scene. The liberal order was a transient one, built in struggle against a past pattern of a strong and economically active state within a largely closed social order. Its moment of triumph was important, giving impetus to the rise of capitalism though it was by no means essential for its development or survival. The liberal order passed away on the basis of the economic and social forces released by its own dynamism, in the very process of its creation. This chapter considers the basic shape of the liberal social order and the relationship it had to capitalism in its period of ascent, the kinds of class organisations and state institutions that went along with it and, most importantly, the various factors that combined to change the political and social organisation of capitalist society. It charts the passage, through war and economic depression, away from a liberal social order.

THE LIBERAL ORDER AS A POLITICAL REGIME

The rise of capitalism destroyed the certainties of the feudal economic and social order. With industrialisation, capitalism transformed the entire economic and demographic character of society. The forces that gave coherence and legitimacy to the old order were destroyed and the question was sharply posed of how the new kind of society would combine class rule, the secured domination of the new and rising class, the bourgeoisie or capital, with dynamic economic growth and accumulation. The liberal order was neither a thought out solution nor a planned accomplishment. It was constructed piecemeal, over a long period and in struggle within and against the assumptions and institutions of the past.

At the heart of the new order was not a conception of the best political system or of the means to create legitimacy and social stability. Rather it was the conditions that enabled the market to dominate both economic and social life that gave meaning to the numerous campaigns to reform and limit the scope of state action and for which the liberal creed of rights and freedoms was so potent. The social prerequisite for market dominance was the separation of a large bulk of the population from the means of social production, from land and from the capital required for industrial production, and the concentration of these assets in the hands of a substantial minority.

The liberal order had at its centre the economic relations of the market and commodity exchange. Goods and services and the ability to work exchanged for money with a formal equality evident in the making of contracts. The major interactions between individuals occurred through market relations of buyers and sellers. It was the market that co-ordinated a diverse society: it was the market that gave a social character to disparate goals and interactions. The political system could enunciate national and social goals but the decisions of weight and consequence were those negotiated in and through the market. Expansion and contraction of industries, the levels of income and the patterns of its distribution and the rate of economic growth were not the results of political choice but of the co-ordinating role of the market.

Over these market relations were constructed ideologies, social creeds, political institutions and limits to state action. Essentially, many of these paralleled the assumptions of the market place and individual responsibility and freedom from the interference of the state was emphasised. Freedoms of speech, assembly (within defined notions of public order) and contract were far more significant than any notion that the state ought to be based in electoral processes of an essentially (or even formally) democratic kind.[1] In France, with the revolution of 1789, the articulation of such liberal rights went furthest, though a liberal-democratic state was not created. In Britain and Germany, freedom of contract was honoured more than the other freedoms and the formal trappings of the liberal and representative state were late additions, so late in the German case that they almost missed the period of capitalist ascent entirely.

Classes

Capitalist development and class formation were interconnected processes. On the one hand, the increasing dominance of capitalism established certain defining class relations in the very processes of production and accumulation. Larger portions of the population came to relate to each other through the market in terms of the commodities that they owned or controlled, means of production or labour-power. In this way, class relations generated a basis for common, class interests but without determining the organisations of classes, their historical character, the ways in which they would conceive of their places in society or the goals that they would pursue. However, the struggles between these forming classes, the experience of market relations and the actions of the state did give classes an organised form and ways of responding to the social consequences of the rise of capitalism.[2] For neither labour nor capital were these organisations of a solid or durable kind, but they were the first stages in a long and complex process of historical development that saw the distinctive character of these classes more firmly etched into the institutions of their everyday interactions.

For capital, their efforts were fragmented and varied. The struggle against the old order and the economic restrictions of the state enforced the development of some organisations combining economic and political demands. The various groups of free traders that campaigned against the corn laws in Britain exemplify such transient beginnings on the passage to more comprehensive and representative class organisations. Market relations, and the patterns of investment, competition and profit were such as to encourage some forms of organisation between individual firms. The frequent calamities that upset smooth expansion, the trade crises that first hinted at the presence of a business cycle, encouraged some firms to organise in the attempt to offset these adverse market conditions. Hence the history of even the earliest periods of capitalist consolidation sees buying and selling agreements amongst businesses to offset problems of supply and sales in uncertain market conditions.[3] Though these frequently collapsed as the scope for profits varied, the onset of bad times promoted new attempts at market-modifying organisations. The greater the dominance of capitalism, the more these organisations came to be permanent features of the economic and social landscape of capitalist societies. Bankruptcy concentrated capital and increased financial centralisation,[4] further undermining the liberal assumptions of the market economy. The need to deal with labour and its attempts to unionise also encouraged more durable forms of business organisation. By the last part of the nineteenth century, cartels, trade associations and employer groups, though not as highly developed as they were later to become, existed in Britain, France and Germany.[5]

For labour, the experience of being without property and subject to the vagaries of the labour market also encouraged organisation. Though the rise of capitalism freed the direct producers from the all embracing control of feudal overlords and guild masters, the freedom of the market still left them subject to the control of those who hired them. Work conditions as well as the practices of hiring and dismissing workers and the setting of wage levels all reinforced the tendencies to organisation and the development of stategies which, at the very least, sought to redress the vulnerability of individual workers in the 'freedom' of the labour market.

It is important to note that the pressures encouraging both labour and capital to organise arose from the operation of market relations themselves. Neither great political vision nor outside forces were needed to start this process of class organisation, simply the experience of the market and the consequences that it had. Both labour and capital, in their different ways, had incentives to avoid the full impact of an unrestricted market. This is significant since it reveals that the social and economic assumptions of the liberal market society were necessarily impermanent. Classes would not remain unorganised, as individuals who 'happened' to share similar market situations. The attraction and necessity for developing forms of class organisation grew out of market relations; the tendency to organisation was immanent *in* market relations from the first. Thus it is that the *ideology* of liberal market society and its superiority as a form of social organisation does not have its most articulate and consistent advocates within market relations as such, though groups within the market may, for a variety of instrumental and non-instrumental reasons, espouse such claims. It is an ideology carried by those on the edges of the market, like the classical political economist, Adam Smith.

The state

The ideology of a liberal state as the best guarantor of individual political and economic freedom has been a potent force throughout the history of industrialised capitalism. Business's frequently reiterated call for *laissez-faire*, for smaller rather than larger state sectors, for freedom to do what is necessary for profit without hindrance from the state, would often seem to be *the* ideology of industrialised capitalism. The same demand has been able to serve two opposed needs. It was the rallying cry for business in its struggle against the old economic order with its restrictive, frequently authoritarian and mercantilist state. On the other side, the slogans retain their potency down to the present day as a way of opposing the innumerable attempts to restrict the free action of business in the pursuit of its private profit by imposing considerations of a social or long term character. Though it is unlikely that business wants the world to be run on liberal assumptions, dismantling cartels, business organisation and ending direct and indirect state assistance, the call for *laissez-faire* can be used to oppose unwelcome attempts at outside regulation of business affairs, and the costs of imposed social programmes.

Despite the longevity of *laissez-faire* as a demand, it must be recognised that the term neither accurately describes what the state did in the liberal era nor the limits that were imposed on the range of state actions.[6] The first qualification concerns the extent of the liberal and representative character of the state. It was only in France, as a result of the revolutionary unheavals against an absolutist monarchy, that anything approaching a liberal and representative state was created and this venture did not last long and needed to be recreated later. In Britain, liberal definitions were attached to existing restrictions on the state and not added to the constitution except by practice and interpretation of common law rights. Whatever else may be said of the state in Germany in this period, it was not liberal, it acknowledged few liberal restraints and its illiberalism did not lessen its contribution to the strengthening of capitalism and the development of industry. Fledgling forms of liberalism and representative institutions appeared only briefly in the Weimar Republic before making way for authoritarian rule.

To the extent that representative institutions existed as part of the structure of the state, they were all based on forms of limited franchise that excluded the bulk of the working population, both men and women.[7] The state was made safe for the rising bourgeoisie on the basis of electoral exclusions of the working population in this initial period of capitalist consolidation. It was only as a result of protracted struggles that the franchise was extended to all adult males and much later to adult females. It is commonplace to note that the representative and formal democratic elements of the modern state were grafted onto existing liberal state structures, though this tends to overstate the political liberalism of this period.

So much for the qualified liberalism of the political form of the state in the era of ascending capitalism, but what of its economic liberalism? The conventional assumptions treat the state in this period as avoiding a direct economic role, preferring (or forced) to confine its efforts to securing the social and liberal framework within which the private economy could flourish.[8] There is an image of the state encouraging competition and free trade, attacking monopoly and protection, setting a supportive legal framework, securing the laws of contract and establishing and protecting a national currency. This view tends to conceal the extensive and varied economic actions of the state at this time. The state did not universally encourage or enforce free trade which now seems to be the prerogative of the strongest capitalist economy. Indeed, in both Germany and France protection was one of the ways in which the state directly encouraged industrialisation.[9] Nor is it clear that the state did act to promote competition and against monopoly, except in its interference with labour organisation.[10] The state of this period certainly tolerated the development of forms of cartel and monopoly organisations amongst businesses. As to the extent of direct economic action by the state, Germany stands as an example of a different path to the same goal, a developed industrialised capitalist economy.[11] In all of these countries the state was quite active in seeking out foreign markets for the products of domestic industry and as sources of raw materials and labour and in the protection of these trading advantages by the use of force. It is possible to identify an ideal type of the liberal state that accords neatly with a model of the requirements of rising and industrialising capitalism but, in reality, the pattern of the economic actions of the state and the limits imposed on state actions shows a great deal of national variation which, though greatly reduced in the years after the Second World War, still persists.

If the image of *laissez-faire* implies that the state did not intervene in the relations between classes it would be completely wrong. The state may have justified its interventions in terms of liberalism (though normally it was inaction that was justified in that way), or of upholding the law of contract or simply the preservation of social peace, law and order, but it consistently acted to prevent working people from combining in an attempt to improve their bargaining power with individual capitalists and in the labour market. The initial history of the labour movements in these three countries is a history of labour struggles against both capital and the state over this issue.[12] The state was opposed to the formation of unions and backed business when it was confronted by industrial action. It took a considerable number of years, many struggles and defeats and substantial changes in the organisation of production before trade unions were accorded both legal recognition and were treated by business as legitimate parts of the social order. In Britain this struggle started to be successful towards the end of the nineteenth century; in Germany, temporarily in Weimar and more permanently after the Second World War; in France, business's refusal to deal with trade unions persisted well past the various times that they were granted legal recognition. Indeed, in both France and Germany there has been a strong undercurrent of anti-union sentiment that affects most business/labour transactions. The determined character of state action against emerging trade unions contrasts with its faint hearted attempts to secure unfettered competition amongst businesses.

The principal features of the state in the liberal era are revealed more by the contrast with what came next. Despite the variety of state actions, both to set the framework for the economic operation of capitalist class relations and to intervene directly in the economy and in the relations between the classes, the boundaries between state and private sectors are quite clear. The state actually occupied very little space within the economy; its share in terms of ownership and output was far outweighed by private enterprises. This was even the case in Germany where the state had played the most economically active role.[13] The operations of the state sector were only loosely co-ordinated and did not compete with the viability of private and profit making enterprises and, indeed, there were many acts of state policy that aided these private firms. On the whole the state accepted the legitimacy and dominance of the private economy and only rarely acted to support a social purpose against the interests of short term profitability. It certainly did not co-ordinate society in ways that supplemented or replaced the operations of the market.

ISSUES IN THE LIBERAL ERA

A great number of different political and economic issues were prominent in this period. Many of these were associated with the consolidation of capitalist class relations and the massive social transformation that accompanied the rise of industry. Conditions and hours of work, public health and urban conditions, the consequences of workers' combination and bankruptcies, free trade and protection were some of the major issues. Underlying these was the basic question of the relationship between the state and economy and the limits of state action appropriate in a society dominated by the pursuit of private profit. The issues of the liberal era that contributed to its passing centred around the form of the state, representation and the extent of the franchise, and the appropriate state response to the problems generated by capital accumulation, the trade cycle and major periods of depression.

Representation and the franchise

With the exception of Germany, in which the authoritarian character of the state and the limited role for the elected assembly made debates about these matters irrelevant,[14] the question of representation and the extent of the franchise were important issues and decisive parts of the passage away from the assumptions on which

Issues in the liberal era 53

the liberal era was based. In many conventional accounts, in which the Victorian age is seen as being characterised by reform and social progress, the reform of parliament and the system of representation appears as the major achievement of the liberal age.[15] Instead, the measures that removed electoral abuses such as the buying and selling of seats, and gradually extended the franchise to adult males were all measures that started to undermine the assumptions of the liberal state and created some of the forces that lead to a change in the political form or character of the state. The liberal era, in its essence, was made possible by preventing the political representation of working people – by confining liberalism and representation to categories of property owners. The attempt by the disenfranchised to reform the system of representation was not just to add some democratic principles to existing liberal practices of the state nor to give its existing pattern of actions a legitimate basis. People struggled for the right to vote so that they could change the *actions* of that state, so that their presence *within* the political system would compel the state to alter the parameters of its action and concern and to reduce the amount of harm that the state, almost without pausing to reflect on the consequences, could do to them.

It has sometimes been argued that the institutions of representative democracy provide the ideal perfect complement to the class relations of capitalism embodied in the processes of production and accumulation, that democracy is capitalism's best political shell.[16] This is a position with both Marxist and free-market variants.[17] The course of developments in Britain, as described above, in France, in the proclamation of universal rights, their loss in periods of dictatorship and their gradual recreation at the end of the nineteenth century, and in Germany, in the even more protracted struggle to get rid of authoritarian rule, suggests that there is no inbuilt relationship between the capitalist organisation of the economy, capitalist class relations and the political form of the state. It is, of course, possible to assert that the representational form of the state has been an effective vehicle for class rule and the preservation of the conditions necessary for profitable private capital accumulation. Or that under some circumstances, dictatorship has proved just as useful. But that is not the same as proving that there is a necessary, as opposed to a historically contingent, association between capitalism and representational democracy.

The extension of the franchise did not occur because it would be a functional solution to problems of class rule, though elements of that were present in Tory reform proposals,[18] but because working-class men and women struggled for the right to vote and were successful in those struggles. Extending the franchise did not end capitalism and its exploitation of labour, a possibility assumed by radical democrats and occasionally by Marx and Engels.[19] This outcome too needs to be explained by considering both struggle and the impact of class relations and the economy on political processes. It can not be simply assumed that the structure of capitalist relations or the logic of accumulation possess magical powers that transform the consequences of political and class struggles so that they serve rather than damage the long-term interests of capital. Within the context of the liberal era with its distinctive combination of state and classes, the struggles of the disenfranchised unleashed within the political system forces and tendencies, such as the development of more efficient forms of party organisation, the potential for executive domination of parliamentary assemblies and changed perspectives for the actions of government, that presaged the passing of that form of capitalist social order. A new political regime was being shaped.

Problems of accumulation

It was not just the political struggles over representation and access to the state conditioning the passage away from a 'liberal' political regime. The economy did not develop smoothly. There were almost periodic economic crises taking the form of a business or trade cycle. The transition from merely bringing together the pre-existing parts of the industrial process under a single roof to a system based on investment in machine-based manufacturing was not without its complications. The working class struggle against the extension of the working day, plus the physical limits to extending the extraction of absolute surplus value, played a part in this transformation of the material basis of production. For capital to initiate such investment, funds needed to be concentrated and control centralised in some ways. Company law, after many bankruptcies and much debate, was changed to allow limited liability and the formation of joint stock companies and these measures helped to overcome some of the problems.

The major factor that undermined the institutional basis of the liberal era and provided the context in which the liberal political regime would pass away was the recurrence of economic downturns, trade slumps and market gluts. The classic form of these was the generalised overproduction of commodities and capital in relation to available consumers. Goods could be sold but not at prices that would realise profits. The prevalence of bankruptcies and the financial collapse of major ventures served both to revalue the capital base of these commodities, enabling them to be sold at lower prices and a profit, and to concentrate the holding of capital resources in fewer and fewer hands, thus serving the process of centralisation and concentration. It was out of such periodic economic crises that the organisations of businesses in cartels and trade associations grew, undermining the institutional basis of the liberal era. The sequence of problems coupled with the changing representative character of the state, created the framework within which liberal assumptions about the role of the state in the economy would no longer hold. Each successive assertion of the trade cycle added to the forces encouraging the state to take a more active role in the economy, to abandon the assumptions of the liberal era and, in doing so, reshape the working of political and economic processes and the relationships between them.

THE PASSING OF THE LIBERAL ORDER

Developments in the economy, in the process of accumulation, and in the political sphere, over the character of the state, combined to make the passing from a liberal to a more co-ordinated and managed capitalist order. For example, the first major extensions in franchise occurred in Britain in the last half of the nineteenth century, by which time similar arrangements were reemerging in France. The extension to include women did not come until much later. In Germany, authoritarian rule prevented such political developments until defeat in the First World War, and these were not really consolidated until the defeat in the Second World War. Nonetheless, in all three countries trade unions were beginning to win a substantial presence in these societies well before that war.[20] This changed some parts of class organisation but had only limited repercussions on the way in which the state acted and the relations between these class organisations and the state. Economic problems had encouraged new forms of class organisation, employer groups, trade associations and attempts to federate and increase the central organisation of industrial and business organisation.[21] Such changes did not, by themselves, alter the character of the connection between classes and the state, between politics and economics. What was decisive in changing the institutional framework within which classes and the state were organised and interacted – the political regime to secure both class rule and accumulation – was two world wars and the period of sharp boom and prolonged economic depression between them. These events, in the context of a rapid development of rival national centres of accumulation, particularly in the United States and Germany, increased imperial tensions between old and new capitalist powers, growing class organisation and perplexed responses by the state to these developments, opened the way for the final abandoning of the liberal workings of the political regime.

The European War of 1914–18 was a new kind of warfare which had a profound impact on the organisation of capitalism in Britain, France and Germany, the major combatants. Although the conflict grew out of diplomatic problems associated with the previous European war and the weakening of the old imperial empires, the struggle between capitals organised within a national framework gave the war its distinctive political character. The kind of war it was, with major confrontations between whole peoples mobilised into massive military combinations to batter each other in endless campaigns of trench warfare, was equally important. It was not just the length of the conflict nor the numbers wounded or killed in it that explains its prodigious consequences. Rather it was the extent to which this kind of war depended on the full mobilisation of economic and social resources. Though fighting the war tended to be based on the state buying what was needed, running up large domestic and international debts and boosting the fortunes of the armaments and related industries, production had to be dramatically increased and sustained. This required co-operation from both business and labour and some rudimentary forms of state co-ordination of production. As such it saw a great increase in the economic and social importance of the state.

The impact of war imperatives on the contending classes was dramatic. For the unions there was the possibility of trading co-operation for a greater degree of involvement in the political life of the nation, acceptability for war effort. It meant, of course, that the trade unions had to abandon any remnants of an international and socialist perspective for the comforts of patriotism and piecemeal reformism though this did not prove too difficult in any of the three countries. For delivering recruits to the war machine, and modifying economic demands, trade union officials were allowed to help run the war economy.[22] There was an equal abundance of rewards for capital, though none was as palatable as the money to be made from war time expansion. To help in its attempts to co-ordinate the economy and boost production the state encouraged those in business who sought the creation of more centralised business representation and strengthened trade associations. New central bodies to represent manufacturing industry were created and strengthened. The link between trade associations and cartels was made more acceptable and durable.[23] A whole new shape was given to the organised presence of business in the political sphere.

As a result of these changes the whole pattern of class and state interactions was transfigured. The state played an enhanced role but it did not replace the market as the main institution co-ordinating and shaping the pattern of economic and social development. Its increased importance was exercised *through* the market, as a consumer. The long term implications of this were less than if the state had ignored existing firms and had produced all the new weapons and military facilities in its own right. Nonetheless, the balance of classes within society was changed in the course of the war, if only for a short time. Labour was more of a force to be reckoned with *inside* capitalist society, and there appeared the possibility that the trade unions would exact a lasting price for their cooperation. Some state officials were emboldened to think that there would be a similarly enhanced role for them in the post-war period.[24] Such ambitions (by both the state and labour) were challenges to the power and dominance of business in the economy, a challenge that had to be met.

Arrangements made in war conditions are fragile and are easily dismantled. In this context business groups began to campaign to have the state return to its previously restricted sphere and to reduce the political importance of trade unions. This was not a straightforward task. In the uncertainty that prevailed and with the image of the Bolshevik revolution before them, business groups wanted to ensure a period of social peace in which they could regroup to reassert their dominant influence on society. In Germany, France and Britain, business groups all negotiated with their respective trade union movements agreements of quite radical kinds, granting trade union recognition, shorter working hours, better working conditions and improved standards of living.[25] These agreements frequently bypassed state structures, and often occurred behind the backs of existing business organisations. When war ended the struggle to weaken labour's ability to make these claims began. In France and Britain, and to a lesser extent, given the novelty of a new republican and representative political system, in Germany, the state returned to its broad liberal assumptions. The succession of rapid boom and equally rapid economic downturn did the rest. The trade unions could be successfully ignored and the agreements became irrelevant. This weakening of the working class can be seen in the rapid erosion of its insurrectionary ambitions symbolised by the breaking of the social implications of the general strike. In France and Britain, trade union attempts to call general strikes failed in 1920 and 1926. In Germany, the tactic was sufficiently effective to prevent the success of the Kapp Putsch with the prospect of a return to authoritarian rule, though the trade unions were either unwilling or unable to impose their reform programme on the new government.[26] From this point, it was a downward path to the success of Hitler and the brief and ignominious attempts to protect their organisations by seeking an accommodation with the Nazi Party.[27]

Even without a major inter-war depression the liberal order was probably doomed. By the time it began, forms of class organisations existed to press for responses to their problems in both the economic and the political sphere. The time of liberal capitalism and unfettered competition between a myriad of capitalist firms was past. The new reality was of cartels, monopolies and trade associations on one side, and on the other, better organised and more centrally co-ordinated trade unions. The state could no longer ignore the consequences of its actions for the bulk of the population as representative institutions were the order of the day. Nonetheless, the simple presence of those factors that rendered the liberal order obsolete were not sufficient for it to pass away. The depression and various government experiments were decisive in moving the system from one form of political regime to another.[28]

The economic depression, though it appeared in different countries at different times, showed surprisingly similar problems had appeared in the process of accumulation.[29] The depression took the form of an intensified collapse of trade – a more dramatic version of the normal downturn of the business cycle. Growth fell, unemployment increased, profits were squeezed, there were a large number of bankruptcies and, in the midst of all this, a few new industries developed and prospered – mostly associated with car production.[30] Within this economic downturn there were many problems about the structure of the capitalist economy and the relations between the various sectors and parts of the production, circulation and accumulation process. The older industries were declining; the technologies employed, the technical efficiency of the plants, the geographic structure of firms were often outmoded and in need of investment, modernisation and rationalisation.[31] Agriculture was a source of major problems, overproducing in competitive markets and involving too much of the labour of the economy. The problems of the depression displaced rural labour and moved it to the cities where it was available to be hired at cheap rates. The exception was France where labour stayed on the small family-owned farms and was sheltered from the direct impact of the recession. This in turn may have contributed to the lack of dynamism in the French economy.[32] The banking system was under pressure: some banks collapsed and others needed government assistance, as in Germany.[33] Problems were also evident in the relationship between banks and the investment and borrowing requirements of industry.[34] Severe problems also appeared in international trade and protection was one response.[35] Though governments responded to the depression in different ways there was one common element. All solutions were designed to boost domestic production and to win a larger share of international trade. In this way internal problems were projected into the international environment and prepared the ground for the Second World War.

In Britain, France and Germany this period saw major experiments, fragmented and contradictory in character, move away from the liberal arrangements of the past. This, coupled with the Second World War, created forces and institutions that broke old patterns of state class relations and made it difficult for the liberal assumptions to be recreated. It is useful to consider the different ways in which the assumptions of the liberal era were abandoned in these years.

In Britain, the post-First World War attempt to recreate the old liberal era was based on a return to the gold standard parity of sterling at its pre-war level. This policy was a failure, aggravating problems in the coal industry and prompting the General Strike and preparing the way for the economy to move into depression.[36] When the gold standard was abandoned so were key assumptions of the liberal era. Free trade was given up as tariffs were granted to particular industries in return for pledges that they would develop adequate cartel and trade association structures to rationalise these industries and boost investment.[37] Here the state intervened in the economy to promote the formation of strongly organised business groups in order to impose a redirection of investment and production. Such efforts, despite the considerable assistance of the Bank of England, were not successful in re-envigorating the economy, though the cartel and trade association policies could secure profits even in hard times. This 'intervention' by the state was neither systematic nor comprehensive and although liberal assumptions were being modified in practice, business sought to preserve as much of them as possible in its campaign for industrial self government.[38] The economic mobilisation for the Second World War, based as it was on close government and business co-operation (including the incorporation of business figures and trade associations into the state structure) and the close involvement of the Labour Party and the trade unions, reinforced those factors that were tending to move society away from the liberal era.[39]

In France the situation was slightly different. The initial government response to the depression was to cut government expenditure and to reduce wages.[40] This did not work. As stagnation continued the polarisation of French politics intensified and various ultra-nationalist groups mobilised against the institutions of the Third Republic. Learning something from the events in Germany, the French trade union movement worked to secure some form of anti-fascist unity and paved the way for the formation of a Popular Front. This was an electoral alliance of the Socialist Party, the Communist Party and the Radical Party designed to block the chances of fascism gaining a hold in the French political system. It came to office in 1936, in the midst of extraordinary scenes as millions of workers occupied their factories and sought major economic and social gains.[41] As a result, Popular Front legislation passed through the hostile upper house and an agreement was reached between union officials and some parts of organised business to recognise trade unions and improve levels of wages and work conditions. The Popular Front government was not seeking to transform capitalism but to find ways to make it work successfully and to ameliorate the social hardship experienced as a result of the depression. Unfortunately, the government did not have a very effective economic programme combining attempts to reduce employment, shorten working hours and not to increase government spending and borrowing.[42] No special attention was paid to the importance of investment and its economic strategy was bound to fail. Faced with incredible problems of balancing its desire for world peace with the need to oppose fascism at home and abroad with an impossible economic programme, the government was bound to fall.

The Popular Front was one of the weakest attempts to try to solve the problems of the depression by altering the relations between classes and the state. Preparation for the Popular Front stressed the importance of trade union organisation and labour unity.[43] The Matignon Agreement encouraged further trade union organisation but the fate of the government lowered morale. The Agreement was seen by significant sections of business as proof of their weakness and encouraged the strengthening of their organisations.[44] Those who had negotiated were repudiated and the central organisation was completely reformed to make it more effective in the political sphere. Business wanted to redress the balance between itself and labour and to have 'revenge' for Matignon.

The capitulation of France and the installation of the collaborationist Vichy regime saw a severe reworking of class-state relations.[45] Nothing was done to alter the defining class relations of capitalism but great attention was paid to their organised expression. Partly on the basis of indigenous trends towards corporatism and partly to ape the fashions of their military masters, the Vichy regime abhorred class conflict and sought to reorganise class and state institutions in such a way that social harmony would prevail. A system of state sponsored business and labour organisations was created under the co-ordination of state officials. The new rulers closed down the old trade unions and attempted to create responsible and subordinate labour organisations.[46] As resistance increased these were colonised by the old trade unions and used as vehicles to press the claims of labour against collaboration. Though the various trade associations and the employers federations were formally closed, business had a very strong presence in the new structures and in the Vichy government itself.[47] In fact, the Vichy period was one in which business was able to improve the effectiveness of its organisation and to reach an accommodation with the state over matters which included planning of output and investment. Kuisel has gone so far as to stress the strong parallels between the plans formulated under Vichy and the actual planning process established by Monnet after the war.[48] The subjection of the French economy to the war needs of the German occupiers partially rationalised the economy and in this way made the post-war transformation of industrial production more possible.[49]

The period of Popular Front government and of Vichy moved the organisation of classes and the relations between them away from the liberal past. The future was not in any sense fixed but there were strong indications that the ways in which classes were organised, the relations between classes and the state, and the parameters of state policy were being reworked.

The Nazi dictatorship in Germany completely opposed the liberal framework of class state relations which they saw as a source of national division and weakness characteristic of the detested Weimar Republic. In power they completely reshaped class organisations and changed the role and power of the state. As the Nazi Party rose to power, the unions sought a compromise[50] but they were destroyed and replaced by hollow organisations subordinate to the party, the state and management.[51] This effectively reduced the political presence of labour within the system. Despite repression, a degree of underground opposition to Hitler continued as did less formal forms of workers' opposition.[52] Leaving aside the debate on the relationship between the rise of Hitler and the actions of various firms and business groups within the New Order,[53] business and its organisations were reshaped to fit the new authoritarian framework, though, as in France, this often worked to improve the professional efficiency of these bodies.[54] The Nazi Party had sought to dominate the economy and big business and to apply the same degree of co-ordination to business as labour. Their dictatorial power was sufficient to guarantee business co-operation though sometimes this interfered with its ability to fulfil efficiently the economic demands of the Nazi state. There are two matters that need to be noted here. Firstly, the Nazi state had to reach an accommodation with business to pursue their social and national ambitions.[55] They had to drop many parts of their avowed purpose and their anti-capitalist rhetoric. This is noted in the literature, frequently on the basis of the Nazis' need to mobilise support from the middle strata of society which, having gained power, they could ignore. In making this interpretation the residual power of private business is lost. Even under the conditions of dictatorship, the Nazis had to reach accommodation with business as a significant social force. Secondly, after protracted, muted disputes, business was able to weaken the application of the 'leadership principle' to their discussions and dealings.[56] This certainly made them different from labour and gave them a different place within the regime.

The Nazi Party altered the way in which the principal classes were organised and the workings of their relationships with the state. Labour was subjugated and subordinated with their autonomous institutions crushed. There may have been some resistance and opposition but insufficient to seriously weaken the German war effort. Even where local Nazi representatives spoke on behalf of workers[57] this was not a way of labour having an 'informal' voice within the system. At its best worker opposition took advantage of the state of the labour market to press for some easing of the pressure. Business, by contrast, was within the system and able to play a political role. It was, for the most part, able to protect its right to private ownership, private control of production and private profitability. It also had the advantage of a workforce that could turn to neither the state nor to its own organisations to pursue its claims in the workplace. This was a security it had not enjoyed in the Weimar Republic. The state had increased its power and its control through dictatorship. It could give orders with the expectation that they would be obeyed and it could certainly shape economic developments to suit its definition of national purpose. It is significant that this dictatorial power was not consistently used against business; on the whole and for most of their rule, it did not need to be.

Some authors see in this new arrangement of class and state, politics and economics the creation of a non-capitalist type of society, with the market completely subjected to the dictates of the state and with capital damaged by the increased power of the state.[58] Though it is true that Nazi party members used their place in the state system to gain control of parts of the economy as their private property,[59] that is they used state position to make themselves private capitalists, and that the state made business invest in areas where they might not otherwise have invested, it is not clear that such actions did great damage to private capital or was against their interests.[60] Losing the war was different but in preparing for and fighting it, private business was guaranteed a quiescent workforce without union leadership and secure levels of profitability. With the memory of Weimar Germany and in the midst of an international depression, these opportunities did not seem unattractive.[61]

The extent to which the state 'took over' the economy can be exaggerated. Direction and purchase were combined and the legitimacy of private profitability was not challenged. Karl Hardach summarises the situation in the following terms:

> Management and risk of business were to be left in the hands of private individuals to maintain personal initiative and enterprise. Excessively egoistic pursuit of private interest was, however, to be restrained by the massive machinery of 'responsible economic self-administration' by an array of state officials watching over compliance with innumerable instructions and orders . . . Though certainly not frictionless, the German economic machine worked and worked quite well, on a narrowly economic level, compared to other economic systems of the time. The organizational setup described enabled planning without a fixed plan and the continued use of the price mechanism as an economic steering device, aiming at a balance between adaptability and stability.[62]

Although Hardach presents this as an attempt to build 'an alternative to capitalism and communism', he describes the political attempt to go beyond liberalism and liberal assumptions which has been identified as characteristic of the political responses to the inter-war depression.

Weimar was such a brief interlude of liberalism between two periods of authoritarian rule. Nonetheless the Nazi alternative was not as substantial a change as is often thought. The state co-ordinated its policies with business and used state purchase as often as other means to get what it wanted from private owners. Further, this alternative to liberalism was unstable and could only work on the basis of conquest and the subjugation of working class organisations.

CONCLUSION

The significance of the incomplete changes of the inter-war period can be seen by considering two other assessments of this period. Fine and Harris present a version of the standard competitive, monopoly, state-monopoly-capitalism account and, in doing so, say something about the passage away from the liberal order. Although Fine and Harris do not illustrate their broad account with too much historical detail, their arguments do have implications for the assessment of the inter-war period.[63] Their approach generates a passage from liberal to monopoly capitalism, to state-monopoly capitalism: the liberal era (in Britain at least) refers to the early years of the nineteenth century and the state-monopoly era to that after the Second World War. Monopoly capitalism then refers to the period between the legal reduction of the working day and the rise of monopolies and the end of the Second World War and hence, embraces the inter-war period. In Fine and Harris's account the development of a 'new stage' depends on a combination of 'the general laws of the accumulation of capital'[64] (the economic) and the political organisation and representation of classes (the political). The form in which this political aspect is discussed is significant.

> ... the transformation of economic relations is not all that is involved. The development of the monopoly stage of capitalism requires that the working class struggles for the limitation of the working day prove successful. This presupposes the political representation of working-class interests and can have the additional effects of moderating class struggle.[65]

At the theoretical level it is not clear that monopoly forms of capitalist organisation do depend upon the political organisation and representation of the working class. The German and Japanese experience suggests that the relationship is not as close as Fine and Harris assume. Fine and Harris's theorising depends on an implicit account of British developments. In this context what is chiefly altered by the political changes they note is the potential range and character of state action. The period between the wars is not best treated as exemplifying a new stage of monopoly capitalism but as a transition period full of fragmented, incoherent, incomplete and unstable attempts to alter the political regime of industrial capitalism, attempts which fail to escape from previous (largely market) forms of social co-ordination. Their account does not take seriously the kinds of political changes that were involved in making this process, the extensive struggles for the vote, for trade unions with a degree of legal protection, for trade union based political parties capable of gaining substantial electoral support. Nor do they appreciate sufficiently the important historical variation and its consequence for the development of new class organisations with their new objectives. Given their view of the state they also miss the significant developments in the political organisation of business and fail to assess the extent to which the problem of business and business demands also showed the passage away from liberal and market forces of social co-ordination.

In 'Breaking with orthodoxy: the politics of economic policy responses to the Depression of the 1930s',[66] Peter Gourevitch has explored the similarities and differences between government responses to the inter-war depression in the United States, Britain, France, Germany and Japan. His explanation is based on the division in national economic activity between a domestic and international orientation and the level of labour intensity. This is then linked to the ability of sections of business and labour to construct coalitions to underpin changed patterns of state activity. Leaving aside this question of explanatory logic which is only lightly sketched, it is instructive to consider how he characterises the crucial changes in economic policy.

Gourevitch sets out the changes in terms of a reorientation of government economic policy necessitated by the failure to find an adequate response to conditions of the depression. In his account there were different (but related) policy responses – economic orthodoxy – neo-orthodoxy ('devaluation of the currency, tariffs, and some corporatistic regulation of domestic markets'), and a more radical departure – 'demand stimulus through deficit spending' or 'state-dominant corporatistic regulation of the domestic economy'.[67]

The successful end product of this interwar experimentation he describes as the 'social democratic' compromise which

... is built around a set of economic policies that combine Keynesian demand management, an open international economy, trade union autonomy in labour markets, private control of capital in both investment and management, and subsidies for agriculture.[68]

His analysis tries to link the sectoral composition of the economy with the situation of various social actors and hence to explain the range of policy options and thus to understand the forces shaping the eventual policy outcomes.[69] In doing so he identifies the key question in these terms:

> Why did some countries stop the policy sequence with neo-orthodoxy while others went on to demand stimulus? Descriptively, this means examining what the support coalitions of Nazi Germany, social-democratic Sweden, and New Deal America have in common that enabled more extensive breaks with orthodoxy than occurred in France (save for a few months of the Blum Government) and the United Kingdom.[70]

The answer he gives is summarised thus:

> The demand-stimulus coalitions of Sweden, the United States, and Germany were, in sum, *cross-sector, cross-class* alliances of groups whose patience with market solutions had run out. In each case farmers made de facto or explicit alliances with certain sectors of business who were themselves seeking to help to break from economic orthodoxy, and with certain elements of labor willing to alter old habits to bring about change. In Sweden and the United States, the labor component of this alliance was provided by the labor organizations themselves. In Germany, of course, it was not, as the union movement was crushed.[71]

Gourevitch emphasises the divisions within both business and labour and sees the policy initiatives taken by government as some expression of coalitions constructed by these 'cross-sector', 'cross-class' alliances. Much is revealed by Gourevitch's comments on the importance of pursuing the assumptions of the 'interest groups' analysis of policy. But Gourevitch goes too far in his usage and devalues the importance of the political process itself. Gourevitch is correct in noting that an understanding of the significance of policy initiatives is enhanced by a knowledge of the 'situations' of social actors. This is so. Knowledge of the problems faced and the alternative strategies which groups propose to respond to these problems does make it easier to assess the significance of the measures introduced by governments. Difficulties occur when the distance between problems and proposed solutions is collapsed to suggest that in practice the actual policies are in fact the sign that coalitions successfully imposed these within the political processes. This weakens the interpretation of the political process and almost completely obscures the role of the state as an institutional entity with problems that flow from its 'situation' in the economy and in society. It is just this weakness that is evident in the summary accounts of each country and the coalitions that support or block the development of the deficit spending policy orientation. This is most clearly evident in the account of Nazi Germany and its treatment of the role of labour and the characterisation of their policy package as one of 'state-dominant corporatistic regulation of the domestic economy'. The formal and rhetorical elements subsume the understanding of the historical struggles, victories and defeats, of groups, class organisations, political parties and the institutions of the state.

The image that Gourevitch uses is that of United States electoral politics in which the nature of the two party system, voluntary voting and regional differences makes it both possible and necessary for different 'interest groups' to form coalitions in the construction of both political parties and electoral victories. Hence the decisive importance of the New Deal coalition constructed by Roosevelt in his victory over Hoover and in his subsequent re-election to the presidency. The political processes in inter-war Britain, France and Germany were not of a similar kind and the coalitions perceived in the change in government economic policy were not 'responsible', in any active sense, for the changes. This is not to deny the importance of classes and class based organisations in the process. Rather, the point must be to stress the extent to which their impact is mediated by the struggles in the electoral and other processes between political parties and the perceptions and concerns of the different parts of the state bureaucracies. It is the complex interactions between these that make the distinctive national responses to the shared problems of the inter-war depression (bearing in mind that that depression came at different times and in different forms to each of the countries under consideration). Only by noting this is it possible to recognise the importance of the Nazi regime's destruction of the trade union movement; or the Blum government's failure to protect the position of French workers against the threat of a war with Germany (despite being committed to anti-fascism); or the consequences of

Conclusion 69

the return to the Gold Standard in Britain and the trade union response to it.

Gourevitch measures the changes through patterns of economic policy summed up in phrases like 'demand stimulus through deficit spending'. But this policy package is, in turn, only a shorthand summary of changes in the size of the state, the range of its actions and its relationship with classes and class organisations. This is the reality behind his 'social-democratic compromise' which is not an attitude to public policy or the range of state action but is a reorganisation of the relationship between classes and the state. It was that reorganisation which was begun in the inter-war period and which was incomplete in all three countries of this study as well as in the United States, whose war-time policies were as important for refining the initiatives of the New Deal as they were in Europe for preparing the way for a more effective reorganisation of political regime.

If the period from the 1840s to the 1940s is considered it is possible to note major changes in the way in which capitalist societies are organised. Although the basic class relations remain the same, quite complex histories give the classes distinctive organisational forms. Labour acquires trade unions and some kind of political representation through the formation of social democratic or labour parties. Capital acquires organisation through cartels, monopolies, trade associations and employer groups. Capital does not normally create a political party in its own image to overcome the problems of the rise of working-class political parties. It either works through existing political groups or relies on its domination of the economy for its influence. The state, too, changes, both in terms of its representative character, with the exception of Nazi Germany, and the scope of its actions in the economy and in society. The hundred year period is one of the progressive undermining of the key economic, political and class characteristics of the liberal era, the appearance of institutions and organisations that are largely incompatible with the liberal era but whose mere fact of existence is not enough to bring it to an end. These elements need to be combined such that the liberal restrictions on the scope of state action are no longer effective with class and state organisations linked in a new and definite pattern. The years since the end of the nineteenth century saw some progress in the search for that distinctive form of class and state organisation, for the establishment of a new political regime that would secure both class rule and accumulation. Two clear departures, Vichy France and Nazi Germany, appeared: neither found the solution, though both contained parts of what was subsequently required to build the new political regime.

NOTES

1. MacPherson (1964; 1978).
2. Thompson (1972); Foster (1974).
3. Hence Adam Smith's celebrated comments on business collusion.
4. It was this which gave Marx's argument over the functional role of periodic crises its potency.
5. The literature on business organisation outlines this pre-history. See Blank (1973), chap. 1; Braunthal (1965), chap. 1; Ehrmann (1957), chap. 1.
6. Taylor (1978).
7. Therborn (1977).
8. See, for example, the account of the liberal state given in Fine and Harris (1979).
9. Henderson (1958); Veblen (1964); Baum (1958); Kindleberger (1964).
10. For accounts of the relationship between the state and cartels and early forms of business organisation in the nineteenth century, see Ehrmann (1957); Brizay (1975), chap. 1.
11. Henderson (1958); Veblen (1964); Stolper (1967), Pt. 1.
12. Abendroth (1972).
13. Stolper (1967), p. 43, notes that 'the Republic thus inherited from the Monarchy a peculiar economic system of mixed ownership in which, in the aggregate, the sector of public ownership did not rank far behind'. But it was largely infrastructural industry and raw material supplies that were in the hands of the state and, though there were state owned industries and state owned farms, private production was predominant.
14. It was not until the rise of the Weimar Republic that adult male franchise came into existence and representative institutions assumed any significance.
15. See Briggs (1969).
16. Jessop (1978) provides an interesting discussion of the problem.
17. See Friedman (1965); Holloway and Picciotto (1978).
18. Miliband (1982), chap. 2.
19. Rosenberg (1965).
20. Kuisel (1981), chap. 1; Braunthal (1978), pp. 31ff; Macdonald (1976), chap. 8.
21. These were not just paper bodies, though not as formidable as they were to become. Nor were they just the creation of governments for administrative convenience. The argument made by Grant and Marsh

for British developments could be applied to the others. See Grant and Marsh (1977), chap. 1.
22. Tivey (ed.), (1925), chap. XII; Wrigley (1976).
23. Kuisel (1981); Turner (1984), pp. 33-49.
24. See Kuisel's account of the fate of the post-war plans of A. Thomas and Etienne Clementel in France, Kuisel (1981), chap. 2.
25. Feldman (1970); For Britain see the attitude of the Labour Committee of the Federation of British Industries in Blank (1973); for later agreements of this type see Milne-Bailey (1929), pp. 430-1; and Brizay (1975), p. 30ff.
26. Braunthal (1978), pp. 42ff.
27. *Ibid.*, pp. 70ff.
28. For two contrasting accounts of government responses to the inter-war depression, see Gourevitch (1984), pp. 95-129; Born (1972).
29. Good discussions of the inter-war depression are rare. See Robbins (1934); Van Der Wee (1972); Flamant and Singer-Kerel (1970), chap. 2.
30. This characteristic feature of depressions can appear as a paradox and give rise to the view that 'bad times were really good': see Stevenson and Cook (1977).
31. Rationalisation, the reorganisation of production along scientific, rational lines to promote efficiency, was a key word of the 1920s and 1930s. See Brady (1933).
32. Kuisel (1981), pp. 94ff; Kemp (1972).
33. Stolper (1967), pp. 123-4.
34. Revealed, for example, in the long enquiry into the Bank of England and its response to the problems of industry; see Sayers (1976), vols 1, 2 and appendixes.
35. Kindleberger (1973); Hodson (1938).
36. For a succinct summary of what the return to the Gold Standard achieved, see Gould, Mills and Stewart (1981), pp. 82-3.
37. The key example was the response to the problems of the iron and steel industry. See Burn (1940), chap. XVI.
38. Brady (1943).
39. For an example of how this worked, see Hurstfield (1953).
40. Kemp (1972).
41. Lefranc (1965); Pickles (1938); Pritt (1941).
42. For a critique of the Popular Front policies, see Kalecki (1938).
43. Ehrmann (1947), chap. II; Lorwin (1966), pp. 67ff.
44. Ehrmann (1957), chap. 1. The text of the agreement is included as an appendix.
45. Kuisel (1981), pp. 128ff.
46. Ehrmann (1947), chaps. X, XII, XIII and IX; Lorwin (1966), chap. VI.
47. Ehrmann (1957), chap. II; Brizay (1975), p. 50ff.
48. Kuisel (1981), p. 155.
49. Freymond (1974); Milward (1970).
50. Braunthal (1978), pp. 70ff; Grebing (1969), p. 137.
51. Brady (1937), chap. IV; Roll (1939), pp. 103ff.
52. Mason (1981) gives an account of evidence which shows a range of

means by which some workers resisted the attempts by the Nazis to increase production in preparation for war. For an account which seeks to interpret this as a form of class resistance, see Salter (1983), pp. 88–116.
53. See especially, Turner (1985).
54. Brady (1937), chaps IX and X.
55. Geyer (1986), pp. 38–9.
56. Geyer (1984), pp. 204ff. Geyer argues that after 1933 industry was able to carve out a sphere of semi-autonomy. See also Grunberger (1971), chap. 12.
57. Mason (1981), p. 123.
58. Milward (1976). For a previous criticism of this view see Neuhman (1942).
59. Woolston (1941), p. 34.
60. For a counter view see Block (1980), pp. 233–4.
61. This is even evident in the account of H. A. Turner whose work seeks to reassess the links between big business and the Nazi Party and to reduce the significance of the relationship that was perceived by opponents of the rise of the Nazi Party at the time. See Turner (1985), Schweitzer (1964).
62. Hardach (1980), pp. 66–7.
63. Fine and Harris (1979), chap. 7.
64. *Ibid.*, p. 106.
65. *Ibid.*, p. 118.
66. Gourevitch (1984), pp. 95–130.
67. *Ibid.*, p. 95.
68. *Ibid.*, p. 63.
69. *Ibid.*, p. 65.
70. *Ibid.*, p. 65.
71. *Ibid.*, p. 66.

3 · THE POST-WAR RECONSTRUCTION OF THE REGIME

In the first five to six years after the end of the Second World War there were major changes in the relations between classes and state and the political and economic systems in western Europe. Aware of what followed the First World War, governments acted to avoid the return to slump conditions. Those factors which weakened liberal assumptions in the inter-war period were significant for the reorganisation of the political regime which now occurred. The ways in which classes were organised into the political process were substantially modified as was the state's relationship with the economy (and the rest of society). This chapter explores the major aspects of this post-war reconstruction and reorganisation of the political regime; the nationalisation of some sectors of the productive economy, the rise of forms of economic (and sometimes, social) planning and the extension of the state provision of welfare. On this basis it is possible to assess the part played by different classes, class organisations and political parties in this profound reshaping of the working relationship between the political order and the process of capital accumulation.

There are a number of problems involved in presenting the argument about this period, mostly caused by the need to explain the distinct paths travelled in the different countries to reach the similar situation of a reconstructed regime. For the purpose of this chapter, I have taken Britain as the point of departure and have added commentaries on what happened in France and Germany to illustrate alternative ways in which the reorganised relationship between the state and classes, the political system and the economy was achieved.

NATIONALISATION

The period of the first majority Labour Government in British politics saw the culmination of a long campaign for the nationalisation of what were treated as the 'commanding heights' of the British economy: the Bank of England, the coal mines, railways and the steel industry.[1] The identification of the 'commanding heights' was strongly conditioned by the experience of the inter-war depression, and those sections of capital which had seemed most responsible for worsening the plight of working people: the Bank of England, whose governor, Montagu Norman, had pressed so strongly for the return to the Gold Standard;[2] the coal mines, whose owners had inflicted such a bitter defeat on the miners in the aftermath of the 1926 General Strike, the railways, whose owners had seemed as indifferent to the problems of their workforce as to the investment requirements of their industry; the iron and steel industry, symbolising the evils of British capitalism as the owners fixed production levels to protect profits while condemning whole regions to high levels of unemployment.[3] Onto these deeply felt grievances had been grafted arguments about the possibility of using state action to modernise and expand the British economy. The writings of Jay and Dalton in the inter-war years suggested linking nationalisation of parts of the economy, justified in terms of achieving socialism, to concerted state efforts to promote economic growth.[4] Within the labour movement, as the long struggle for nationalisation went on, this second strand came to predominate in the argument about what nationalisation was for, how nationalised enterprises should be staffed, organised and conducted, especially in regard to other, still privately owned, capitalist enterprises. The bitter memories of the Depression were harnessed to the Morrisonian conception of the 'public corporation' and the attempts to revitalise the British economy on the basis of state action to assist private capital.[5]

The actual nationalisations undertaken by the Labour Government reveal an important pattern. The Bank of England was nationalised only to the extent that it was given official status as a central and reserve bank.[6] It was still the central pivot of the private banking structure and although the governor was appointed by the government, the Bank retained considerable independence. The quasi-nationalisation of the Bank of England did not end the

Bank's ability to press for orthodox financial policies. Indeed, the long experience of Bank advice since then would tend to suggest the nationalisation has had little impact on the policy attitudes of the banking system. What nationalisation did achieve was a modernisation and centralisation of the banking system which did not attune it to the needs of domestic industry. A number of energy sources were taken from fragmented municipal and private hands and centralised under the guise of nationalisation. Electricity and gas generation were the main examples – but water supply was treated in a similar manner.[7] Key parts of the transport system were nationalised, basically the railways and road transport (later denationalised).[8] The coal industry was nationalised as, at a much later date, and after a major struggle, was the iron and steel industry.[9] The steel industry was denationalised in the 1950s.

This pattern of state initiative represented a major movement by the state into the production and circulation of commodities in a capitalist economy *without* challenging the dominance of private ownership. Nationalisation only affected a small percentage of total industrial production and left the major parts of the financial, manufacturing and retail systems in private hands. Compensation was always adequate and often generous.[10] Those industries taken over were unprofitable and often required extensive investment to modernise their facilities. The exceptions were road transport and parts of the steel industry, both of which were denationalised. All industries nationalised produced either goods or services for private firms in other parts of the economy. As such, the nationalisation programme created a situation in which the state increased its presence in the economy through the ownership of some parts of the *infrastructure* of that economy. The organisational structure of the nationalised industries did nothing to reduce the separation of labour from management and did little to increase the role of workers in the running of the state owned concerns.[11] The rules under which they traded were designed to ensure that consumers of products, most importantly private business, were not exploited.[12] These industries were funded so that they could undertake large investment programmes on the basis of access to their tax revenue and state guaranteed loans.[13] Pricing policy was used to transfer resources to the private sector at less than their economic cost as a form of indirect subsidy.[14] The relationship between the state and private sectors was not antagonistic: the state sought to co-ordinate the efforts of its sector with the needs and requirements of private capital. Even though nationalisation reduced the area in which private capital could be invested, the state sector remained subordinate to the private sector and serviced some of its more general needs.

In France the expansion of state ownership happened in a different way. French business, with its close links to the Vichy Regime and the occupying Nazi authorities, was in a weak position to oppose Resistance demands that the state take over significant sections of the economy.[15] The desire to punish collaboration and to control the commanding heights of the French economy combined in unusual ways.[16] The Renault car firm was nationalised, without compensation, as retribution for the Renault family's flirtations with Nazism, and so the state had an immediate, though isolated, presence in manufacturing industry. The major banks and financial institutions were taken, giving a certain coherence to the financial structure, and parts of the infrastructure of energy and transport were also nationalised. Despite this different pattern of state ownership, the total size of the state owned sector was no greater than in Britain. The fragmented patterns of state ownership with its financial and manufacturing concerns meant that the relationship between the private and public sectors of the economy could not be as neat and simple as in Britain. The potential for greater state intervention in the private economy was there but the rules under which state owned enterprises were run ensured that such concerted efforts were infrequent.[17] Nationalised firms were to be run as much like private firms as possible and indeed state-owned firms could spend any financial surpluses earned in any way they liked with only occasional instances of state direction. Whereas in Britain the very rules for the conduct of the state owned sector revealed the basis for the co-ordination of the two sectors of the economy, in France the emphasis was displaced onto the system of 'indicative' planning.

For Germany, the whole discussion is complicated by the heritage of Weimar collapse and the Nazi dictatorship. It is not a matter of considering the way in which the state *expanded* into the economy but the extent and character of its *withdrawal*. The close relationship between industry and the banks, coupled with the state guarantees for the banking system in the Weimar period, meant that, when the banks collapsed, the state was left in possession of large sections of the German financial and industrial economy.[18] The Nazi era saw a consolidation of the state's position in the economy with a degree of 'reprivatisation' into the hands of party figures and trusted associates. State direction of the economy was extensive in the Nazi era and as the war deteriorated state controls on production, investment and consumption became increasingly evident. Hence, at the end of the war, with the destruction of the Nazi Party and with business discredited for its support of the regime, it could have been a simple matter for a socialist trade union movement to have consolidated its position and for the state to be run along socialist lines. Nothing so obvious or simple occurred. Germany was split in half by the occupation of the allies and in the western sectors the dominant part in the anti-Russian coalition was played by the United States of America.[19] The whole western zone was dismembered and reconstructed and business once more secured its place in West German society. Though denazification ought to have had some impact on the structure of the private economy, especially with the removal of Nazis and their business supporters, it did not. For example, the great arms manufacturers, Krupps, did not lose their economic position, nor did the great chemical combines, though they were forced to divest some of their more unsavoury and/or blatant military activities.[20] The Nazi era's extension of the power and role of the state was treated as the key evil of its age and hence policy was designed to reduce the size of the state sector and to limit its influence on the economy. Reconstruction was undertaken on the basis of 'neo-liberalism' and the creation of a 'social-market economy'.[21]

How far was the role of the state reduced in the economy and in society? Did the commitment to 'neo-liberalism' recreate or, given the history of capitalist development in Germany, create a society in which market relations dominated all economic activity with the state reduced to some minor part? The evidence is incomplete but what there is suggests that the policies of neo-liberalism in Germany, the selling off of state owned assets, reduced the presence of the state in the German economy to the same level reached by the increased size of the state through nationalisation in Britain and France. Wallich, in *Mainsprings of the German Revival*, notes that in the early 1950s the state consumed, transferred and invested some 35 per cent of the GDP.[22] He lists the ingredients of the nationalised sector in the following way:

... it includes the railroads and the most local transportation, a large part of the utilities, telegraph, telephone, and radio, the savings banks, and quite a few industrial enterprises, including Germany's star performer of recent years, the Volkswagen Works.[23] The number of workers employed by the industrial enterprises alone exceeds 200,000.[24]

Such a state owned sector is not radically different from that in either Britain or France. Its formal structure may have lacked coherence, complicated as it was by federalism and the relatively greater role given to local government. What does make the situation in Germany different is the ideology used to frame government policy over investment and public sector policies. Neo-liberalism as a doctrine made it difficult for the state to justify massive investments in basic industries when other forms of more direct assistance could be turned into profits by private firms.[25] As regards the size of the economic activities of the state and its owernship of the different parts of the economy, a rough equivalence was created in the years after 1945 in Britain, France and Germany.

ECONOMIC PLANNING

The fact of an increase in the size of the state owned sector, though important in itself, is not so significant as the way in which it was connected to the dominant, privately-owned part of the capitalist economy. To what extent did the increased size of the state sector increase the influence of the state on the economy as a whole? Did state action replace the market as the major form of social co-ordination? If it did not, how was state action co-ordinated with a predominant market mechanism? Further, how did this reworking of the relationship between the political and economic systems affect class organisations and their relationship with the state? Given that the most distinctive changes occurred in France, it is useful to start with that example.

In the period after the Second World War, a new system of planning was introduced in France that was neither centralised nor based on authoritative commands. The frequent use of the name 'indicative planning' emphasised the extent to which the Commissariat du Plan suggested targets and policies without being able to demand compliance with them. In theory, the system worked on the basis of a statistical survey of enterprises with this information related to a given set of growth targets. Policies were then suggested to make these targets more easily obtainable.[26] Business was involved in the discussions at all times; trade unions had much less influence and their attitudes to the planning process varied greatly.[27] The Plan existed as a document without legal backing and with no body of officials to see that its decisions were respected. The Plan's supporters see the dramatic improvement in the rate of growth and the level of investment as proof that the Plan successfully combined market forces with state persuasion.[28] The remarkable record that saw the virtual re-industrialisation of the French economy after the war and a surprisingly sustained period of high growth[29] gave indicative planning a very good image. But what of the reality?

There are two sides to the assessment of the planning experience in France. On the one hand there is the assessment of the role of the state. Was planning an example of state co-ordination supplanting the market mechanism? Such is the view of the Plan's detractors who see the state's actions as a confirmation of a 'dirigiste' tradition in France, further undermining and weakening the power of the market.[30] Though this position overstates the case, there is a sense in which the state played a greater role in securing compliance with targets than appears in the conventional account. With its control of the credit system, the state was able to direct investment funds in line with the plan and to deny funds to those that opposed it.[31] There are few examples of such direct action, but sufficient to undermine the view that the plan worked on the basis of statistical expertise and abstract persuasion. On the other hand, there is the assessment of how much the state actually contributed to the high levels of growth and the reorientation of the economy. Certainly there is within France a revisionist interpretation that stresses the limited contribution of the plan and emphasises in its turn the adaptive power of capital in circumstances of altered investment opportunities.[32] Certainly nationalisation and the changed shape of the post war European and world economy provided new incentives for private capital to invest in manufacturing and the relative backwardness of French industry encouraged the introduction of new technologies. Nonetheless, the state's contribution to the modernisation of the basic infrastructural industries was of great significance, as were the general incentives provided by the state to encourage productive investment.

The confusion arises from the treatment of the role of the state. Despite the eulogies of the planners, the state did not move to the centre of the economic stage at the end of the Second World War. Its decisions were important but they were not based on a sufficient share of national production or such rigorous control of the finance system that they displaced private capital from its position of dominance. Just as the rules for the conduct of state owned firms in Britain revealed the subordinate role of that sector, so the basic planning procedures in France revealed the continued dominance of the private sector and of market relations. The planning of the state was an adjunct to, and further encouraged, the tendency for planning in privately owned enterprises, for the amalgamation of firms and the improved efficiency of cartel arrangements that had forms of indicative planning already inscribed in them.[33] The transformation and modernisation of the French economy was neither the product of state initiative nor market discipline but of the distinctive way in which the actions of state were co-ordinated with the market evading organisations of French business.[34]

On the surface, the contrast between French and German approaches to planning could not be more marked. In the formative years of the Federal Republic, the government was committed to reducing the size of the state sector and reducing the influence of the state on the conduct of the economy. The 'neo-liberal' vision owed its intellectual force to the work of Austrian economists in the interwar years who rejected socialism, planning and all other collectivist perversions.[35] In Germany there was no attempt to remake a past liberal order but to create a situation in which authoritative rules would bind state initiative, limit discretionary intervention, and allow the greatest scope to private initiative and market relations. The dramatic recovery of the German economy in the 1950s, much as the French successes endorsed indicative planning, won extensive praise for both the industrious German workers and the policy precepts of neo-liberalism.[36]

How 'neo-liberal' was state policy? How limited were the economic actions of the state? Once again there is a substantial gap between what happened and the claims about it. The German state operated an extensive set of subsidies, tax concessions and profit boosting arrangements all designed to improve the position of private business. Apart from enriching business, the purpose was to make more funds available for investment.[37] To complement this lapse from neo-liberal theory was an equal failure to make any significant increase in the degree of competition in the heavily cartelised German economy. Neo-liberalism did not include determined state action to break up cartels or regulate monopolies that sought to limit production or sales. Wallich sums up the mixed achievements of neo-liberalism in these terms:

> Large sectors of the economy are still kept, or were kept for a long time, under controls. The government has continued to play a preponderant role through its large budget, through the indirect control exercised over investment by means of the tax system, through ownership and operation of important industries, and through its somewhat paternalistic habits. A not inconsiderable volume of investment has been centrally planned. From the side of private enterprise, too, freedom of the market remains restricted. Cartels and other restrictive trade practices have been eliminated only in part. In many cases they have merely been driven underground at a time when, because of favorable economic conditions, they would not have been very active in any case. These are the things to give us pause when one thinks of Germany as the test case of a 'free' economy. Its freedom has been only relative, by comparison with the preceding period of monolithic control. It is only by virtue of a major shift in emphasis that Germany may be regarded as a protagonist of a free economy.[38]

Thus, for Germany, as for France, the post-war period saw a state sector formally subservient to the accumulation of capital in private hands. The market was recreated and existed in alliance with a strong state sector, and what was significant was the way in which the two were combined.

There is very little that needs to be said about planning mechanisms in the British economy in this period. The Attlee Labour Government inherited war-time controls and rationing and these were progressively removed.[39] As Brady has shown, the basic institutions for a planning system linking labour, capital and the state, somewhat like the French system, were created in Britain but were never activated.[40] Business opposed the setting up of elemental Development Councils and all moves to introduce forms of state planning. The Labour government preferred to allow the experiment to lapse rather than intensify already strong business opposition.[41] The situation inherited by the Conservatives after 1951 lacked formal procedures for even government-business consultation and no attempt was made to set production and investment targets.[42] The normal array of measures to support private business existed and lacked any guiding coherence. The only other possibility for co-ordination existed through the production and pricing policies of the nationalised industries, already discussed.

The three countries travelled different paths in terms of changes in the size of the state sector and the way in which the state sectors were combined with private sectors. Though the mechanisms and strategies that linked the two sectors were conceived in starkly contrasting ways they all expressed the general subordination of the state to the accumulation of capital in private hands. The strategic differences enshrined in each position, mixed economy, indicative planning and neo-liberalism, had consequences for the rate of growth and the patterns of development that occurred but all left market relations as the dominant means of economic and social co-ordination: state action was a supplement to, and not a substitute for, the market. The state remained on the fringes of the productive economy; its choices were marginal, though in terms of boosting investment or encouraging some developments more than others, such decisions were, sometimes, of great importance. The reality did not match the assumptions of the new orthodoxy of Keynesian economics that treated these marginal choices of government as the key determinants of national economic performance. For the policy advisors these were the only ones they could influence directly, which is not the same as being the factors which actually determined the way the whole system worked. Nonetheless, each of these positions implied changes in both the ways in which classes were organised and the presence that they had in the political processes managing these marginal actions of government. Before considering this aspect it is necessary to consider one further extension of the state's role.

WELFARE POLICY

After the Second World War, in each of the three countries, there were substantial changes in state provision of health, education, pensions and unemployment benefits and housing; and the growth of what has been described as a welfare state.[43] The speed at which the state assumed these additional tasks varied, as did the doctrines that justified the change, but the general similarity of the achievements must be noted.[44] For Britain, the dramatic nature of increased state provision was most marked. The nationalisation of medicine through the creation of a free, non-means tested National Health Service was the most compelling symbol. Of equal significance were the moves to increase state spending on housing, reform of the education system, increasing pension benefits, and improvements in provision for the unemployed, those without income on a more permanent basis and others who were socially disadvantaged. Though neither France nor Germany nationalised medicine, they both introduced a range of measures to increase state provision. There were degrees of national variation in how needs were identified and the way in which the state responded but the general pattern is similar.

The debate on the nature of the welfare system has been extensive and has focused on the extent to which the increase in state provision was a triumph for the struggles of the working class[45] or was a concession granted by capital as welfare provision was functional to either its social[46] or economic requirements.[47] It is important to note that once again state action did not replace the market as the main determinant of the welfare. The amount or quality of health care, education, housing and other provision was still largely determined by participation in the market, through the commodities traded, the type of work done, or indeed, whether work could be found at all. (The commitment to full employment was the most significant welfare contribution in all three countries.) State welfare provision was a supplement to income earned in market relations. It did not come in sufficient quantities and in such extensive forms as to be an alternative to work derived earnings. That some people did live on the benefits provided by the state does not prove that it was an alternative for them, only that the choice was not available. Further, the welfare system worked through a system of income transfers which largely meant that the working class paid for their own welfare in a more collective way. As such it did not mean that the welfare system served as a means of promoting greater social equality, or to reduce the benefits of capital ownership.[48] Nonetheless, increased state welfare provision did improve the material standards of those on the margins of the labour market and did have an important impact on working-class children and old people. It did not mean an end to poverty, social inequality, the social consequences of unemployment, or exploitation. In a similar manner to the other increases in the role of the state, increased state welfare provision confirmed the subordinate role of the state and the dominance of market relations.

CLASSES IN THE CONSTRUCTION OF THE NEW ORDER

The changes in France, Germany and Britain had a significant impact on the ways that classes interacted and fought out their continual battles over the production and distribution of surplus. The changes also involved new ways for classes to relate to the state and to be involved in its policy-making processes. It is necessary to assess both the character of these new patterns of interaction and the extent to which the different classes, class organisations and political parties were involved in the creation of this new political regime.

The issues are relatively simple, even if the answers are not. Was the reconstruction of the institutional order a result of successful pressure for reform from the organised working class, who clearly had called for the measures of nationalisation, economic planning and increased welfare provision, as argued by people like John Urry and Geoff Hodgson?[49] Or, was this new institutional order a response by capital (and the state) to the threats potentially posed by organised labour, a concession designed to entrap the labour movement and its political representatives in loyal and constructive opposition and co-operation with the powerful in society, as argued by Miliband?[50] Or, a variant on this second position, were the changes necessary adjuncts to those occurring in the accumulation process itself, a social accommodation to the implications of a new stage in the process of capital accumulation, as argued by people like David Yaffe, Ben Fine and Laurence Harris?[51] An assessment of these positions turns on the ways in which the different classes and their associated organisations and political parties were involved in this process of reconstruction. For example, in all three cases, the labour movement, the combination of trade unions and a social democratic political party, played a significant part in generating the ideas and programmes upon which the reconstruction would take place. The labour movement in Britain had developed the basic notion of the mixed economy during the dissarray of the 1930s.[52] In France, the trade unions and the failure of the Popular Front coupled with the experience of the Resistance were important parts of the process by which both nationalisation and planning came to be central parts of French reconstruction.[53] As is obvious, events in Germany were complicated. It is true that the German trade union movement had been of great importance during the rise and fall of the Weimar Republic. Its significance was greatly reduced by the Nazi regime and its organisations were destroyed. After the war, the old unions were not simply revived by the occupying powers. Instead, the trade union movement was reformed. Industry wide and general unions were created to replace old sectional and craft unions. As part of the reform, laws defining the legitimate forms of union action were also introduced, effectively limiting the right to strike and the right to organise. As the war ended, the old unions pressed for social changes to destroy the social base of fascism which, of course, meant breaking the social power of heavy industry. The role of the USA in the occupying forces and the rise of the cold war with the Soviet Union left the unions with little part to play. In part this was needed to overcome the depredations of the Nazi era. Nonetheless, the decision not to campaign for nationalisation but to support 'co-determination', in which workers' representatives were given a place on the managing boards of basic industries, was made by the trade unions and expressed a continuation of the same approach that had seen the setting up of works councils in the Weimar period.[54] Still, that was but one part of the pattern of post-war reconstruction in Germany and the trade unions can be neither praised nor blamed for their acquiescence in the general institutions of the social market economy that were supported by the allies and proposed by the Christian Democrats.

A similar pattern can be seen in the involvement of business organisations. In Britain, the Federation of British Industries did not welcome the nationalisation programme of the Labour Government but was largely willing to acquiesce in it.[55] Opposition only mounted when the Labour Government strayed into profitable areas of the economy. Its most successful campaign was the one waged against the setting up of an authoritative planning system to co-ordinate investment in the private sector.[56] In that pattern of trade union and business acquiescence lies the essence of the institutional arrangement of state and economy in Britain – a nationalised sector linked to the private economy through its investment, supply and pricing policy, without an active policy of co-ordinating the investment plans for the private sector. For France a similar pattern is evident. Business, heavily implicated by its collaboration during the Second World War, lacked the strength to prevent nationalisation as a form of retaliation. It also lacked the strength to prevent the setting up of the planning system which it saw as a threat to freedom and private enterprise.[57] Only experience showed them the beneficial side effects of this state intrusion into their affairs. Though it was partly the weakness of business that allowed some elements of the trade unions and the Resistance to press for this programme to modernise French capitalism and industry, business and its political allies were strong enough to ensure that planning remained a voluntary and not a compulsory matter and that the logic of the accommodation between the state and private sectors was never translated into a policy to challenge the general and broad dominance of private capital. As is obvious, the situation in Germany is different. Business as well as trade unions were weakened by the Nazi regime and the defeat in the Second World War. The impact of occupation in the western sectors reorganised the trade unions and purged its communist and militant members but rehabilitated business and restored it to a position of pre-eminence. Thus business was well pleased with the philosophy of neo-liberalism and especially with the incomplete way in which the doctrine was applied. It would be wrong, however, to see the creation of the social market economy as an instance of business power. Rather it was a product of the particular circumstances and of the way in which conservative German politicians cooperated with the occupying authorities in the western zone.

As a reflection of the pattern of initiative between the classes and class organisations there are the varying roles of the different political parties in shaping this new order. In Britain, it was most clear that the social-democratic British Labour Party was the principal architect of the reorganisation.[58] Though it based many of its initiatives on the practices of the Conservative dominated wartime coalition government, and could cite numerous commissions of inquiry and government sponsored reports to support its moves, it was the Labour government's election that made for the reorganisation of the political regime. Nothing supports the view that a Conservative government would have implemented such a set of nationalisations. Churchill's inclinations tended towards a 'neo-liberal' strategy and his subsequent accommodation to the mixed economy is not the same as evidence that he would have acted to create it. In France, the crucial actions that changed the framework of government, business and labour relations were set by the end of war coalition dominated by social democrats and a minority of communists. Though, as in Britain, conservative political forces once again came to dominate, they too accepted and worked through the pattern of class–state relations created in these formative post-war years. Germany is the exception. Conservative forces were dominant from the start and social democracy's major role was in reconciling the labour movement to the limited reforms and sacrifices of the economic miracle.

On this basis it is possible to assess the significant pattern of initiatives behind the construction of the new form of political regime. Firstly, working-class initiative was of great significance in breaking the old stagnation and providing the ideas and impetus for the reorganisation of the link between the state and economy and between classes and state. In the one case where working-class initiatives were not important, it was the effects of military defeat and the character of the occupation that supplanted internal factors. Secondly, there was a sense in which the new political regime was a response by the combination of state and dominant class to the increased power and presence of the working classes, a concession designed to preserve the basic source of the power, material privilege and dominance of the class of capital. What is as noticeable as the importance of working-class initiative is the fact that this initiative never became a significant challenge to the continued dominance of private capital. Partly this is to be explained by the counter pressure of business and the conservative character of the state and partly by the social democratic form given to working-class grievances – a form which always stressed the limited nature of the challenge to capitalism and promoted the maximum amount of co-operation with it. Thirdly, it should be noted that the new institutional order created by this reorganisation of the political regime proved to be most appropriate to a new period of economic expansion and to the new organisational shape of the industrialised capitalist economy. Indeed, the act of constructing the new political regime either aided the creation of the new shape of the economy or consolidated those tendencies characteristic of the new organisation of the economy.

This was a situation in which the three possible explanations for the historical, institutional development of capitalist society are essentially combined. The combination is best approached in the following manner: war, victory and defeat provided the framework within which the political regime of industrialised capitalism could be reorganised so that there was a greater harmony between the operations of the economic and political systems. In this new situation, working-class initiative provided the impetus for this transformation but it did not make the transformation in ways that decisively changed the balance of class power between labour and capital. Instead, it was private capital, social democratic and conservative political parties, and state officials that gave form and substance to the reorganisation. Much as political representation was extended to the working classes in stages and with restrictions and conditions, containing the radical impetus behind the demand, so the new institutional order of industrialised capitalism was created.

THE CHARACTER AND LOGIC OF THE NEW POLITICAL REGIME

The new form of the political regime, organised in the aftermath of the Second World War, has several significant dimensions which brought together many of the separate strands analysed in the previous discussion of the passing of the liberal order. Class organisation, for both labour and capital, consolidated the tendencies evident in the inter-war years. The competence of the organisations increased with more emphasis given to professional staff. Both the trade unions and trade associations became more organised and more centralised in their operations. Attempts were made to make both labour organisations and business organisations more comprehensive, that is embracing more members and sections of the classes in central, co-ordinating bodies. Though some progress was made in this direction, it was never fully successful. Large sections of workers in retail, service and small enterprises remained un-unionised in all three countries.

Similarly, there were clear divisions within business over participation in co-ordinating business organisations. Some large firms stood aside from organised representation, preferring to rely on their own direct dealings with government and the state bureaucracy, and many small firms gained little from their participation. And the division between finance and industry still existed as a problem for business organisation in Britain. It was of far less significance in France, owing to the nationalisation of the banks, and in Germany, owing to the close relationship between banks and industry – a tendency reinforced by government policies and tax incentives.

The organisation of the state, and the range of state actions, was also changed in this period. As with class organisation, greater emphasis was placed on improved organisational efficiency to match the increased range of state actions. The combination of increased state actions with the changed relations between the political system and the economy affected the ways in which classes and the state were related in this new phase of industrialised capitalist development. Despite variations, the question of how classes were organised into politics and the concomitant concern with how the political process affected accumulation was posed by these changes. Trade unions won a degree of increased participation in making political decisions in the sense that they were given more positions on representative, tripartite bodies and that they were consulted, especially on those matters where their co-operation was important, as over wage restraint. Business groups had their position within the system, already strong, consolidated. In addition to the informal consultations that are a commonplace part of the relationship between business and government or the state bureaucracy, the scope and frequency of formal consultation also increased. Nowhere was this more evident than in France with the newly-formulated planning procedures.

To give a brief summary of the character of the new arrangements it is necessary to set them off against the pattern of the past, incomplete passage from a liberal order. The political form of the state remained constant, still based on representation and electoral politics important for authorising the formation of new governments. (For Germany this was a new departure, and in France under the Fourth Republic the frequent changes in government ought not obscure the continuity at the heart of the state system.)[59]

Within the state, the position of the executive and the administration was consolidated. Assemblies were little more than the procedural accoutrements of constitutional rule. The most significant changes were in the relations between classes and the state. Here class organisations were brought into closer relations with state institutions and the political (that is, within the political system) decision-making process. Planning, the mixed economy, nationalisation, and even their seeming opposite, neo-liberalism and the social market economy all involved moving market and the state closer together, to an articulation in which the market was the more important and state decisions tended to be subordinate to, or service the needs of, private capital in general. Business was more closely involved than the trade unions. In some parts of the system, in some countries, elements of tripartite institutions, ones that linked in discussion though not binding agreements, the organisations of labour, capital and appropriate parts of the state, appeared. Again France provides the clearest examples, but even here the participation of trade unions declined as the emphasis on business co-operation increased. Despite the appearance of these bodies, they were not at the heart of the new regime, being largely confined to minor and/or routine matters. National economic policy was still the province of private capital in the market and the government making subordinate, marginal decisions.

The logic of the new political regime, the new way of linking politics and economics/class and the state, was, at the time of its creation, unclear. Much depended upon its success in combining class rule and accumulation. In retrospect, any radical challenge from working class organisations was quite rapidly contained and the new arrangements, coupled with the ideological pressures of the cold war, made a firm basis for social stability. These arrangements, once given the impetus of a change in US trade policy, a new international financial system managed through the International Monetary Fund, and the cold war urge to rearm and boost the European economies, provided a sound basis for an unprecedented period of economic expansion.[60] This in its turn contributed to social stability, as some of this expansion resulted in improved material conditions for working people. Despite these advantages for the new political regime, there were tendencies and problems inherent in it that could lead to its passing from the scene in the same way that the liberal order had done. The increased scope of state action opened the way for more state action, raising questions about the relationship between the state and the privately owned sectors of the capitalist economy. Closer relations between state and class organisations also posed the possibility of even closer ties, of even greater direct participation by class organisations in the political process. What limited the prospect of further increases in state action and changes in the parameters of state and class interactions was the prospect of growth and accumulation. So long as the economic system expanded and delivered sufficient profits to private capital, adequate taxation to the state and reasonable wages to the working population then the pressure to change the role of the state and the relations between classes and the state could be contained. But what would happen if growth began to slow down, if problems of accumulation came to the fore, or if the pattern of class strength and weakness, initiative and resistance, was to alter? What kind of rearrangement of the political regime would be made to balance class rule and accumulation?

NOTES

1. Barry (1965).
2. Sayers (1976); Clay (1957); Boyle (1967).
3. It was the actions of the steel cartel in association with the Bank of England that ended the attempt to site a steel works at Jarrow and formed the basis for one of the most powerful symbols of unemployment in inter-war Britain. See Wilkinson (1939).
4. For examples of these arguments, see Dalton (1935) and Jay (1938). For an account of the Labour Party at the time of these changes, and one which is not trapped by the mythology of the red decade, see Miliband (1973). For a more rigorous exposition of similar views see Kalecki (1971).
5. Herbert Morrison (1933) had devised an organisational form for state-owned ventures to insulate them from 'political' influence, defusing the social and political impact of nationalisation.
6. Robson (1960); Spiegelberg (1973), chap.6.
7. Tivey (1973), chap.3.
8. See Schneker (1963); Richardson (1971).
9. Ross (1965).
10. Joy (1950).
11. Robson (1950)
12. See the discussion of the terms for the operation of the nationalised industry in McEachern (1980), chap.4.

13. Hughes (1973).
14. Pryke (1971).
15. For an account of the Resistance programme, see Kuisel (1981), chap.6.
16. *ibid.*, chap.7; Sheahan (1963); Einaudi, Bye, and Rossi (1955).
17. See Sheahan (1963); for an alternative see Baum (1958), also Kindleberger (1964), chap.9.
18. Stolper (1967), chaps. IV and V.
19. The nature of this influence has been extensively debated. See Merritt (1976), pp.91-103.
20. Manchester (1969).
21. See Erhard (1960); also Hallett (1973).
22. Wallich (1955), p. 141.
23. The Volkswagen Works were eventually denationalised – or at least shares were made available to the public. See Grosser (1974), p. 287.
24. Wallich (1955), p. 143.
25. *ibid.*, p. 165.
26. Bauchet (1964). As a former advisor to the Commissariat du Plan, Bauchet gives a most enthusiastic account of the process.
27. Of the initial period, in which the flavour of French planning was established, Kuisel notes that it produced an 'économie concertée' of business and the state, but not labour. Kuisel (1981), p. 259.
28. For a general overview of the achievements of the Plan, see Ardagh (1977), chaps 1-3.
29. Fohlen (1980), vol.6, no.1, pp.100ff.
30. Baum (1958).
31. Shonfield (1965), pp. 166-170.
32. Carré, Dubois and Malinvaud (1975), chap.14; Caron (1979), chap.14. Also see McArthur and Scott (1969).
33. Cohen (1977).
34. Ehrmann (1957), chap.V.
35. See Hayek (1935).
36. Arndt (1966). There are, of course, alternative explanations for the 'economic miracle' that stress the legacy of the Nazi era, the restricted consumption of working people, the influx of labour as refugee and 'guest workers'; see Wallich (1955); and Minnerup (1976).
37. Denton, Forsyth and Maclennan (1968); Fels (1976).
38. Wallich (1955), p.150.
39. Budd (1978), chap.1.
40. Brady (1950).
41. Rogow (1955), pp.41ff.
42. Hence the complaint of the Federation of British Industries over the distant relations between them and government in the early 1950s. See Blank (1973), p.123; Kipping (1972), pp.92ff. For an account of the changing attitude within the Conservative Party see Harris (1973), chaps. 12 and 13.
43. The term 'Welfare State' is a misnomer, exaggerating the extent and significance of state provision. The term denotes the increased role of

the state with the same kind of inaccuracy as 'mixed economy'. The image of the caring state was a necessary complement to the image of the more powerful state.
44. Flora and Heidenheimer (1981).
45. As seen in Urry (1981), pp. 114–15.
46. Piven and Cloward (1972).
47. Gough (1979).
48. Townsend (1979).
49. Urry (1981); Hodgson (1984).
50. Miliband (1982).
51. Fine and Harris (1979).
52. Attlee (1937) gives a clear account of what was actually done by the first majority Labour Government in terms of the policy goals of the 1930s.
53. Kuisel (1981) traces, with other factors, the contributions of the labour movement to the eventual success of the campaign for planning.
54. Shuchman (1957).
55. Blank (1973), chap.4.
56. *Ibid.*, pp.85ff.
57. Kuisel (1981), pp. 249–50.
58. Rogow (1955) provides a clear account of the pattern of its actions in the shape of the mixed economy.
59. Williams (1972).
60. For an account of the period of boom and its complications, see Armstrong, Glyn and Harrison (1984); also see Cipolla (1980), chap.6, pts I and II.

4 · BETWEEN BOOM AND RECESSION

The post-war settlement reordered the relations between classes and the state and established a new political regime. It is important to consider how this new regime 'worked': how classes, their organisations and the political parties responded to the logic of their new situation; how the state responded to its new position. This political regime had been constructed, in part, as a response to problems of the inter-war depression and the sacrifices of the Second World War symbolised by the commitment to full employment and growth. Full employment implies a change in the labour market and, related to this, some change in the working of the relations between labour and capital. This meant that growth was always problematic within the new regime. So long as growth was assured then solutions could be found. But what happened when the prospects of growth became uncertain? What did the state do and how did the classes and their organisations react? These are the broad issues discussed in this chapter.

RESPONSES TO THE NEW REGIME

Economic growth and full employment were intended to be the consequences of the new regime. If that is so then the record for the 1950s indicates success. Growth rates were higher and sustained for longer than before in all three countries. Both France and Germany experienced their own forms of 'economic miracles' with rapid rates of growth, averaging almost 6–7 per cent for the 1950s and 1960s. This was dramatically higher than in Britain but, in its own terms, Britain, with a growth rate over 2 per cent was doing better than its historical average.[1] Such rapid economic expansion, even when it involved improvements in technical efficiency, increased the demand for labour and the levels of unemployment declined to record peace time lows. Indeed, for much of this time there was a shortage of labour which was imported from overseas, from former colonies or from poorer countries in the area.[2]

If, in terms of broad economic indicators, the post-war rearrangement of the political regime worked, how did the various class organisations and the political parties respond to the changed situation?

One of the significant indicators of the changes which had occurred can be seen in actions of trade unions and their social democratic political parties. In both Britain and Germany, the political parties responded by defining their acceptance of the new order and formulating their policy ambitions in its terms. In Britain, there was the conscious social democratic re-evaluation of the politics of the Labour Party. A good example of this can be found in Crosland, *The Future of Socialism*.[3] In this book Crosland argues that the creation of the mixed economy and Keynesian economics removed the question of property ownership from the political agenda. There was no need to nationalise or to extend state management of the economy. The Attlee Government had created all that was needed for an effective social democratic response to the residual problems of a capitalist economy. The emphasis had moved from equality to equality of opportunity and the need to eliminate remaining incidental areas of disadvantage and poverty.

Despite the eloquence of Crosland's reformulation, the party as a whole was not converted to its optimistic and quiescent view. The 'revisionist' controversy highlighted the degree of unease that remained.[4] Here was a concerted campaign to prevent the modernisation of the language of the party's 'socialist' commitment. The symbolic centre of the dispute was focused on Clause 4 of the party's constitution. The revisionists lost the battle of the symbols but won the battle on the party's orientation.

In West Germany the situation was different. The German Social Democratic Party (SPD) had not *made* the post-war settlement and had battled to preserve its history against the Nazi past and the proclivities of the occuping powers.[5] Hence it had campaigned, and lost, its electoral battles with a programme marked by the properly revisionist position of Bernstein's era. Even this was too socialist for the new political arrangement, with too much Marxist language and too many explicit class claims. And so began the struggle to modernise the party's programme.

As with the revisionist controversy in Britain, the task for the SPD was to accept the new order and to devise policy claims in its terms.[6] Unlike Britain, the debate was much more overtly theoretical and sought to assess the significance of the changes wrought by the occupying powers and the era of growth ushered in by the social market economy. Again the emphasis moved away from a programme of nationalisation, but in Germany the SPD explicitly embraced the efficiency of the market as superior to political or state intervention. Once the distribution of productive property had been accepted, then problems were residual and more simply solved and, again, equality had been replaced by equality of opportunity.

In this revision of the party programme greater attention had to be paid to questions of international politics. The party had to abandon its hostility to the United States and accept the legitimacy of the cold war as an appropriate frame of reference. In its own way it had to learn to stop worrying and to love the bomb. Interestingly, this debate did have a parallel in Britain. There Gaitskill, as leader of the party in opposition, wanted the party to adopt a more supportive position towards nuclear weapons and the United States. In this he also failed but vowed to 'fight, fight and fight again' to modernise his party's position. Interestingly, both questions, of nuclear weapons and nationalisation have not been finally resolved in Britain throughout Labour's post war history. In Germany, the questions have been basically resolved within the SPD but they have remained, in other political forces, continuing issues for German politics.

In both Britain and Germany, then, the social democratic political parties, and with them, their trade union bases, adjusted to the new political regime, accepted its logic and its claims and sought to work within them. Indeed, as a result both parties spent considerable time in office managing the workings of the new political regime.

The symbolic core of the SPD's reorientation was the Bad Godesburg conference of 1959 where a new party constitution was adopted. The substance of the new position had been debated for two years and was a direct response to the party's electoral failure. It was a self-conscious attempt to shed the past. Gone was the desire to extend the influence of labour through nationalisation.

Instead, the party accepted the achievements of the social-market economy as the basis for growth, rising standards of living, full employment and individual freedom.

Events in France were shaped by a different logic. The relationship between the trade union movements and political parties was quite different and this complicated matters.[7] The major labour union, the Confédération Generale du Travail (CGT) and the French Communist Party (PCF) were linked. Though not a revolutionary combine, they certainly shared a 'workerist' approach to the politics of the Fourth Republic. They did not adjust to the new situation, though they behaved as if they were a social democratic party, without its beliefs. The other, more social democratic party, the SFIO, had a weak connection to its trade union base. This party took a fuller role in the Fourth Republic but was poorly organised and always under threat. It did not modernise its position in a way that paralleled social democratic parties in Britain and Germany. With an electorally significant Communist Party to its left, and with the remnants of a revolutionary tradition around, it did not give up more direct class appeals and criticisms of capitalist society. The change in the electoral system in the Fifth Republic encouraged co-operation between the two parties. The need to exchange votes to win office meant it was necessary to devise a common programme preserving the rhetoric of a working class based social transformation. Policy reformulation had to wait until the formation of the Partie Socialiste (PS) and the election of Mitterrand as President in 1981 with a weakened position for the PCF. Managing the recession displaced this tradition. Even then it did not break fully with the rhetoric of socialism. It still favoured nationalisation and the extension of planning and the transformation of the social order. This kind of reorientation will be considered in its place, in the context of prolonged recession.

On the other side of politics, the conservative side, the reorganisation of the political regime also required some kind of adjustment. Here the increased role and scope of the state and the increased legitimacy of trade unions was some kind of challenge to prewar assumptions about the proper relations between political, economic and social power.

In Britain, the basic dimensions of the new regime had been created by the Labour Government and its trade union base. Although there had been a degree of consensus over some of the changes, as a total package they were under threat from a revised Conservative Party. After winning the 1951 election, the Conservatives did not dismantle the post-war settlement. The road transport industry was denationalised and, over time, most of the steel industry returned to private ownership. As that was done it was possible to set out the ways in which the 'mixed economy' was to be run without a planning mechanism and no significant government co-ordination of investment.

This change affected the Conservative Party itself and gave increasing prominence to those who embraced a co-operative, corporatist model of society.[8] Thus, people like Macmillan, who had advocated an expanded role for the state in the inter-war years, came to the fore. The alternative strands within the party, which embraced free markets and a reduced role for government, were effectively marginalised. At best they provided a whispered criticism of the long term consequences of the incremental expansion of government, one ear attuned to the voice of Hayek, the other to ministerial preferment.

The close relationship between the Conservative Party and sections of business dissolved in the new period. From the point of view of the Conservative Party, business had been freed of uncertainty and could now compete happily in the market place without any need for a dialogue on economic policy. At first this was accepted with enthusiam.

In Germany, the conservative forces required little adjustment to the new order as they had been responsible for its design. German business was also well pleased with the new order as it restored private ownership and did not significantly break down cartels or concentration of ownership. Further, the new situation was not favourable to trade unions. Co-determination was, at worst, an irritant, and had secured the return of the coal and steel industries to private hands. The problems business was to face were two-fold. One set concerned the application of social market principles to the lack of competition in the economy. Here they tried to prevent the application of the anti-cartel law by having it declared non-constitutional. Although this failed it delayed the law by many years. When it was declared constitutional, the law was more of a symbol than a means to promote competition in the heavily controlled German economy.

In France, business and conservative political forces had to make some adjustment. This largely involved coming to terms with the planning system. Once the trade unions withdrew their enthusiastic support for planning and the economic benefits became more apparent, then business could reach an accommodation with the process. The political parties were more concerned with the logic of electoral struggle in the Fourth Republic than with devising policies to fit the new forms of class state interaction. Only in the Fifth Republic did this become more important – more after the events of 1968 than before.

To ask the same question of the state as of parties and class organisations is slightly inappropriate. The actions of the state in this period were the expression of the management strategies inherent in the form of the post-war settlement and the new political regime. To understand how the scope of state action had been transformed by the new political regime it is best to look at what happened when the assumptions of the new regime began to be worked through, when the state had to do its part in managing the consequences of sustained full employment and promoting continued levels of growth.

At this stage it is useful to consider the role of ideas in setting up the policy frameworks that would shape policy in the management by the state. It has assumed the status of an axiom that the long boom created by the post-war settlement was a triumph for Keynesian economics.[9] This was not the case. In Britain bits of the Keynesian policy prescription were pressed in to service the fiscal strategies of the state but there was no far reaching 'Keynesian revolution'. The main symbol was the freedom from the need to work with balanced state budgets and the possibility of using broad fiscal means to promote (or curtail) growth. In Germany the ideas of Keynes were irrelevant. Post-war reconstruction was shaped by neo-liberal economic doctrines and the state was obliged by the constitution to balance the budget. Nonetheless, within the confines of the social market economy the state still found ways of promoting economic growth, though it was denied the means to select or co-ordinate its efforts with the private sector. In France, the ideas of Keynes were not important. Instead, planning helped the French state find means to manage the new situation and to promote economic growth.

PROBLEMS IN THE PURSUIT OF GROWTH

Although there had been a stop-go pattern to growth throughout the 1950s and early 1960s, it was only in the middle 1960s that the tendency to unrestrained growth came to an end. In Germany, the decline was quite marked with the years 1966 and 1967 standing out as a period of low growth. Real GDP grew at only 2.5 per cent in 1966 and declined by 0.2 per cent in 1967.[10] In France, the years 1967 and 1968 show lower rates of growth than the years surrounding them, being 4.7 per cent in 1967 and 4.3 per cent in 1968. In the years on either side, the rate of increase was 5.2 per cent and 7.0 per cent respectively. For Britain the rate of growth was down to 1.5 per cent in 1969, but in the previous year it had been 4.1 per cent, and the normal situation was for growth to be slightly over 2 per cent. Indeed, for Britain it can be argued that the long boom ended earlier and that the economy, though expanding at a rate higher than the historical average, fell further and further behind its European and international rivals.[11]

Was this downturn in growth and the social unrest which accompanied it related to the dynamics unleashed by the reordered political regime? It would seem so. Full employment had increased both the bargaining strength of trade unions and the sense that workers had not had their share of the benefits of the long boom. This theme was certainly present in the 1968 strikes and the vehement rejection of the Grenelle agreement in France, and in the unofficial strike wave in Germany.[12] In Britain, the rise of a more militant style of unionism and the hostility to attempts to reduce their bargaining power indicates some of the same resentments were at work.[13] Further, the demands made by students in Paris in May 1968 echoed in Britain and Germany, and highlighted suspicion about the increased power of the state, the limited democratic practices of the more affluent society and the quality of life assured by the long boom and the more technocratic age.[14]

To pursue these questions it is necessary to ask what the state was doing to respond to the social consequences of full employment and the challenge to find new sources of growth now that the certainty of economic expansion was gone. This brings into consideration the period between the ending of the long boom and the onset of the present period of prolonged recession. To understand this period it is necessary to concentrate on a number of related changes. Firstly, there are the changes that occurred in the range of state actions and in the size of the state's share in economic and social life. Did the state intervene more than it previously did? In what sorts of areas and why? Secondly, did the state set up new institutions to co-ordinate economic activity and to secure the co-operation of the major class organisations of labour and capital? Were these new co-operative institutions more formal than real, gestures towards possible future co-operation? How did the state, and the class organisations, respond to the increased tension surrounding the levels of wages, profits and the level of new investment? Were attempts made to control or reduce the levels of real income and to boost the profitability of private firms by direct and indirect means? And finally, how did the state and class organisations respond to the problems of the increasingly international scope of investment and production?

Britain

In Britain the long boom was less dramatic then elsewhere; and growth problems emerged earlier, towards the late 1950s rather than the middle 1960s. There was time for far more experimentation in the attempts to regain growth. The relatively poor performance of the British economy also encouraged an analytical growth industry as all kinds of writers sought to diagnose the ills of the British system and propose new courses that would release unexpected dynamism. There emerged a fairly steady pattern of state initiative supplementing private enterprise, seeking to boost investment and to increase the amount of co-operation and co-ordination in the economic and political system. With the election of the Conservative Party to office in 1951 the parameters of state ownership and private enterprise were set, government initiative was minimal and the system ran along conventional lines. The failure to find sustained growth led to a number of responses from business, labour and the state. The literature on business organisations reveals that they initially welcomed the Conservatives' 'hands off' approach to the economy until it started to create problems for them. At that point they began to discuss ways to strengthen their organisations and to improve relations with government, and to a lesser extent, with the trade unions.[15]

For Conservative policy makers, the problem of low growth was related to the strength of trade unions and the level of wage settlements. Responding to this began the sequence of government initiatives on pay restraint. In 1954-5, the Conservative Government set up institutions to monitor pay increases and the trade unions refused to co-operate. Recognising that union co-operation would be hard to obtain, the Government started an 'imitate French planning' campaign and created a series of tripartite bodies to discuss policies for the co-ordinated economic expansion and development of particular industries and for the industrial economy as a whole.[16] A peak version of these tripartite bodies, the National Economic Development Organisation was set up to consider the longer term development of the economy. Under the Conservatives these bodies were largely form without content, though they did act in certain cases, often with the assistance of sums of government money, to restructure some of the older, least economically viable industries such as textiles.[17] Here, in an embryonic form, was the linking of pay restraint with the pursuit of economic growth, a combination which would, after almost fifteen years of experimentation, produce the Social Contract. In its more elemental forms there are two versions of pay restraint linked to growth. The first equation is shaped by the desire to avoid the inflationary consequences of full employment. In this version pay restraint eases the pressure on prices and produces a lower rate of inflation which may, in its turn, encourage growth and employment. The connections between each stage of the equation were only loosely sketched. The second equation tries to show the steps by which wage restraint may be an effective response to the problem of low growth. In this equation, wage restraint eases the pressure on prices and paves the way for greater profitability, greater profits fuel investment making for growth and higher levels of future employment. In the early stages the connections between pay restraint and forms of planning to promote growth were very imprecise but they became more obvious as both governments and labour learnt from each successive relative failure.

In 1965 the Labour Party, under Wilson, campaigned on a growth strategy that depended on government initiative.[18] The campaign slogan concerning the 'white heat' of technological change summed up a programme of state action to fund and promote high technology research and then to encourage private business to adopt and commercially exploit that development. Like so much under the Wilson Government the white heat cooled to a low rhetorical glow and the problems of the British economy increased. New technologies and new applications for technology were made, but they rarely became a potent force in the British economy.

Also during the Wilson Labour Government an attempt was made to revitalise tripartite structures to give them a meaningful role in the context of a National Plan.[19] The National Plan was meant to represent a new approach to the pursuit of growth in Britain. It broke down on the basis of business opposition and the very severe problems involving the value of sterling and Britain's balance of payments which undermined any assumption that government policy could generate a significant improvement in the rate of growth.

The whole question of the co-ordination of economic effort within the private sector and between the private sector and the state sector was left unresolved. The setting up of tripartite formal structures and the giving of money as an incentive to rationalise the shape of production was not the only state response to the problems of the economy. Despite initial reluctance, the Wilson Labour Government managed to re-nationalise the main sections of the steel industry while leaving a small, profitable privately owned sector.[20] With planning put to one side, the emphasis was once again on getting unions not to use the bargaining strength given by full employment. The Wilson Government set up boards to monitor both prices and incomes and tried to promote a policy of voluntary wage restraint.[21] Once again the unions refused to co-operate and so a compulsory pay freeze was imposed (followed by rapid pay increases once it was lifted). With the failure of both wage restraint and the state efforts to boost investment, attention came to focus on trade unions and their ability to win major wage increases. It was assumed that if the trade unions could be reformed, the rank and file would be more easily controlled by their official leaders and the incidence of unexpected unofficial strikes would be reduced. This is what lay behind the enquiry into industrial organisation and *In Place of Strife*.[22] Though the limits to be imposed on trade unions were slight, *In Place of Strife* was defeated by the revolt of

104 Between Boom and Recession

significant sections of the parliamentary Labour Party with trade union connections.

The Wilson Government saw all its initiatives to resolve the problem of low growth defeated. Industrialists would not co-operate in the National Plan, trade unions would not co-operate in either wage restraint or trade union reform and the problems in the economy were increasingly obvious and severe. The response of the Heath Government was directly tied to the pattern of Labour's failure. Heath wanted to return to free market forces and to escape from the political need to respond to the weakness of the British economy.[23] As a result Heath made the symbolic gesture of de-nationalising a number of state-owned properties. In industrial relations the Government sought to use the law to win the reforms that co-operation with the unions could not bring.[24] First Heath introduced an Industrial Relations Act to define legitimate trade union practices and to bring the conduct of disputes under the control of a labour court. The trade unions refused to co-operate and faced punitive fines for refusing to register with the court. In the end the Act was quietly put to one side as it exacerbated rather than improved industrial relations.

After the failure of imposed trade union reform, the Heath government decided to solve the problem through a statutory pay policy. The calculations remained the same. It was hoped that such regulation would moderate wage increases and add a degree of predictability to the situation. If the trade unions refused to co-operate they would be guilty of breaking the law and resultant strikes would increase the electoral difficulties of the Labour Party.

Events did not work like that. Trade unions chose to ignore the system. At first this made little difference as the pay norms were suitably flexible. The National Union of Mineworkers challenged the system in 1973 in an effort to restore their position in the hierarchy of manual working wages. They were buoyed up in their demands by the artificially inflated economy of the Barber Boom. The oil crises only added strength to their short-term position. Heath pushed to spread the pain of the stoppage by putting Britain onto a three day working week. When he called a 'who rules the country' election he lost.

During the period in opposition, the labour movement was considering their position. Some had come to recognise the possibility of trading off wage-restraint for planning policies to ensure growth and to improve the welfare of the old, ill, unemployed and the young. The thinking was: if the future is like the past a Labour Government will want some form of prices and incomes policy. Let's use our strength, which is sufficient to break such a policy to make it work *and* to deliver significant economic and social benefits. Two books reveal the dimension of the problem and response. Andrew Glyn and Bob Sutcliffe published their influential book *British Capitalism, Workers and the Profit Squeeze* which showed the sources of trade union strength and its potential in such a period.[25] For them, British trade unions were well organised, strong and boosted by full employment; British capital was weak – caught between international competitition and the trade union movements with a squeeze on their profits. In such circumstances the system was ripe for transformation. The other book was Michael Barrat Brown's *From Labourism to Socialism* which set out an account of the nature of the British economy with a discussion of how labour was now placed to use its strength to bargain for a more socially significant role.[26]

The period between the ending of the long boom and the onset of persistent recession did not solve the problems in the economy. Political and economic developments, however, combined to set the scene for another attempt at reworking the political regime, building on the incremental consequences of the post-war change.

France

In France, the long boom weakened rather than collapsed and there were other severe problems in the relationship between class and state in the period between boom and the onset of the recession. The problem of growth appeared in a different way. The whole of the French economy had to be transformed and production modernised so that it could compete with European and international rivals.

The planning system constructed in the postwar years has been at the centre of debates over the heightened rates of growth in the French economy. Its indicative rather than command character and its emphasis on consultation with all social partners in the modernisation commissions has been distinctive. In the initial stages, the emphasis was on a process of 'concertation' of interests through lengthy consultation, negotiation and discussion.[27] It was this act of 'concertation' that made central direction unnecessary and gave the plan the social basis for success. Admittedly, not all 'interests' were equally weighed in the process; small business was less favoured than large firms and the involvement of the trade unions was somewhat intermittent.[28] But this form of planning changed as the problems faced by the French economy changed and the environment in which these major firms had to operate became more complex.

The succession of plans approach the problems in the economy in a number of stages, some of which have implications for an assessment of the way in which class organisations were represented in the political process.[29] In the first period, the emphasis was on post-war reconstruction and creating the economic infrastructure within which dynamic enterprises could triumph. Starting with largely state owned heavy industry, the plan provided modernisation of the economy. In the second period, the emphasis changed. With the construction of the European Economic Community and the increased presence of US firms, the need to make French business responsive to international competition became important. Planning then concentrated on encouraging the formation of larger, more efficient firms to compete with their foreign rivals and so the state encouraged mergers and concentration.[30] The state also provided support for the levels of investment needed for this task.[31] The emphasis was on closer relations with the big firms, and resulted, in the view of one author, with the civil service acting as the political voice of big business.[32] The last plan of this stage, the fifth, covered the years of the weakening of the boom, 1965-70. The sixth plan showed the rise of a new econometric planning model and an attempt to generate a complex interlocking map of all economic activity in France. As such it was a prelude to a decline in the comprehensive ambitions of French planning. Along with the concern with increasing the competitiveness of French business there was an increasing emphasis on improving the social infrastructure of French life, especially in the areas of housing, health and education.[33]

In the period between the ending of the boom and the onset of recession there occurred a reorientation of the planning process. State inducements were concentrated on a smaller number of very large firms in an effort to make them internationally viable. Not all efforts were successful in this regard and US firms gained a strong presence in some of the key areas of new technology.[34] (This concentration on particular firms may not have been as significant as sometimes thought since the heavily cartelised and monopolised character of the French economy/business had always meant that in dealing with sectors the state dealt most frequently with a few, large firms.)[35] The character of state investment and the operation of public sector firms also changed and there was an attempt to internalise the discipline of the market in the state sector.[36] This largely meant that the state sector was encouraged to have greater internal coherence than had previously been the case.

In the initial stages the planning process had ignored the labour market in terms of both the supply of labour and the level of incomes. As expansion and modernisation became the norm these concerns were added. By the time of the fifth plan, there was some attempt to address the needed social infrastructure for future expansion. Part of that emphasis was on reforming the education system to produce a technically competent elite as well as mass educated technicians. Another part sought to extend planning to cover wages. The emphasis here was on using a pay policy to slow the rate of wage increases (already lagging behind the rate of growth) to counter inflationary pressures in the planning process. In their own ways these two emphases combined to influence the May events.

Although the dip in growth in 1967 and 1968 was slight, it signalled uncertainty about the future. Such uncertainty and the planning initiatives helped set the scene for the explosive public protests of May–June. These protests had two sides. On one side, student protests closed the universities and brought into the open questions about the nature of society generated by the planning process.[37] One of the themes in their revolt concerned the reform of the universities, to make them more selective and more tied to the economic needs of France. Another theme focused on the lack of democracy in French society and in the schools and universities. On the other side were the massive strikes and factory occupations, involving at one stage more than ten million workers. These strikes set out to reduce the imbalance in the distribution of the rewards of planning and sustained growth. In their turn, too, they exposed the undemocratic structure of both the work place (in the call for *autogestion*) and in trade union structures. The Grenelle Agreement, initially rejected, granted extensive pay rises and improved work conditions. The pace and character of educational reform changed with a much greater emphasis on 'participation'.

After the May events, business modernised its organisations and considered what it needed to successfully combat the militant mood in the trade unions.[38] It did not abandon those who had negotiated the agreements, nor did it seek a 'revenge' to parallel that after Matignon. The trade unions sought to improve their organisational efficiency, to exploit the gains they had made and to press for a greater involvement of workers in the running of the workplace and the trade unions in the running of society.

As in Britain, these questions were not finally resolved in the period between the ending of the long boom and the onset of the recession but the stage was set for further experiments in the workings of the relations between class organisations and the state.

Federal Republic of Germany

In Germany, the end of the long boom was marked by a short but comparatively severe recession. In 1966–7, economic growth slowed dramatically, migrant labour was repatriated, unemployment rose, the utilisation of industrial capacity dropped and the combination of these factors made a stark contrast with the almost uninterrupted economic expansion of the post-war era.[39] Though probably not directly related to this downturn, there developed a quite strong extra-parliamentary left politics, some sections of which went into armed opposition to the existing state. In a well-prepared response to this development, the German state resorted to a more authoritarian posture, both in its police moves to destroy the 'terrorist' wing of the opposition movement but also in its surveillance of the population as a whole, and in the restrictions placed on the political affiliations of government employees.[40] These developments, though significantly affecting the social and political climate in the Federal Repulic, are a side issue in the major response of the state to the events of the recession and the political actions of the trade unions and business organisations.

With the gradual rise of the Social Democratic Party to prominence the parameters of state action were adjusted to respond to the situation caused by the ending of the long boom.[41] Though the role of the state had been considerable in the era dominated by the neo-liberal theories of the Frieberg school, the rules under which state policy operated did restrict the scope for state intervention into the conduct of the economy.[42] In the aftermath of the recession and with the appointment of Schiller to the post of Economics Minister (further consolidated when the post of Finance Minister was subsequently added), neo-liberalism gave way to a much more Keynesian oriented state policy with a clear counter-cyclical intent.[43] Though denied the possibility of an unbalanced Federal Budget, the government had recourse to a 'special investment budget', which could run a deficit,[44] to boost the levels of investment through the use of state funds and guaranteed loans.[45] The state used its position to encourage mergers so that West German business could compete on the international market[46] and its funds to encourage research and development in newer technologies, further improving the quality of industrial production.[47] Such initiatives brought large business and the state even more closely together than had previously been the case.[48] It is perhaps characteristic that the Federal Government, dominated by the SPD, did not extend its presence into the economy in a more direct or more controlled way and that it did not contemplate the extension of state ownership even in those areas that required greatest state assistance.

In a manner parallel to the changed orientation of state economic policy went a series of measures that sought to maintain social stability through the greater participation of trade unions in negotiations over national economic policy.[49] As a response to the 1966–7 recession, the government proposed that the major 'interest' groups in society should meet to consider the impact of 'orientation' data on their intended economic behaviour.[50] In effect, it meant consultation between the major representative groups for business and labour with economic experts and state officials. This proposal was supported by the trade unions who thought about it in terms of the post-war demand for 'co-determination' at the economic level.[51] Moves in that direction had been blocked by the Adenauer Government and it looked as if there was a chance to re-establish the union movement's claims. The trade unions wanted to trade co-operation and wage restraint for influence over the management of the national economy.

The main business organisation, the BDA, also recognised the old theme reborn and, at first, resisted the government's call. Nonetheless, they came to recognise the scope of these proposals.

As is so often the case, different participants in the process made different assumptions about its purpose. Both the government and the BDA seemed keen to use the objectively provided 'orientation' data and the sharing of discussion to encourage wage restraint and hence rehabilitate profitability and investment.[52] For a time this strategy succeeded and wage demands were well below the levels of economic recovery and profits grew dramatically.[53] The gap between wage levels and the boosted profits was obvious and workers responded with unofficial strike actions, forcing a rapid increase in money wages to redress the situation.[54] The trade union movement was increasingly frustrated about the way in which Concerted Action worked. They sought to put the management of the national economy on the agenda but this was either ignored, postponed or resisted by business and government. What the trade unions wanted was an open discussion about the distribution of wealth in society, about the levels of profits, about investment and future employment. It became clear that Concerted Action was only a device for securing wage restraint and, from that time, the meetings declined in importance for all participants.

This raises the third issue in the context of the period that passed between boom and the onset of the recession, an incomes policy. Events in the response to the downturn of 1966–7 show that the levels of wages in the economy were appearing as a problem to government and, given the still buoyant state of the economy, trade unions and workers were well placed to resist some of the moves to lower the rate of wage increases. After the initial success of Concerted Action, its failures as a wage restraint policy led to a downgrading in the significance of this discussion and the pressures for an incomes policy were transferred to other parts of the political economic system. The arrival of Helmut Schmidt as Economic and Finance Minister saw the emphasis shift to an indirect incomes policy with most pressure being exerted where it could be most effective, on public sector workers.[55] Neither complicity in tripartite negotiations that were not extended to include levels of profitability[56] nor an indirect policy in conditions of a still expanding economy were likely to solve wages as a problem for business and the state. Rather, such moves formed a logical prelude to the initial conflicts of the recession when it did arrive.

CONCLUSION

In Britain, Germany and France the ending of the long boom ushered in a period dominated by attempts to find secure sources of growth. These all involved a reorientation of state policy, a more active posture on promoting investment and research on technology and its adoption for industrial production. The size of the state increased, and in Britain there was an increase in the size of the state owned sector of the productive economy. In all cases a new form of an old problem was appearing for business and government, namely the way to gain some control over the rate and levels of wage increases so as to boost private profitability and to increase the levels of private investment. With problems of falling domestic demand and an outflow of capital, especially from the Federal Republic,[57] for investment in commodity production, oil and industrial production, there was a rise in international competition, further squeezing the margins within which companies had to operate. It is in the sense that none of these problems, of the balance of full employment, secure growth, protected profits and high levels of investment (especially private investment), were adequately resolved that the period after the end of the long boom was the prelude to a period of persistent recession.

The policy initiatives between boom and recession did not reorder the relations between classes and the state which were characteristic of the political regime established in the post-war settlement. The increased range of state action remained within the confines of that agreement. The state-owned sector did not reach much beyond infrastructural sectors and certainly did not threaten to displace the dominance of privately owned firms from the manufacturing economy. The attempts to tie workers into state initiatives to promote growth extended assumptions made in the post-war settlement rather than changed, in any qualitative way, the processes linking business, labour and the state. The political regime remained unchanged. Nonetheless, this period was also an interlude in terms of the development of the political regime in the sense that trade union experience of near full employment and the restraints sought by business and the state in the face of the task of maintaining sustained levels of growth, prompted them to rethink the tactical and strategic options open to them. Between boom and recession class-based organisations rethought the terms in which they would co-operate with each other in the pursuit of growth, and the concessions that labour would require for moderating its wage demands.

NOTES

1. Cipolla (1980), vol. 6, pt.1, pp. 100-1, 132-5, 221-3; for the general situation see Armstrong, Glyn and Harrison (1984), chap.8.
2. Paine (1974), esp. Pt. 1, pp. 5-36; Castles and Kosack (1973) and (1972); Kindleberger (1967).
3. This was the basic assumption in Crosland (1956); see also Shonfield (1965).
4. For an excellent account of the internal diversity of the Labour Party see Warde (1982).
5. See Braunthal (1983), chap.1.
6. *Ibid.*, chap.8; Chalmers (1964); see also Paterson (1976).
7. Ross (1982); see also Smith (1981).
8. Harris (1973).
9. Tomlinson (1981), pp. 72-87; Schott (1982), pp. 68-81.
10. These, and the following figures, come from OECD, *Economic Outlook*, December 1980, p. 134 and July 1981, p. 132.
11. Youngson (1980).
12. Cullingford (1976); Markovits and Allen (1980); OECD *Economic Survey: Germany*, 1968, 1969, 1970.
13. Dorfman (1979); Panitch (1976); Crouch and Pizzorno (1978), vols 1 and 2.
14. The literature on the May events of 1968 is extensive but for an overview see Posner (1970); Cohn-Bendit (1969).
15. Blank (1973), pp. 123ff and chap. 5.
16. Budd (1978); Harris (1973).
17. Turner (1969), chap. 3 and pp. 69ff; Kipping (1972), pp. 92ff.
18. For accounts of what this meant see Wilson (1974); Foot (1968); Coates (1975); Warde (1982), chap. 5.
19. Budd (1978), chap. 6; Brown (1972), chaps 5 and 6.
20. McEachern (1980), chap. 8.
21. See Jones (1973); Crouch (1982), chap. 2; Panitch (1976); Soskice and Ullman (1983).
22. Moran (1977).
23. Andrew Roth (1972), p. 217.
24. Moran (1977), chap. 3.
25. Glyn and Sutcliffe (1972).
26. Brown (1972).
27. Carre (1975), p. 486; Bonnaud (1975), p. 94.
28. Cohen (1977).
29. Hough (1982), pp. 111-15 for a summary of the eight plans.

30. Michalet (1974), p. 107.
31. *Ibid.*, pp. 108ff.
32. Birnbaum (1980), p. 107.
33. Hough (1982), p. 114; Ardagh (1977).
34. Caron (1979), pp. 342–3; see also Servan-Schreiber (1968).
35. Caron (1979), p. 336.
36. Michalet (1974), p. 118.
37. Posner (1970); Cohn-Bendit (1969); Brown (1974).
38. Brizay (1975), chap.3; see also Bunel and Saglio (1984).
39. OECD, *Economic Survey: Germany*, 1967, 1968, 1969, and 1970. These provide details on the economic dimensions of the recession as well as a commentary on the policy moves undertaken by the government as a response. In particular note their criticisms of the way in which the Federal Government was unable to develop an adequate counter-cyclical response in the terms of the then prevailing orthodoxy. For an account of the gradually declining growth rate and the business cycles of the post-war period see Hardach (1980), pp.226ff.
40. The case that the Federal Republic had prepared itself with wide ranging powers to counter the left has been argued by Cobler (1978). Gordon Smith's rejection of Cobler's contention takes no account of the fact that the Federal Republic did not have to add any procedures to its existing arsenal of state powers to respond to the Red Army Faction. See Smith (1979), note 16, p. 217.
41. Lieberman (1977), p. 196.
42. Note the commentary on this in the OECD, *Economic Survey: Germany*, 1968, 1970; Küster (1974), pp. 66ff.
43. Lieberman (1977), p. 208.
44. *Ibid.*, p. 209.
45. For details of these economic measures see OECD, *Economic Surveys: Germany*, 1967, 1968, pp. 13ff.
46. Küster (1974), pp. 80ff.
47. Hirsch (1980), p. 123.
48. *Ibid.*, pp.123–4.
49. Markovits and Allen (1984), part 3.
50. For a detailed account of Concerted Action see Clark (1979), pp.242–58.
51. See Braunthal (1976); also Clark (1979) p.245.
52. Clark examines the extent to which participation in Concerted Action discussions and the debate of provided data may have lowered the level of wage demands, *ibid.*, pp. 248ff.
53. As Clark observes, 'What is undisputed is that during the first two years of Concerted Action, real wages lagged behind the overall real growth rate of the economy (7.3 per cent in 1968) and a long way behind increases in company profits.' *Ibid.*, p. 249, also see OECD, *Economic Survey: Germany* 1968, p. 23; 1969, p. 13.
54. OECD *Economic Survey: Germany*, 1970, pp. 14–16; 1971, pp. 5, 6, 8, 9–10, 12, 14, 16 and 30; Clark (1979), pp. 249ff.

55. Clark (1979), pp. 253-4.
56. *Ibid.*, pp. 147, 252, 253.
57. OECD, *Economic Surveys: Germany,* 1969, p.18; 1970, p.20.

5 · WITH THE STATE – INTO THE RECESSION

INTRODUCTION

Although growth rates recovered after 1969 the underlying economic problems were not solved. Political attempts to control wages were not successful nor did they improve the strength of the economies in these individual countries. The dramatic booms in 1973 were without real foundations, only increasing the likelihood of recession. As things transpired, the collapse was much more dramatic than could have been foreseen on the basis of standard business or trade cycle calculations, lasted far longer and was of quite a different kind from previous periods of economic downturn since the end of the Second World War.

The incident that triggered the recession was the oil crisis of 1973. The rise of OPEC, the success of its cartel policies and the oil embargo that accompanied the 1973 Middle East War, reduced supplies and dramatically increased the price of oil. Given the dependence of modern industry on oil for energy and as a raw material, it was likely that output would fall and prices would rise. After ten years of recession, it is possible to see that this downturn was more like the inter-war depression than any of the previous, temporary periods of low growth.

There are numerous differences between these two periods of major economic downturn and these help isolate the distinctive features of this contemporary recession. The differences in length and intensity of the downturn provide clues about the significant changes that have occurred in the intervening years. The depression of the 1930s, even though it lingered on, was at its most dramatic for about two years at the most. A very major reduction in output occurred as well as a substantial increase in unemployment but the worst was confined to these years. This time, much the same has taken far longer to happen, suggesting that the changed size and role of the state has been able to delay the onset of such cyclical downturns, modify the extent of the collapse but not shorten their duration or final consequences.

The changed role of the state can be seen in other distinctive aspects of the present recession. The unique and largely unexpected combination of inflation and declining output (stagflation) has also been blamed on the monetary and fiscal policies of the expanded state. Monetarists see inflation as a result of the state's willingness to expand the money supply to boost production in all the trade cycles of the post-war era, with more funds needed each time to stave off downturns until the point was reached where inflation became uncontrolled and growth declined.[1] A similar story is told by those who argue that stagflation was a result of the fiscal, credit and tax policies of post-war governments which used Keynesian policies to prolong booms and shorten recessions. Such interpretations have both right and left wing variation. Mattick and Yaffe both argue that the increased role of the state, in the name of a Keynesian orthodoxy, would only stave off the day of reckoning, that crisis could be postponed but not avoided.[2] Events have fallen out much as these diverse accounts suggest but this does not confirm their interpretations, though their coincident emphasis on the state is not accidental.

Despite the neat fit between analysis and outcomes, none of the basic models could account for the character and duration of the recession. Keynesian analysis was confounded by the very co-existence of inflation and recession, for inflation ought to have generated a degree of economic growth, or reduced the rate of decline in output. Monetarist accounts fail since the relationship between an expansion of the money supply and inflation is not a direct, causal one and the truth of the analysis is not proved by the truth of its reverse, that a constriction of money supply leads to a reduction in the rate of inflation, since it is the intervention of economic recession that 'causes' the decline in the rate of inflation.

The recession that started in 1973–4 poses a number of important questions about the developing role of the state, its economic consequences and its relations with class organisations. Did the economic actions of the state cause this recession? This could have been the effect of the increased use of economic resources by the state itself, the cost of state administration or through diverting resources from the productive sectors of the economy. (Note that 'productive' does not refer to those sectors that are privately owned. The real distinction is between those parts of the economy involved in the production and circulation of commodities and those which are not.) In such a view fiscal and monetary policies are more adjuncts to the process than the determinants of its consequences. Some emphasis needs to be paid to these economic questions since this recession has been primarily economic in character. The social implications flow from the economic conditions and the questions of political responses have been largely conditioned by the economic circumstances of low growth, low profitability, low investment, high inflation and high unemployment. The urgency with which each of these components has been tackled reflects the political assessment of their priority but not their actual historical significance or contributions to the problems confronting industrial capitalism in this last quarter of the twentieth century.

The onset of recession and uncertainty posed a series of problems for the contending class organisations and for the state. For labour and the trade unions the problems were quite marked. Inflation was a threat to real incomes and measures were needed to adjust salary increases to changes in the real costs faced by labour. A variety of policy options were open: the only imperative in the situation was a need to respond. The decline in output implied an end to full employment and certainly raised the prospects of increasing unemployment, increasing problems for the maintenance of real wages. The range of alternatives was limited. In the past, state policy countering recession restored full employment. Traditionally, trade unions were in a poor position to maintain employment in the face of a major recession and, certainly, would have problems seeking to maintain both employment and real wages.

For business, some of the problems were obvious and shared but others were specific to particular parts of the economy. Inflation, especially as it affected raw material prices, created problems for industry and retail sectors. With the international market saturated with surplus products, the possibility of offsetting the consequences of domestic recession was reduced. For finance, inflation caused acute problems since it was unusual for interest rates to be as high as the escalating rates of inflation. Hence, bank investments and loans were producing low or no yields, an obvious problem. The decline in production was not in itself a cause, it was a response to the difficulties of financing production, selling goods and earning sufficient profits to make investment attractive. For finance, the decline in domestic production simply increased the attractiveness of overseas investments and loans and, to the extent that there were barriers in the way of an unrestricted outflow of capital, there were policy choices to be argued. None of this should be taken to mean that business did not face severe problems in the persistent recession. The longer it went on, and the more severe the decline, the greater the strain placed on individual firms. Though the system as a whole may emerge from a severe downturn or economic crisis with improved health after the purging of inefficient, unworthy, wasteful enterprises, those parts being purged can not be so sanguine about the process. Business wanted an end to the recession but its enthusiasm and support varied with the political, economic and social costs of the particular strategy being implemented.

Recession and inflation both posed problems for the state as a social and economic entity in its own right. Without indexation tax revenue increased with inflation, at least in money terms as rising incomes increase the amounts of taxation paid. But recession reduces economic transactions and reduces the tax base. Unemployment and the social dislocation associated with prolonged recession increases financial demands on the state and how to finance state expenditures is a problem. In addition, the state's own share of the 'mixed' economy was also in trouble. In manufacturing it was as much squeezed as any private firm, and in the infrastructural areas, the demands for its products were reduced as the industrial economy contracted. These economic problems posed the problem of the relationship of revenue to expenditure as a 'fiscal' crisis for the state.[3] The distance between income and expenditure can be reduced by a number of measures: borrowing, increasing taxes or reducing expenditure. Any single measure or combination of measures has extensive effects on the wider economy, the different sections of business and on labour. The economy did not generate an imperative that compelled, in any authoritative manner, a particular response. Rather it created problems which required some form of state action.

The economic dimension is not the only one involved. The state is also concerned with the question of stability and with the need to preserve a degree of social cohesion, especially in a major recession with high unemployment. After a lengthy period of full employment and rising standards of living, with trade unions well organised and developing socially challenging schemes there is no guarantee that those disadvantaged by recession will simply accept their fate. Some schemes are cheap, others expensive, either to increase welfare provision or to boost the powers of the police and armed forces. Such increased costs must be offset by expenditure cuts somewhere else.

The recession set up a series of economic and social problems for the contending class organisations and the state. This chapter explores the initial response to economic downturn, in which the normal post-war counter cyclical measures were applied in a more vigorous manner to what was a more severe downturn. This response reveals the implicit logic of the post-war settlement and exposes the way in which the years of growth and government intervention not only altered the environment in which classes confronted each other but also changed the balance of forces between them.

CLASS AND STATE RESPONSES TO THE ONSET OF RECESSION

Once it became clear that the recession was not going to disappear the state was forced to respond. The problems generated for the two major classes meant that there were great clamours for action, at the very least to control inflation and then to restore conditions of growth, stable profits and full employment.

In Britain, the circumstances surrounding the sudden 1972–3 boom and the attempt to limit wage increases by statutory means precipitated a political and (only secondly) an economic 'crisis'.[4] It appeared, both to the trade unions, and certainly to business, that the trade unions were in a position of strength. The long years of near full employment had re-enforced their position: their members were relatively united and, led by the miners, relatively militant over pay claims. In social affairs, their successes in opposing incomes policies and the legislated reform of trade union affairs had encouraged trade unions to have a broader vision of what was possible and desirable in existing circumstances. This period of trade union confidence was evident in the negotiations between the Labour Party and the trade unions over a voluntary policy of income restraint. The politics of the general situation made it necessary to strike some bargain between the party and the trade unions: pay restraint would need to be agreed, but the strength of the trade unions was such that non-wage demands would have to be traded for such agreement. The repeal of the Heath government's Industrial Relations Act was an obvious first step. In the context of what had happened in the labour movement, symbolised most vividly by the arguments of Michael Barratt Brown in *From Labourism to Socialism*,[5] 'concessions' would be in the areas of social expenditure, education, health and welfare. It should be noted that although the trade unions called for substantial increases in the size and role of the public sector, which should be borne in mind for subsequent discussions, there was no new major commitment to nationalisation as such.[6] The emphasis was on Planning Agreements that would open up company plans and records for long-term scrutiny by both state officials and trade union representatives, and extend the presence of the state into the more potentially dynamic sectors of the then privately owned economy.

Such ideas were a response to two related experiences. The first concerned the post-war wave of nationalisation. Though these measures had given the state a presence in the economy which it had previously lacked, they had not brought substantial financial benefits to the working class, nor had they altered the power relations between managers and workers in either the public or private sectors of the economy. The new strategy, with its emphasis on opening the books and a greater state and trade union role in the conduct of private firms, was a limited response to the situation created by the previous nationalisation campaign. The second relevant experience was of the failure of private capital to provide for sufficient investment, structural reform and dynamism to secure a high growth economy and full employment. That is why the trade unions wanted the state to extend its planning role, so that it could offset the clear deficiencies of the private sector. The critique of Britain's industrial failure, its concern with the operations of the City of London as an institution for financing industrial development, its concern with promoting investment in risky but high technology ventures were all the product of a desire to preserve a strong British economy and the economic conditions which, under capitalism, would secure the best standards of living for the working population as a whole. As such, this new pattern of ideas was a studied response to the problems facing the British economy which would consolidate the position of the trade union movement and the working class *within* the system as it existed. Though the rhetoric of the campaign was socialist, and the demands were sometimes presented as part of transition towards a socialist economy, the actual focus of the programme was to strengthen the position of labour within capitalist economic and social relations and to recapture growth at minimal cost to labour.

Business, industry in particular, had also changed its analysis of the role of the state in the conduct of the advanced, industrial capitalist economy. Though large sections still thought in terms of free enterprise and a minimal role for the state, the representatives of the larger firms and the professional officers of the CBI had come to see a more positive role for the state. This affected their assessment of the contributions of the two major political parties. The failure of the Heath government's statutory incomes policies made some more favourably inclined towards a Labour Government than they would have been in other circumstances.[7] The major problem confronting business, outranking both inflation and recession, was the militancy of the trade unions and the prospects of continued industrial strife. Paradoxically, the Labour Party's commitment to a voluntary accord was seen by some as preferable to a statutory policy because it reduced the direct presence of the state in economic matters. What was needed was a set of policies that would restrain wage increases and contain the thrust of the labour movement. At the very least this would give a breathing space within which the class relations of capitalist production could be secured before the consequences of the recession could be tackled by more conventional means. Although the trade unions did not seek to challenge the class power of capital, they were too strong to be simply brushed aside. Indeed the act of confronting trade union strength may have been a trigger that would have pushed the unions into even more militant policies. Questions of profits and reinvestment took a second place to the question of countering inflation in a way that would contain trade union agitations and secure the long term social position of capital.

This combination of inflation, recession and class conflict was the environment within which the state had to act. The strategy for the state's response was strongly conditioned by the electoral success of the Labour Party in 1974. Although the Party's electoral programme had not been designed for the circumstances in which it was elected, it did have as a key concern the setting up of institutional structures to promote growth in a low growth economy. The connection between the Party and the trade unions made the prospect of a managed response to inflation much more likely than it had been under the Conservative Party. In the next section, I will consider the programmes of the 1974-9 Labour Governments under two main headings. The first section will deal with the Government's policies on the links between planning, investment and growth, the second, with policies on incomes and the state's social expenditures. It is very convenient that the policies of the Government very neatly divide around such a point, nonetheless, the social mission of the Government was to be achieved through the combination of these two sets of programmes. These two dimensions are also relevant to the consideration of events in France and Germany at this time and the account of the forces at work in Britain will be related to those present in France and Germany.

INVESTMENT, PLANNING AND GROWTH

An important part of the Keynesian orthodoxy was that the state should respond to economic downturns by measures to boost aggregate demand. In the context of the recession which started in the seventies, this was only partially an option. The traditional indifference to the source and pattern of expanded demand was undermined by inflation and the marked weakness of the domestic economy. In a strategy to preserve domestic industry, boost demand and shorten the duration of the recession, the state sought to promote both private and public investment. Given that the recession inevitably reduced the levels of private investment, this meant that the state increased its share in total investment and gained more importance in planning the pattern of future growth. It was not just the counter-cyclical urge that increased the role of the state. In some countries, most notably Britain, the political forces that came to prominence were convinced that the recession illustrated the prior failures of private investment and urged state action, not just to supplement the deficiencies, but to take the initiative. Hence, moves to rescue recession-hit firms from financial failure through nationalisation, guaranteed loans or tariff protection were often linked to attempts to strengthen the position of the state within the economy and to give it more scope for economic direction. Since the recession most adversely affected manufacturing industry, this 'rescue' strategy moved the state directly and indirectly into manufacturing and beyond the more strictly infrastructural areas of the mixed economy. The combination of financial pressure on state firms, the increased significance of state investment, and the role of the state in supporting and rescuing endangered industries, raised significant questions about the role of the state in the economy and the appropriate boundaries between the state and privately owned sectors. On its own, this would have been a significant development, capable of distressing private business but it happened in the context of trade union demands that increased their presence in the political process and, worse still, urged this very expansion of the state's role.

Britain

Let us consider Britain first. In opposition, the Labour Party had reworked its approach to planning and investment. After dismantling direct economic controls at the end of the Second World War the Labour Party had very little to say about the state's role in promoting and directing investment. With its weakened commitment to nationalisation it was left gesturing in the direction of planning but without any substantial resolve. This can be seen in the fiasco surrounding the so called 'National Plan' and the rapid dwindling of the 'white heat of technology' phase of the Wilson Government. After the ending of the long boom and the years of failure to rediscover sources of sustained growth, the Party adopted the idea of a National Enterprise Board to link the public and private sectors of the economy together in a strategy that would promote growth without resorting to deadening bureaucratic controls.

The National Enterprise Board (NEB) was an adaptation of ideas that had been in the Labour Party since its reform after the First World War (in the call for a National Investment Board) and of Holland's analysis of the inappropriateness of French-style indicative planning in low growth economies such as Britain.[8] The NEB was to be a state share-owning body that would act to boost investment in areas of great risk but with potential to provide long-term growth and increase British exports.[9] The onset of the recession changed, to a certain degree, the logic of its initiatives. The financial problems of firms made them less able to resist the Board's overtures and the price of rescue was often a significant government shareholding and state appointed directors on the board to oversee the modernisation plans funded or guaranteed by the state. For these and a number of other reasons, private business was strongly opposed to the NEB, its abstract conception and its practical role.[10] Its opposition was increased through hostility to Tony Benn, the Secretary of State for Industry and a passionate advocate of the Board's modernising and innovative role. Private business mounted a determined campaign to be rid of Benn and to emasculate the National Enterprise Board to stop it reaching further into the private economy. For business, Benn came to symbolise the thrust of the trade unions into the arena of political decision making about the economy – since his actions stressed the importance of democratising, if only in limited ways, the management of companies in which the state invested, and the attempt to expand the economic leverage of the state. Business was successful in its campaign and the removal of Benn from Industry to Energy was a symbol of the change of emphasis in Labour's approach to business and the recession. It is not as if the NEB strategy was a deliberate challenge to the prerogatives of management and private capital. Indeed, the whole life of the NEB was one of compromise, commercial judgement and state assistance to private industry; it could not be interpreted as the state imposing an alien strategy on business. The state was, however, taking more initiatives than it had before to see that funds given to private firms were used to achieve the intended goals. The NEB and the strategy of promoting industrial investment and modernisation through state encouragement and initiative was a failure.

Labour's other attempt to increase the ability of the state to monitor economic development, the Planning Agreement, also failed.[11] Planning Agreements were meant to be quasi-legal documents setting out a company's plans for development, expansion or contraction over a number of years. They were meant to be seen by trade union representatives and, when the government had provided funds for expansion, by state officials. Their purpose was to give trade unions a much greater sense of involvement in their companies, to remove the element of surprise from a company's redundancy announcements and to provide a mechanism for the state to monitor the uses to which its funds were being put. The Planning Agreement was a much greater annoyance to private business than any other proposal, apart from nationalisation.[12] It was seen as a direct encroachment on managerial rights undermining the dynamism and commercial viability of firms. The most objectionable part of the planning agreement was that it would give trade unions an oversight role. Knowledge about a company's intentions could be used by the trade unions to plan their campaigns to have maximum effect. The negotiation of planning agreements between the state and the recipients of state funds was a situation that worried business but against which it had no sound defence, apart from arguing for general and not specific assistance and for a minimal role for the state.[13] The extent of opposition to planning agreements can be gauged from the fact that only one was ever signed and that was between Chrysler and the government.[14] Although it outlined impressive guidelines for the investment/ rescue strategy, these were not followed and the firm eventually withdrew from the British scene, selling off its assets to a European consortium.

The weaknesses that existed in the areas of investment and planning seriously undermined the coherence of the Labour government's efforts to link patterns of wage restraint with an investment strategy to ensure recovery and stable long term growth. In effect, the failures in this area left the situation much as it was, with the traditional institutions of the British system of private capital intact and able to continue their failure into a new era. The financial institutions would still operate to ship funds away from the industrial sector and to boost the value of sterling with little regard for its impact on British exports. Britain's industrialists would still fail to make the extensive and radical investment commitments that would be needed to modernise the productive base of the British economy.

France

The potential impact of the oil crisis on France was greater than on Britain, since France was so heavily dependent on imports for its energy requirements. Although it is true that inflation and declining output were the immediate consequences of the 1973–4 situation,

France was not so badly affected.[15] The immediate response, as elsewhere, was to continue with the tested methods to counter the effects of the downturn and to promote investment and consolidate the chances of recovery. Though the French measures were criticised for exaggerating cyclical movements rather than countering them,[16] the overall tendency, in the years up to 1976, was to use state spending to offset the weakness in private investment. In the context of the changes in French planning, with the emphasis moving towards a greater sophistication in the modelling of the economy and a more discriminatory package of supports and assistance,[17] and the moves to 'stabilise' the situation – the role of price controls will be discussed below – the state's share in total investment increased while that of private investment declined.[18] As Shonfield remarks, in assessing the difference between the seventh and eighth plans:

> If the trend of the VIIth Plan were for example simply extrapolated into the VIIIth, this would imply a significant change in the balance between the private and public sectors of the economy.[19]

Though the weakness of such a simple-minded projection is easily exposed, it does point to the common problem caused by state sponsored investment and the contraction of private investment in the period of protracted recession. Such a development paved the way for the substantial reassessment of macro-economic policy that accompanied the rise of Raymond Barre to prominence in the making of economic policy.

The state continued with its efforts to promote the formation of larger economic units more capable of competing in European and world markets. It also continued its efforts to promote the modernisation of backward sectors of the French economy and to promote increased research and development in the fields of new technology. Despite the fact that the French planning mechanisms were probably the most sophisticated and most comprehensive available in Europe, these measures were not a marked success, and paved the way for a change in policy direction, that came in 1976, earlier than in most other countries. The Giscard Presidency was marked by a desire to reduce the importance of the state in economic life and a strong wish to strengthen the place of market forces in the making of industrial policy. Despite this ambition, as Dianna Green comments 'This regime, then, which had nailed its colours to the mast of economic liberalism, created, *prima facie,* the means of devising and carrying out the most coherent, systematic and detailed industrial policy ever seen in France'.[20] Despite the rhetoric it was still a matter of the state trying to pick winners and losers. Such changes did raise questions about the boundaries between the state and privately owned sectors of the economy and the pattern of initiative between the two.

Government, in the first phase of the recession in France, was dominated by conservative political forces, and as a result trade unions were in no position to be influential. They had no shortage of ideas about what should be done about the level of investment, even though they had no effective political vehicle to advance their goals. This was the era of the Common Programme in which the PCF and the PS negotiated a joint approach to government which involved a commitment to significant nationalisation and democratic planning to solve the problems of investment and industrial renewal. This document was supported by the CGT, but initially opposed by the CFDT. The CFDT had developed a distinctive approach to the political role of trade unions and the difficult relations with competing political parties.[21] It promoted a vision of 'autogestion' as a strategy for the transformation of the social order avoiding the revolution/incorporation dichotomy. For them, the Common Programme's focus on nationalisation and state power missed the vital question of how new enterprises were to be managed and society transformed. The dynamics of the political and industrial situation were such that they came to negotiate a common action position with the CGT and to campaign for the electoral success of the PS and PCF as the best way of solving problems facing workers. The unions were, however, caught up in the dynamic of PS and PCF conflict over election tactics. With the split both unions reassessed what they had been doing and how they should respond to persistent recession and the political situation.[22] They made their 'trade union' contribution to a future government strategy while not being 'influential' in this period. The most significant developments for a political response to the economy came not from the trade unions but from the disputes between the parties on the left. The breakdown of the Common Programme strategy (where it did not depend on the calculation of electoral advantage and the balance of power between the two parties) turned around two different conceptions of the size of the public sector and its role. The PCF favoured a centralised planning system with an extensive, publicly owned core and the PS favoured a more open, looser, management of relations between an enhanced but by no means dominant public sector and a significant private sector with significant market relations.[23]

With conservative forces dominating and the whole tone of the Government's response, the organisations of business had little scope for concern. They would have been happier if the strategy had worked and the French recovery had been sustained. The obvious long-term failure caused them some anxiety. In this period this was kept under control by their hostility to the trade unions and the forces of the left. The CNPF openly supported the right in the elections in the seventies as a response to, what was for them, the threat from the left. The emphasis on nationalisation and an extension of planning in the Common Programme was seen as a danger to the rights of management and property. The extension of the role of the state, under the control of a conservative government did not cause them as much anxiety as parallel events in Britain. That had to wait until after Mitterrand's election in 1981.

Federal Republic of Germany

The oil price increase and the cyclical pattern of economic growth combined in the Federal Republic of Germany to produce a recession in output which had only a slight impact on inflation and the trading position of the economy.[24] As with France and Britain, the tendency was to respond to the economic downturn with the particular array of counter-cyclical measures developed in the preceding years. In Germany's case, this meant a concern to use state policy to encourage private investment, largely through a manipulation of the pattern of taxation and tax concessions, so that private firms would invest in new plant, technologies or rationalise and modernise old equipment.[25] As in previous downturns, it was possible for the state to modify the impact of the recession on the levels of unemployment by encouraging 'guest workers' to leave or not to return. Unlike before, this was less effective, partly because the number of guest workers had already been reduced, partly because the economic position of immigrant labour was such that it could not easily be replaced by German workers (the structure of employment had changed) and partly because the EEC had started to set strict rules over the repatriation of labour and the conditions under which immigrant labour could be employed.[26] It is clear that in the initial period of the recession, it was the state which took the initiative in promoting investment in depressed conditions and used both deficit financing and positive state action to boost the domestic economy.

Given the slightly different configuration of the recession in the Federal Republic, it is less easy to assess the consequences of these state actions. It is possible to see that the state's share in investment outstripped that of the private sector in this period but it is less clear that this represented any lasting change to the overall balance between the state and privately owned sectors of the economy. State assistance to private industry was fairly indiscriminate in its application and the state lacked the means to direct or co-ordinate the investment which occurred as a result of its generosity. The significance of this indifference did not appear as a problem until much later in the recession, by which time the possibility of a more determined effort by the state had already passed.

The situation in Germany ought to have had strong parallels with events in Britain. When the oil crisis hit, a coalition government of the Social Democratic Party and the Free Democratic Party was in office. The Social Democratic Party had close relations with most parts of the trade union movement and the two had some experience of working together when hard times hit. Further, the DGB had, like the TUC, been developing a response to economic management of an industrialised capitalist society which emphasised an increased role for trade unions and the state. In the Federal Republic it took the characteristic form of a demand for an extension of co-determination and the pursuit of parity on co-determination boards. There was, as in Britain, a critique of the deficiencies of private capital, willing to make profits but unwilling to make job-securing investments. As Markovits and Allen summarised the position: 'In numerous studies, the DGB is intent on showing how capital's profits continue to increase without any effects on productive growth: profits are used for rationalisation, for deposits in foreign bank accounts and investments in foreign countries.' [27] In this context demands were made for the state to take a greater role in economic planning. There was every sign that the trade union movement recognised its strength and wanted to see some changes in the way the system worked to protect the position of workers and to preserve full employment.[28]

The trade union movement made almost no progress on their demands for a greater state role in planning or supervision of the private economy. It had a similar range of ambitions as the British Labour Party. Indeed, in some areas its vision was greater and in others it was more directly concerned to have the trade union movement play a part in the supervision of private investment, or to accumulate funds under its own control. Nonetheless, it did not have the equivalent of the Social Contract to fuel its push for the introduction of these changes. Crouch, in his influential article 'Varieties of Trade Union Weakness', argues that union strategy in West Germany was based on promoting high investment by moderating its wage demands and thus ensuring high rates of profit.[29] This may have been true of the period of the boom but in conditions of renewed recession with investment down and jobs being shed the unions needed more than moderation to secure their position. Whatever tension existed between capital and labour, or between capital and the state, they were not backed by significant state action to introduce these union demands in the first stage of recession. Indeed, the German labour movement acquiesced in the strategies proposed by business and government on the basis of a share in the decision making within various 'crisis cartels' despite the fact that they did not win the kind of social role in planning that they generally sought.[30] German business can have had little cause to complain about the government's response to the onset of recession. Trade unions did not gain a significant advantage from the government of the Social Democratic Party and certainly did not use their influence to increase pressures for a state supervision of private firms or state direction of investment in the private sector. The question of trade union attempts to extend co-determination, which did antagonise business, is discussed below.

The general pattern of state initiatives over investment, planning and growth in this the first stage of the recession reveals a common attempt to boost the levels of total investment and private investment. There was also a common concern to encourage the modernisation of the productive process and the introduction of new technologies. The particular character of these initiatives reflected the different techniques already developed to offset periodic cyclical downturns. It was a case of more of the same. It was only in Britain that an attempt was made to expand the significance of state initiative in the operation of the economy. Nonetheless, the constricting impact of recession on business profitability and its willingness to invest, meant that the state's investment initiatives incresased in comparison with those of the private sector, and in some cases, this appeared to be of long-term, decisive significance. Only in the case of Britain could this be interpreted as an encroachment on the prerogatives of management and private capital, though the broad question of the relationship between private and state initiatives was raised in other countries, if in a less dramatic form. Again, Britain was unique as this move to expand the state's economic role was explicitly related to the changed presence of the trade unions in the political system, since the trade unions provided the essential social support for the moves taken by the state.

WAGES, PRICES AND PROFITS

In analysing the different forces that combined to make this period of economic downturn worse than its postwar cyclical predecessors, the connection between wages and profits is significant. As a political issue it came to prominence after the ending of the long boom and, from the perspective of private capital and the state, the failure to contain trade union wage demands. Sometimes the analysis of the link between wages and future growth was fairly subtle, as in the case of Glyn and Sutcliffe. In *British Capitalism, Workers and the Profits Squeeze,* they argue that it was not trade union militancy and the high rate of wage settlements that endangered the levels of private profitability and hence the levels of investment and future growth, as was popularly argued by political and business figures.[31] Rather, it was trade union strength in a situation where Britain was being squeezed in the world market, and hence could not increase prices to pass off wage rises to consumers. In these circumstances the struggle between labour and capital was expressed as a profit squeeze and a steady decline in the profitability of manufacturing firms. The OECD, in their analysis of Germany at the onset of this recession, gave a far more prosaic account of the same process.[32]

Any tendency towards a squeeze on profits is greatly accentuated by recession, in which over-production acts as an additional barrier.[33] In such circumstances, restricting wage increases becomes even more important and in Britain, France and Germany determined efforts were made to control wages as part of a counter-inflation policy. In almost all cases the initial emphasis was on placating trade union demands with some gesture of state action. Sometimes the trade-off was between wage increases and the supervision of price increases, or between wage increases and the level of state spending on welfare and social provision. The most comprehensive example was the Social Contract negotiated in Britain between the Labour Party/Government and the TUC.[34] In France, the moves were less dramatic, being carried out by an essentially conservative and neo-liberal government, but still they sought to combine wage restraint, income transfers to the least well-off and forms of price control.[35] In Germany, the structure of concerted action was maintained but much less emphasis was placed on the social regulation of profits (through price surveillance mechanisms) or state welfare supplements; all this despite a social democratic government.[36]

Britain

The Social Contract was, in part, a mechanism for slowing the rate of wage increases which depended on a commitment to increase state spending on the provision of welfare, pensions, schools and benefits for those not in the labour market. It was negotiated between the Labour Party and the TUC in opposition to the Heath Government's statutory wage restraint. Voluntary wage restraint was possible if the government acted to offset the consequences of inflation for the young, old and ill. Measures of price surveillance, food subsidies and profit and dividend restraint were part of the package. The importance of these latter measures should not be exaggerated. Oversupply often worked to restrain the rate of price increases and sometimes the price surveillance procedures were one way of securing price increases in these economically difficult times. Similarly, dividend restraint was only a minor inconvenience to the majority of economically significant firms.[37]

It is not necessary to go into the fine print of the agreement, nor the complex patterns of negotiations and trade offs that varied from year to year as the levels of real wages were reduced and the government modified its commitments to social expenditure.[38] Suffice it to note that the strategy had certain immediate benefits. At the end of the Heath Government the trade unions were mounting increasingly militant and more socially oriented strategies (of which the Social Contract was but one example); the combination of Labour rule and a continuing recession meant that trade unions were neither so militant nor socially ambitious. The rate of inflation gradually dropped and later, with the second 'oil shock', had only risen slightly. The levels of industrial output had begun to recover as had the profits earned by industrial firms. By contrast, banks and other financial institutions had suffered as a result of the high rates of inflation and the relatively low rates of interest, leading to low or negative earnings on their loans and investments measured in real terms. The international position of the British economy, its competitive weakness, the consequences of joining the EEC, its financial indebtedness to the International Monetary Fund revealed the severity of the long-term problems confronting the British economy. These, coupled with the absence of any sign that the Social Contract strategy had increased domestic industrial investment, or made an end to the recession more likely, paved the way for a major change in the strategy, centred on the relationship between the state and the economy and, predicated on that change, in the relationship between classes, class organisations and the state. Though what happened in the last years of the Labour Government appears quite tame by contrast with the Thatcher era; in the context of the period after the end of the long boom, it marked an important reassessment of the way in which that growth strategy had worked.

The two sets of class organisations of labour and capital show contrasting patterns in their rejection of the 'Social Contract' approach to managing the impact of the recession. The main body of the trade unions came, gradually, to understand that the strategy did not protect their wages or their employment, that the government was not fulfilling its promises on social expenditure, and that the state lacked determination to press private capital to invest in the face of a prolonged recession. The question of wage differentials eroded trade union unity and the slight upturn in the economy reduced the TUC's willingness to endorse another year of unrewarded wage restraint. The real problems in the relations between the TUC and the Labour Government came in the so called Winter of Discontent, when public sector workers sought to force the government to be more generous in its round of wage settlements and not to erode further their real standards of living. These workers had been affected by all parts of the government's strategy. The failure to increase public provisions at a time when the demands for welfare assistance were increased by the recession, the tight control over public sector wage increases, as part of the campaign to reduce the budget's borrowing requirements, all increased the problems faced by public sector workers. The collapse of the relationship between the TUC and the Labour Party/ Government paved the way for its subsequent electoral defeat. This is not surprising since the Party had come to office on the basis of its greater ability to manage trade union/government relations.

For business organisations the period represented a major challenge to their views on the proper relationship between the state and the economy and between political parties and class organisations. During the long boom, the CBI had abandoned industry's traditional *laissez-faire* rhetoric in favour of a constructive accommodation between business and the state in the mixed economy. This new period of state action challenged the established logic of the mixed economy and strained the relationship between the state and private business. For business, the package of trade union consultation and restraint in return for state action was the very essence of the Social Contract period. Whereas left criticism of the Labour Party stresses the extent to which labour was constrained by these empty agreements,[39] for business they represented a major increase in the power of trade unions and a reduction in the political system's ability to protect their (business) interests. It was the expanded role of the trade unions which was decisive in changing the attitude of the CBI towards government action and the Labour Party.[40] From being concerned that the balance of the mixed economy had been altered,[41] the CBI came to reject the whole 'managerialist' perspective. It reverted to business's more traditional views; monetarism, lower taxes, smaller state, free-market forces, reduced role for trade unions, and for business to rely on its relationship with a reformed Conservative Party.[42] It should be noted that the changes in business attitudes were as much promoted by a concern with the social relations between labour and capital as they were with the success or otherwise of Labour's economic strategy. Also, these changes in attitude would be effective only to the extent that the Conservative Party rejected the 'managerial' perspective which had been its stance since the time of Harold Macmillan. The needed changes occurred, fairly much at the same time, with the selection of Margaret Thatcher to replace Ted Heath as the leader of the Conservative Party.[43] It would be wrong to see any direct link between the two changes; indeed, they were both responses to the changed social and political landscape wrought by trade union/Labour Party negotiations in this, the first stage of the recession.

France

Though a similar array of measures were also adopted in France to counter inflation, the package lacked both the drama and the social implications of the British events. The fact that the measures were imposed by a conservative government, with trade unions as excluded from the economic decision making process as ever, explains this lack of social challenge. The French strategy had three related parts. Firstly, there were the moves to contain the rates of wage increases through negotiated contractual agreements in both the public and private sectors.[44] Secondly, there were strengthened measures of price control and a tax on inflation generated profits obviously undermining calls for wage increases.[45] Thirdly, there were further reforms of the social security system, to increase payments to the poorer sections of the population and to those most adversely affected by increased inflation.[46] In outline, the package was not all that different from the Social Contract in Britain, except that it lacked coherence and the formal negotiations with the social partners to set its parameters. Despite the apparent lack of a social challenge by labour, strengthened by the electoral weaknesss of the Union of the Left, this strategy paved the way for a new era of monetarism and neo-liberal policies.

After it became clear that this was no normal cyclical downturn, the French trade unions developed an analysis of what the recession meant and responded to the problems of reduced output and inflation. Their views were surprisingly similar to trade unions in both Britain and Germany. The recession persisted because of international and domestic problems and an insufficiency of demand.[47] Increasing wages and shortening working hours would improve the situation by boosting domestic demand and reducing the pool of unemployed. To the extent that inflation was a problem it should be tackled by controlling prices and, perhaps, in that context, levels of wage restraint could be considered. Some of this programme was under the control of trade unions themselves ... they could press for higher pay, improved work conditions and shorter hours directly in their dealings with business, and this they did. In addition they could encourage 'their' political parties to adopt programmes that accommodated these demands. In this period they were squeezed by the electoral politics of the union of the left and their lack of political success. At best they could press for changes in the Common Programme and pave the way for a future government response.

Business responses to the situation were conditioned by their concern over the possible revival of leftwing political forces and by the way in which government acted, increasing the size and role of the state. Unlike in Britain and Germany, their response was not conditioned by direct hostility to the increased political presence of trade unions coupled with an expansion of the state. On the whole they had only to contend with the expansion of the state. Their situation was complicated by the apparent failure of the Government's economic strategy. In the initial period, counter-cyclical policies did not make the recession go away. In the second phase of neo-liberal experiment, success was not overwhelmingly obvious. It is not that the strategy conspicuously failed in economic terms. True, depressed conditions persisted but the major economic indices for output, inflation and employment showed improvements and the impact of the recession in France was less than in its rivals. In the French case it can only be the increased initiatives of the state, the heightening of international competition in a period of generalised overproduction and the comparative competitive weakness, that paved the way for the rejection of the 'contractual' approach and the return of French neo-liberalism in the person of Raymond Barre, appointed Prime Minister by Giscard d'Estaing in 1976.

Federal Republic of Germany

In Germany, consistent with its history, the moves over wages, prices, profits and government expenditure showed deference to private business. Thus, unlike Britain and France, there were no attempts to restrain price increases as the profitability of private investment was seen as being dependent on such increases. On the wages front, the Concerted Action machinery remained intact and useful. The onset of the recession meant that there was even less emphasis on negotiated reductions in wage increases; rather Schmidt's rise produced a more authoritarian determination process.[48] In Germany, the trade union movement was well aware of the problems generated by persistent recession. As recession hit they responded with a successful wage compaign winning large increases in 1974. They then agreed to wage restraint over the next couple of years even though they were concerned to protect the levels of real wages and employment. Broadly they were concerned by the export-oriented strategy pursued by their government and would have preferred a greater emphasis on the home market. They too wanted higher wages, shorter hours and improved work conditions. On their own they could press for these in the context of normal industrial relations. Real problems existed in their relationship with the SPD/FDP Government and its economic strategy which favoured profits and sought to restrict wage growth.[49] They had no effective means to trade wage restraint for the economic and social change they thought desirable. In only one area did their relationship with SPD make a significant difference. Unlike the British trade unions, the DGB had a strategy designed to increase the presence and power of trade unions within private enterprise through the extension of co-determination.[50]

The DGB pressed for an extension of co-determination to increase the number of firms covered by the programme. The unions also pressed to have parity in the numbers of workers' representatives on the board. Neither of these proposals were supported by employers who struggled against them both.[51] For them, the extension of co-determination was a direct inflation of the presence of workers within, not the political process, which would have been bad enough, but within the economic process. It was in the midst of this struggle that the Concerted Action programme ended when the trade unions withdrew as a response to business's appeal to the constitutional court to render invalid the new co-determination laws.[52] The extension of co-determination was upheld and then the law was implemented. The extension of co-determination did not alter the balance of control in privately owned enterprise,[53] but it was a powerful symbol of a potential for a future trade union challenge and a cause of concern for private business in the system.

In Germany business did not face the same situation as in Britain. It is true that trade unions were increasing their presence both in the political and economic fields and that the size and the scope of state action was increasing. Nonetheless, in Germany the connection between these two processes was not as intimately connected as it was in Britain. True, the state enacted the legislation to extend co-determination but that extension was not related to the expansion in size and scope of state action. The state remained an enthusiastic defender of the economic position of private business. It was seeking ways of strengthening the profitability of firms as a way out of the present recession and it avoided supporting trade union demands to reorient the government's strategy away from its focus on exports and the world economy. Business faced ambiguity and uncertainty from the actions of the trade unions and would seek government action to reduce that but it did not have to confront the SDP/FDP government as such. The government conceded the economic importance of private enterprise and the social market economy and pursued degrees of monetary control, neo-liberal precepts and austerity. Though German business was upset, it was not as upset as British business.

The general response of governments in Britain, France and Germany to the relationship between wages, prices and profits was consistent with the history of their post-war counter-cyclical initiatives. In each case the extent of wage increases was seen as an economic problem needing a state response. In each case there was an attempt to persuade trade unions to accept some erosion of their real incomes in return for some increase in the levels of private investment to secure the economic future and, perhaps, generate long-term growth and employment. Since such a reward was only in the (distant) future, governments acted to placate trade union suspicion by giving some state assistance to the poorer and more exposed sections of the population. Similarly, the state acted to monitor price increases, an apparent parallel to the regulation of wages. In all cases, the persistence of the recession undermined this approach; revenues were reduced and governments claimed they could no longer afford the promised increased social expenditure; the trade unions became increasingly reluctant to agree to the steady erosion of their living standards, especially when there were signs of a minor improvement in economic conditions towards the end of the period. To a certain extent, though strongly conditioned by the particular circumstances of each country, the relative powerof the trade unions, as measured by their presence in the political decision making process, had been increased in the years since the ending of the long boom. Such an increase had either been accentuated or consolidated by government strategy in this period. It was this social dimension, coupled with the persistence of the recession, which caused private business organisations to re-evaluate their approaches to the mixed economy, the role of government in the economy and their attitudes towards the trade unions. The implications of this social perspective were most evident in their subsequent support for monetarism and neo-liberal policies.

THE NEO-CORPORATIST PHASE

On the basis of the preceding account of state initiatives over the relationship between wages, prices, profits and investment, it is possible to evaluate the relevance of the neo-corporatist arguments that flourished in this period. For the neo-corporatist, this period appears as the fulfilment of a long process in the historical development of the institutional relations between labour, capital and state. The partial adoption of tripartite planning institutions after the ending of the long boom was completed by their wholesale adoption, especially in the area of incomes policies, in the first period of the recession. These developments were presented as if, at the very least, a new stage in the accumulation process and a new social order had been created.[54] For sceptics, this raised the question of the difference between a new stage in capitalism and a strategy that can be used by the state in particular circumstances, a strategy that passes away when circumstances change. Some aspects of this difference will be explored below.

When looking at what happened, it is surprising how few significant tripartite institutions were actually created.[55] The celebrated example of the British Social Contract reveals the misconceptions involved. The Social Contract was a bipartite arrangement between trade unions and the Labour Party/Government: the organisations of private capital were not involved at all. Indeed, the exclusiveness of the negotiations was one aspect which antagonised private business. Even such institutions as the National Enterprise Board, which arose out of the Social Contract and affected private capital, was not the product of tripartite agreement. Perhaps if it had been, it would have proved more durable. It is only through the government and its separate negotiations with the two sets of class organisations that there is any sense of tri-partitism at all. To be generous, the neo-corporatists did not rely on such strict formalism to support their cases.

The implication of their arguments is that times and circumstances have changed. Unlike in the inter-war years, violence and state power are no longer necessary to persuade unions to participate. The unions, as a result of a long period of education in the realities of the politics and economics of developed, industrialised capitalism, actively seek incorporation and the creation of tripartite bodies as the best arenas in which they can express their social power. In a similar way business hostility to the state and co-operation with unions has been broken down. The pragmatic acceptance of such co-operation, over time, comes to be part of business routine. Out of the experience and increasing co-operation of class organisations and the state comes a degree of formalisation in flourishing neo-corporate bodies.

To present the developments in this way is to confuse notions of a new phase in capitalist development with a strategic initiative dependent, it is true, on the institutional changes that have occurred in the post-war period. It was a limited response to difficulties that could not be solved in any other way. The presence of trade unions strengthened as a result of sustained full employment is the problem. Their increased bargaining power was not destroyed simply by the onset of recession. The classical response to recession, increase unemployment and cut wages, is not easily available, certainly not without the prospect of substantial social disruption. When it is clear that the recession will persist, then classical measures are more attractive to both business and the state. The growth of so-called neo-corporatist institutions in the first phase in the recession is a strategic response by the state to the power and potential of trade unions. That is why the state in all these countries sought to operate different kinds of incomes policies, involve the trade unions (that is the cost of the scheme) and gradually regulate the rate of wage increases until inflation began to cut their real incomes. It is a strategy that lasts only so long as there is no other effective response to the social consequences of the recession. As soon as the recession starts to undermine the organisationalstrength of the trade unions and their morale, the strategy can be modified and, finally, abandoned. The classical consequences of recession then take over from quasi-neo-corporatist institutions. The varying degrees to which British, French and German governments adopted such a strategy provides a measure of the presence of trade unions in the particular system.

THE RECESSION GOES ON

It is clear that the strategies adopted by different class organisations and the state did not work to end the recession. The so called 'second oil shock' of 1978 was only a complicating factor in an already difficult situation. Though the economy had shown some signs of recovery, there was never any indication that it would produce a return to full employment and sustained growth. The logic of global overproduction was beginning to be felt, as manufactured goods flowed into Europe from Japan and, to a lesser degree, the newly industrialising countries of East Asia and Latin America. The persistence of recession intensified the problems for classes. For labour, levels of imcome, employment and state supplements, in the form of welfare provisions were all under threat. For capital, both the recession and the state responses created their difficulties. Industry was threatened by inflation, international competition and the level of wage settlement. Finance was hurt by the low levels of real earnings and the uncertainties of international loan and investment policies. All parts of capital felt threatened by the political and social gains made by labour since the inter-war depression: a question of class power as much as economics. Similarly, most parts of capital viewed the combination of trade union presence and the expanding significance of state action, especially in manufacturing industry, as a major barrier to their future economic and social security. The persistence of recession set the scene for a major reworking of the relationship between class organisations and the state and between the state and the economy.

NOTES

1. Brittan (1975); Harris and Seldon (1977); Seldon (ed.) (1979).
2. Mattick (1971); Yaffe (1973).
3. O'Connor (1973).
4. The word 'crisis' – widely used at the time – was inappropriate. The situation was a difficult one for the state management of industrial relations but there was no sense in which the viability of the system was called into question or challenged. The image of powerful unions was highlighted by the political ineptitude of the Heath government in seeking to contain wage increases in an artificially sustained, short sharp boom. To combine this management failure with a call for a 'who runs the country' election was an act of political bravado that compounded the failure and boosted trade union confidence to a very great degree. It was as much this problem that confronted the 1974 Wilson Labour Government as that of high inflation or low output.
5. Brown (1972).
6. For an account of what the proposal implied see Holland (1975).
7. Grant and Marsh (1975), pp. 90–104.
8. For an account of arguments that sought alternative patterns of state action to secure growth, see Holland (1972). This article reveals some of the thinking behind Holland's advocacy of the National Enterprise Board for Britain, and the initiatives taken by Tony Benn when he was Secretary of State for Industry.
9. Coates (1980), chap.3.
10. CBI, (1976), p. 56; CBI (1977), p. 25.
11. Coates (1980), pp. 100ff.
12. CBI (1976), chap.VII.
13. CBI (1977), p. 25.
14. Coates (1980), pp. 102–6.
15. OECD, *Economic Outlook*, December 1980, p. 134.
16. OECD, *Economic Surveys: France*, 1977, pp. 28ff.
17. For accounts of these changes, see Green (1978), pp.60–76; Collis (1979), pp.256–61; Hough (1982), chap.5.
18. OECD, *Economic Surveys: France*, 1977, p. 36.
19. Shonfield (1980), p. 833.
20. Green (1984), p. 147.
21. For information on the CFDT, see Hayward (1979), pp. 53–67.
22. See Ross (1982) for a detailed account of the positions each took and the relations between them, pp. 38–64.
23. Green (1979), pp. 81–96.
24. OECD, *Economic Outlook*, December 1980, pp. 134–6.
25. OECD, *Economic Survey, Germany*, 1974 and 1978 for accounts of the internal debates over economic strategy and the various financial assistance schemes introduced.
26. Castles (1984).
27. Markovits and Allen (1980), p. 77.

28. Braunthal (1983), chaps. 6, 8 and 13.
29. Crouch (1980), p. 94.
30. Esser and Fach with Dyson (1983), p. 110.
31. Glyn and Sutcliffe (1972).
32. OECD, *Economic Survey: Germany*, 1974, pp. 20, 37–8.
33. *Ibid.*, pp. 20, 34ff. There is clearly a problem with this since we know that prices were increased – at least to offset oil price increases. They claim that the increases were never enough to offset the full impact of labour and raw material costs.
34. Bornstein and Gourevitch (1984), pp. 42–5.
35. OECD, *Economic Survey: France*, 1974, 1975 and 1976.
36. Clark (1979).
37. CBI, (1976), pp. 9, 19–20, 39; CBI(1977), p. 19.
38. See Coates (1980); Thomson (1981), pp. 27–63.
39. Cliff (1975).
40. CBI (1977; 1980).
41. CBI (1976), pp. 8ff.
42. CBI (1977; 1987).
43. Behrens (1980).
44. Hough (1982), pp. 146–7; OECD, *Economic Survey: France*, 1974, pp. 61, 48.
45. Hough (1982), pp. 136 and 145–6; OECD, *Economy Survey: France*, 1974, pp. 22–3.
46. OECD, *Economic Survey: France*, 1974, pp. 21–34; OECD, *Economic Survey: France*, 1977, p. 36; see also Cohen and Coldfinger (1975).
47. Ross (1982), pp. 45–51 gives an account of the positions developed by the CGT and CFDT. They both agree on the need to increase minimum wage levels and to boost domestic demand.
48. Clark, (1979), p. 253.
49. Braunthal (1983), pp. 121–2.
50. Müller-Jentsch (1981), pp. 105–22; see also Markovits and Allen (1980), pp. 68–86.
51. Braunthal (1976) gives a detailed account of the legislative and political manoeuvres slowing the introduction of these changes.
52. For an account of business hostility to the extension of co-determination see Bunn (1984), pp. 178–9; Clark (1979), p. 256; Markovits and Allen (1984), pp. 162–4.
53. Braunthal (1976), p. 245, comments: 'The crucial question that cannot be answered yet is whether parity co-determination in all German companies will tilt the power relationship between workers and managers by curbing the economic power of the latter. Two decades of parity co-determination in coal, iron, and steel industries, and partial co-determination in other industries, as the performance of works councils, shows no proof so far.' For a similar evaluation from a more radical perspective, see Markovits and Allen (1980), pp. 80–2.
54. Pahl and Winkler (1974).

55. There were many tripartite bodies set up, but few were of great significance. For an account of the British situation, see Thomson (1981).

6 · WITH THE RECESSION – AGAINST THE STATE

As the recession continued, and it appeared that the expanded state response had failed, governments and political parties began to change their responses. In France, Giscard remained President but the appointment of Raymond Barre as Prime Minister in 1976 signalled a change. In Germany, the Social Democratic Party remained in government and all that happened was a gradual shift in emphasis. In Britain, although the outlines of the new policy had been given by the Chancellor, Denis Healey, after the balance of payment difficulties in 1975–6, it was the election of a transformed Conservative Party in 1979 that gave the distinctive character to the neo-liberal experiment. There is no unambiguous economic trigger for these changes, even though the second oil shock of 1978–9 was a common reference point, reflected in the OECD's discussions of the changed policy framework.[1] The character of the changed policy perspective is starkly revealed against the pattern of developing class and state relations in the post-war world. Up until this point the emphasis had been on expanding both the size and the scope of the state and creating closer organisational links between class organisations and the state in an effort to maintain both accumulation and social cohesion. The neo-liberals rejected this consensus and, indeed, saw such developments as the cause of inflation and prolonged economic recession. In contrast they proclaimed the need to reduce the size of the state and the scope of its actions and to increase the distance between the state and formal class organisations.

Such a changed state strategy, in rhetoric and reality, throws into relief the logic of post-war developments. It also suggests questions about the forces underlying the steadily increasing role for the state. The argument so far has suggested that the expansion of the state was related to, if not essentially functional for, securing social cohesion while seeking new avenues for economic growth. The challenge is posed: is it possible to explain the rise of a neo-liberal response in terms of the developing class–state relations, or is such an emphasis misplaced in this new political era?

THE POPULAR POLITICAL EXPLANATION

Political figures used a number of related arguments to justify such a dramatic change in the pattern of state action. Here I want to set out the terms in which the post-war development is presented and the different kinds of claims made to support the change in state policy. In doing so I want to show what underlay the political sensitivities of the neo-liberals as they came to approach the task of managing the state in an era of prolonged recession. To illustrate the popular political case I have used the speeches of Margaret Thatcher in the years between her neo-liberal conversion and her electoral success, as she explicitly identifies the key problems and their appropriate neo-liberal solutions.[2]

The growth of the state

A key theme in all neo-liberal arguments is that the state had grown too large and that this had bad economic, political and social effects. Taxation has increased to the point where it limits the profitability and undermines entrepreneurial initiative.[3] The state wastefully consumes resources that would be better left in the hands of the private, wealth-creating sector. The balance of the 'mixed economy' has tipped too far in favour of the state which now dominates and stifles economic growth.[4] State expansion is also linked, via taxation, to increased wage demands and inflation.[5] Socially, the expansion of the state in the welfare area has weakened the character of the population, undermining self reliance and personal initiative, rewarding unequally the indigent and the careful.[6] Inequality is needed for proper incentives for full human development.

> Opportunity means nothing unless it includes the right to be unequal – and the freedom to be different . . . I say: 'Let *our children* grow tall – and some grow taller than others, if they have it in them to do so.' We must build a society in which each citizen can develop his full potential

both for his own benefit and for the community as a whole; in which originality, skill, energy and thrift are rewarded; in which we encourage rather than restrict the variety and richness of human nature.[7]

Politically, the state expands to meet popular demands, and, by responding to calls for greater equality, weakens the efficiency of the economy.[8] Governments need to restrain, not respond to, the demands of citizens where they are likely to damage the economic efficiency of the market system.

Such a criticism of the role of the state suggests a ready cure. The size of the state needs to be reduced and the scope of the state actions limited. Governments should reduce both taxes and expenditure and cut damaging budget deficits. The state should sell its economic assets. Its essential tasks, primarily for defence and administration, should be performed as cost effectively as possible. The welfare system needs to be restructured to give greater scope to the family and self reliance. It is through a programme of this kind that the economy will become free again, enterprise will flourish and economic recovery will follow.

Such a vision of a reduced state leaves the point at which the process will stop unstated. It is not clear that the intention *is* to return to the situation before the steady encroachment began, that is, to the situation before the inter-war depression, although that is what the vehemence of the rhetoric suggests. The implication could be that it is only necessary to restore the relationship between the state and private sector to that which existed before the onset of the recession, when the state remained largely confined to an infrastructural, mixed economy role.[9] Such a position would fit the specific case made against state expansion if not the tone of the argument.

The trade unions

Linked to the argument about the state is a claim about the increased power of trade unions in the post-war period. They are seen as inordinately powerful, seeking to exercise an illegitimate veto over government policy.[10] For the Conservative Party, this 'inflation' of trade union power had been vividly expressed in the 1973 miners' strike and was confirmed by the privileged relationship between the TUC and the Labour Government in the Social Contract. In economic terms, this trade union power increased wages, squeezed profit margins, forced up prices and inflation, reduced levels of investment, reduced international competitiveness and was an important barrier to escaping from recession. On a social level, trade unions were seen as infringing the rights of citizens through strike action and the closed shop.[11] The 'special' legal protection of trade unions was also seen as having serious economic and social consequences. In political terms, it was the relationship of trade unions to the Labour Party that was the source of the problems.

As with the argument over the expanded role of the state, this case too suggests clear and simple remedies. The power of trade unions had to be reduced and this could be done by removing legal protection and ending the closed shop provisions. Laws could be enacted to restrict the right to strike and to provide penalties for breaches of the law. Trade union reforms could also be given the sanction of law, enforcing ballots before strike action and certain standards for internal trade union organisation. The political significance of the trade unions could be reduced by the election of a Conservative Government determined not to be involved in any bipartite arrangements over prices and incomes policies or tripartite negotiations over national economic policy. Little could be done over the organisational and policy links between the trade union movement and the Labour Party, but the old tactic of attacking the trade union financial support for the Labour Party through an explicit 'opting in' provision could be tried. The combined effects of these legislative initiatives would be to reduce the ability of trade unions to protect employment, wages and work conditions.

This argument reveals acute class sensitivity as it identifies class organisation and the balance of class forces between labour and capital as having a significant part to play in the recession. Altering that balance, by changing the legal circumstances for labour organisation, is seen as an important part of the strategy for promoting renewed profitable private accumulation. Legally constrained trade unions would not be able to use economic recovery or a return to full employment to increase the bargaining power of labour.

Business

In the popular political account, there is little criticism of the conduct of private industry or the role of private businesses in general. When private business is mentioned it is to praise its innovative and wealth creating role.[12] There is no suggestion that the business sector has, by its actions or attitudes, contributed to its own difficulties. The problems faced by business are created by others, either the state or trade unions. Finance favouring overseas investment or industrial investors leaving Britain, is explained by reference to the restrictive, innovation destroying policies of the state.[13] This is curious, given the part the low investment and the failure to introduce modern production facilities and techniques has played in creating the relative backwardness of British industry.

Given this analytical map of what was wrong with the economic, social and political situation in Britain, it is easy to understand the appeal of monetarist and small-state policies. They would reduce the size of the state and restore the pre-eminence of the private sector. Further, they would remove any doctrinal basis for state intervention to counter unemployment or falling output. So long as the rate of increase in the money supply was contained, inflation would fall and the real economy could revitalise itself solely on the basis of accurately perceiving market signals. The money supply in its role as the teacher of economic truths, would make it possible to take politics out of the determination of wage increases and any increase in unemployment would encourage workers and their trade unions to learn realism. There would be no need for government to try to devise incomes or prices policy and only a limited need to respond to increases in unemployment. Thus, the state would no longer be an illegitimate and harmful power in the economic and political life of the nation. Britain would be great again.

Though there is such a close fit between the diagnosed ills and the suggested cures for the nation, this does not remove the major problems that face this account of the recession and its genesis in the postwar developments in the role of state and its relationship with class organisations. These analytical problems come in two kinds. The first concerns the role of the state as an active force in social development. Neo-liberal analysis recognises vested interests that state staff have in protecting the size of the state. Indeed, that is one major part of their explanation for why the state grows so steadily. If that is so, why would the state come to change its whole perspective in economic and social development and begin to act against a continued pattern of economic and social expansion? Was it assumed that the political will of a Thatcher Government would be all that was required to make state officials give up old habits? Is it possible that there already existed in the institutions of the state, forces and problems that could produce an alliance between some parts of the state and just such a neo-liberal government in support of reducing its own size and significance? This is a matter that needs to be explored further.

The second question concerns the adequacy of the monetarist and small state strategy to achieve the economic, social and political goals set it by the popular political arguments advanced in its favour. Could such a strategy end the recession and find paths towards a higher rate of growth? Was there, in fact, an industrial strategy that could produce a thriving private- enterprise- based manufacturing sector able to generate high (if not full) employment which would not be dependent on state support, either through direct action or taxation concessions? Was it possible to permanently reverse the growth of the state? Although monetarism and small state strategies directly face the social and political ambiguities raised by the state's expansion during the first phase of the recession, what kind of changes could they make to resolve such ambiguities and not engender social disruption or economic catastrophe? The most appropriate way to approach these questions is by considering the range of economic, social and political problems set for the various classes, their organisations and the state by the experience of the initial response to the onset of the recession.

THE PROBLEMS OF PROLONGED RECESSION

The prolonged recession created major problems for business, labour and the state.

The state

In the course of the first phase of the recession, the state expanded dramatically, when measured in terms of its share of Gross Domestic Product, its place in the total economy, or the significance of its economic and social decisions. Such an expansion, especially at a time of economic recession, poses the question of where the money is to come from to fund its expanded role. The state can raise money in a number of ways. It can increase taxes on income and spending. It can tax capital gains, capital transfers and wealth. It can 'print' money or borrow more from private sector banks. It can run itself more efficiently and charge profit making prices for the products of the nationalised sector and use its monopoly position to make these self financing. It can extend its ownership into profitable areas of the economy, either directly through nationalisation or in partnership with private firms, and syphon these funds into its various economic and social programmes. To make any or all these moves would signal that the state was seeking to consolidate its expanded role; indeed, the logical consequence of some of these efforts at financial security would necessitate a further expansion of the state.

There is an alternative response to the problems of state finance. The state could see that continuing recession must squeeze state revenues and that alternative sources of funds would be hard to come by, or that the pursuit of independent state finance would cause major social problems in terms of the relationship between the state and private capital. On this basis, the state would seek limited ways to increase its revenue (minor tax changes) while economising on its own operations. The range of state actions could be reduced, increases in welfare spending contained, activities unnecessary for its essential role could be sold off, scrapped or reduced. The state could withdraw from its expanded position and consolidate its finances and functions.

Here then is a schematic view of the economic problems confronted by the state and a sketch of two different ways in which these problems could be faced. The options are contradictory: contract the state or consolidate its increased position.

Business

In Britain, there is a division between finance and industry and the impact of the first phase of the recession was different for each sector. Finance was hard hit by the high inflation rates coupled with stagnating outputs. So long as the rates of interest remained below the levels of inflation then financial assets were under great pressure. Finance would clearly welcome any policy change to allow for high interest rates, equal to or in excess of the rate of inflation. It should be mentioned in passing that finance is the one section of capital that is not so badly hit by increasing budget deficits to the extent that they are financed by borrowing, since such demand will bid up the price of credit and turn to private advantage the commercial transactions of the state.

Industry was also affected by inflation, stagnating output and bankruptcy. Inflation may have lessened the burden of debt on industry, but rising prices of raw materials and energy certainly squeezed its profit margins, as recessed conditions made sales harder in crowded markets. Funds were needed for investment requiring increased profits, cheaper sources of credit and, perhaps, less government spending to increase the funds available to industry. (Less spending, that is, on things other than infrastructure and financial support for industry.) Such a pattern of industrial concerns indicates the source of tensions with finance which are only increased by the consideration of such matters as the value of sterling (finance helped by a high value which would weaken industry's ability to compete with imports in the home market and impair export chances).

These economic differences between finance and industry may be subsumed under a wider shared consensus over the problems created by the expanded state strategy in the first phase of the recession. Capital as a class faced the ambiguities created by the expansion of the state beyond its confined infrastructural role. To what extent was the state able to consolidate its position and constrict the operations of private capital? Although the state had not as yet acted in this way, did it now have a potential to replace the market as the main force behind economic and social co-ordination? Similarly, all sections of capital were equally threatened by the increased social and political presence of the trade unions. Hence, both finance and industry could be expected to support state strategies that would return trade unions to a less political and less significant role.

Labour

The problems for labour were of a different kind from those of business and the state, though closely related to the fact of business failure. The persistence of recession and the workings of the Social Contract, forced labour onto the defensive. Gone was the broad social vision and militant action. It is true that the rhetoric of a greater role for the trade unions remained, and support for increased state action in the private economy, but what had been destroyed was the vehicle by which the trade union movement could pursue those goals. The offer to trade wage restraint for influence and the expanded role of the state had been nullified by the increasingly limited wage restraint role of the Social Contract and the trade union movement's relations with the Labour Government. In the absence of the Social Contract, the labour movement had no organised strategic initiative to support. The fact of recession and rising unemployment and the declining belief that recovery was near, weakened the trade union movement. The key issues were now wages, work conditions and employment, but the means to fight over these issues were eroded by unemployment. Although the experience of the Social Contract may have, at least temporarily, undermined support for the wage restraint-trade off approach, it could only have strengthened the demand for increased state action over investment.

This schematic view of the problems caused by persistent recession and the initial expansion of the state, and of the options opened up for the different classes and their associated organisations, makes it possible to see the basis for an alliance between the state and capital, within the confines of a particular economic, political and social strategy. In the interpretation of the significance of the monetarist small state strategy, the distance between the initial position and the state's actual strategy will be used to expose the balance of power between the state and private capital at this stage in the development of British capitalism. If the vehicles for capital's political representation were changed so that they no longer sought to accommodate business to an expanded state sector, then there was scope for a monetarist, small state strategy. As we know, the CBI and the Conservative Party did reject the post-war consensus position on the role of the state and reverted to forms of neo-liberal analysis, an analysis which was still the ruling assumption in some parts of the state. The alliance between the state and business could help both to solve their economic, class and political problems, strengthening the historic relationship between the two.

Such a possible alliance is matched by an alternative, that of an alliance of the state with Labour and the trade unions for a consolidated, stronger state with a potential to move further against the position of private business. Indeed, this prospect as much as anything else must have strengthened business' resolve to act decisively against the post-war consensus that legitimated such state expansion.

THE STRATEGY IN PRACTICE

Having set out the popular arguments for the strategy and the abstract and schematic concerns upon which a class–state alliance for its introduction could be based, it is now possible to consider what happened when the monetarist, small state strategy was applied. The strategy as implemented by the Thatcher Government was neither identical with the arguments popularly presented nor did it simply embrace and represent the economic and class concerns of business in any uncomplicated way. Though not in any sense pragmatic, the actual government initiatives in many areas were less substantial than the rhetoric and reflected some assessment of the class circumstances in which it was operating. This is not to deny that the changes of policy were not great, just that they were not as dramatic as implied by the rhetoric. In assessing the impact of the strategy it is necessary to consider the economic, political and social effects separately, since it can not be assumed that these are automatically harmonised, nor, that if they were, this would mean success.

Economic considerations

In considering who gained from the economics of the small state/monetarist programme, it is necessary to make judgements over the broad success of the strategy in overcoming the recession and its characteristic problems. It would be easy to debunk the claims made for this approach by reference to the distance between what was promised and what happened, or, to the extent that the economic consequences were unanticipated, to suggest that a 'true' small state/monetarist programme was never even tried.[14] This would not be useful. In Britain, the initial effects of the strategy were to boost the level of inflation to a dramatic extent, partly the product of the second round of oil price increases and partly a result of the changes from direct to indirect taxation.[15] Levels of output fell as the recession moved into renewed recession, of an even greater severity than in the first stage in the 1970s. Along with renewed recession went a decline in the viability of the industrial economy and a decline in the levels of private industrial investment. Reflecting the industrial recession was a steady, sustained, dramatic increase in the levels of unemployment, reaching a post-war high in 1982.[16] The level of unemployment only began to fall in 1987, despite a much earlier reduction in the rate of inflation and an upturn in economic activity. The recovery that started in late 1982 has not been so solidly based as to overcome the problems facing the industrial economy.[17] Even after the rapid industrial growth in 1987-8, British industry was still vulnerable to competitive imports.

In such a bald sketch of the economic consequences of the strategy there are matters that need further elaboration. For much of the time industry did not fare well. This opens up a question since the CBI had changed its own perspectives during the Social Contract period and had come to support the same small-state/monetarist policies. Interestingly, the CBI seems to have been aware that such an approach would increase interest rates. As they commented in 1976:

> We recognise that this policy would lead initially to higher interest rates than would arise if the money supply were allowed to increase at a faster rate. Any such increase in interest rates would be unwelcome to industry, just as the high rates of interest charged in the recent past have been unwelcome and have discouraged plans for expansion. But, while industry desires lower interest rates in the future, it is fully aware that this cannot be achieved until the UK's rate of inflation is significantly reduced, both absolutely and in relation to those recorded by our competitors. We would prefer a consistent monetary policy appropriate to the fight against inflation, even at the cost of relatively high interest rates, rather than reversion to lax monetary policy bringing cheaper money but also threatening additional inflationary pressures in the future.[18]

Despite such prescience, the CBI became disenchanted with the impact of the strategy on the industrial economy, and advocated various forms of reflationary policies.[19]

It was not just the high interest rates which caused problems for industry. The value of the pound was so high that industry was over priced in its export markets and vulnerable to imports. Though the value of sterling was not the only factor, industry lost ground in both areas. The CBI's response to the problems of 'overvalued' sterling was divided by the different perspectives of different parts of industry. At the 1982 CBI annual conference, the organisation sought to have endorsed a motion, mildly critical of government policy and calling for a decline in the value of sterling.[20] This was defeated after a strong 'rank and file' opposition, expressed as often in terms of national pride as in terms of business advantage. It is not clear that the high value of sterling was intended (or was necessary) as part of the small state/monetarist strategy; a greater value for the pound, greater stability in its value, but not a pound so strong and sound that it undermined the viability of Britain's already exposed industry. Significantly, in the run up to the 1983 election, the government acted to encourage some downward drift in the value of the pound[21] which was followed by some limited improvement in the economy. Even when industrial production recovered, British manufacturers were still vulnerable to imports and weak in export markets.

The impact of the combination of high interest rates and the value of sterling on industry suggests that the class of capital was not affected equally in all parts of their economic operations. Finance was helped by just those consequences of the policy that harmed industry. The high interest rates, sustained despite nominal falls in 1982, compensated finance for the low interest rates in the first phase of the recession and the squeeze on operating margins. The strength of sterling enhanced the position of British institutions in the world financial markets, especially in terms of recycling the still large stocks of petro-dollars. If this were the only evidence, then it would be possible to argue that the small state/monetarist policies were of special significance for finance capital and that industry was largely wrong to have identified with the strategy before the 1979 election and perverse in their guarded support for it afterwards. To understand the basis for more or less unified business support for the monetarist small state strategy it is necessary to consider the social and political circumstances within which the strategy was implemented.

The economics of the strategy touched many other areas. In the initial phase of intensified recession there was a marked increase in labour productivity as output fell and unemployment rose. Though this was welcomed by business and economic commentators, it was not a sign of rapid improvement in the competitiveness of British industry.[22] Indeed, there was no possibility of this unless investment in industrial equipment increased substantially and for much of the period levels of industrial investment remained low. In terms of wage settlements, most commentators saw a 'new realism' in pay determination. This meant that initially pay increases fell behind the rate of inflation and represented a reduction in levels of real wages.[23] How far this represented some permanent alteration in the relations between wages and profits in national income and just how much reflected the stage of downturn in the economic cycle is unclear. By 1987-8 wage increases were again in excess of the expected rate of inflation and the government had to use general deflation as a response.

The most dramatic aspect of the Thatcher Government's radical attempt to reduce the significance of the state has been its extensive privatisation policy. From modest beginnings it has grown to a full-scale attempt to get rid of all the state's assets that can be made profitable or attractive to potential private sector buyers. From small arms manufacturers to major companies such as BP, British Telecom, British Gas, the move is away from state ownership and nationalisation. The programme stands as a vivid signal of the changed direction of government policy. Sometimes shares have been sold below their values, at other times government has had to act to make the purchase more attractive than it would otherwise be. Nonetheless, the sales have been significant, increasing the number of people who own shares and providing a significant boost to state revenues, freeing the way for tax cuts and other alterations in economic preferences. At the present the Government plans to raise about four billion pounds sterling every year through sales and this is a significant part of its fiscal calculations. Of course, there will come a time when the state has no more assets to sell and, by then, the equations will have to be calculated differently.

In the context of such significant sales of state assets and the cuts in public provision, it is surprising how difficult it has proved for the Conservative Government to reduce the size of the state (as measured as a percentage of GDP) to below the level it was when they won office in 1979.[24]

The increase in welfare expenditure as the recession deepened and unemployment increased more than offset cuts in other areas.[25] As a result, despite the intentions of the strategy, the size of the state as measured against the total of domestic production did not decline.[26] Even after five years of economic growth, the size of the state only declined slowly and by 1987 had not fallen below the 1979 level.[27] It was hoped that continued rapid growth in 1988 would affect the awaited change in ratios. What is significant is the length of time that it took and the amount of effort that was necessary. The initial attempt to reduce the overall levels of taxation was not conspicuously successful, even though the tax cuts were regressive in character and, to the extent that they increased inequality, may have promoted further investment. Later tax cuts have been significant and regressive, far more important for the better off and far less impressive for the poorer sections of the community. In their own way, the pattern of tax cuts helped increase the inequality in the distribution of national income which has been a significant feature of the Thatcher Government's years in office[28] and a reversal of a long running tendency, a reversal far more effective than the attempt to reduce the size of the state. It is clear that the Government's economic policies have reduced the economic weight of the state as the budget has been nearly balanced and the public sector borrowing requirement has been reduced to zero, and indeed, some government debt has been repaid.[29] It is not clear that this change has altered the significance of state action or reduced the importance of its decisions on the private economy as a whole. It is not clear that these moves reduced the economic effects of the state in the economy, even though the size of the public sector borrowing requirement was reduced. The policy-making role of the state and the significance of these moves will be discussed below.

The economics of the small state/monetarist strategy did have an impact on the conditions of working people. As the recession intensified, manufacturing contracted and unemployment increased dramatically until it stood at almost 13 per cent of the work-force in 1986.[30] With such a change, long-term unemployment became a significant fact of life in working-class communities,[31] especially in the depressed areas of the north. It was only after a lengthy period of growth that unemployment began to fall and in 1988 had been reduced to about 9 per cent (after a major revision in the way in which unemployment is calculated).[32] On OECD basis, unemployment still stood at around 11 per cent of the work-force. At times, unionisation was seen as a barrier to the generalisation of the economic advantages of unemployment: the problem was seen not as a hard core of unemployment, but a hard core of employment.[33]

The benefits that were thought to flow from unemployment were not directly economic, but rather the social consequences that unemployment would have on the willingness of employees to strike for significant wage increases. As such the impact has been discussed below.

Political considerations

Economic considerations alone are not enough to explain support for this strategy. It is necessary to turn to political and social aspects where the political role of trade unions is important. Under the Social Contract strategy, the political role of the trade unions had been substantially increased. The impact of prolonged recession, especially as symbolised by increasing unemployment, undermined the basis for trade unions to demand representation in these national economic decisions. Unions still remained the organised representatives of labour in the country but unemployment weakened the ability of the trade unions to press that claim. No longer could trade unions use their strength to challenge national economic policies. Further, the electoral success of the Conservative Party and the fact that significant numbers of trade unionists voted for the Conservative Party, weakened the claim that the trade union leadership was sufficiently in tune with the attitudes of their members.

The Conservative Government embraced a strategy designed to reduce the political and social role of the trade unions. Trade union laws have been reformed, limiting the rights of unions to picket and regulating the conduct of strikes. The cumulative effect of the reforms has been significantly to weaken their organisational strength and their ability to take concerted and effective action. Equally significant have been the two major industrial confrontations and their ramifications. The preparation for and defeat of the 1984 Miners' Strike was a very important symbol that the role of militant trade unions would be limited. The confrontations at Wapping over Murdoch's introduction of new technology and the mass sackings of workers further emphasised that trade unions would face the full weight of the police and the law in their efforts to conduct industrial relations as usual. The rise of a new style of unionism, signing single union deals with no strike clauses, has split the trade union movement and undermined the scope for effective union opposition to Thatcherism in the immediate future. In these circumstances it is not surprising to note that industrial disputes have decreased to record low levels. This is made more significant when it is remembered that in the recent period, employed workers have been enjoying very significant real wage increases, lessening in their own way the image of trade unions as necessary to win benefits for their members. So the consequences of the Thatcher Government's policies and the economic circumstances combined to reduce the political presence of the trade unions and to confine them to a very minor role. The image of militancy and social vision has been dimmed. The decision of the TUC not to negotiate with the Thatcher Government was of little real significance, since under Thatcher any negotiations that took place would never have resembled those that resulted in the formation of the Social Contract.

It is far harder to trace the political relations between business and the Conservative Government, though there is some evidence to suggest that business has not enjoyed the same kind of access that it had before. It is evident that even if access has been preserved, the formal organisations of industry have, at times, not been pleased with the direction of policy and the rebuffs that they were given for suggesting changes. In 1982 the CBI was severely criticised for pressing for a more reflationary fiscal stance than that approved by the government.[34] The very success of the Thatcher Government in reducing the role of the trade unions has weakened the need for the CBI to be consulted or very politically active.[35] It no longer has to fight to be heard, to counter the influence of the TUC and as such its presence and role has diminished. In this sense, the formal representation of business organisations has been constricted during the Thatcher years. Still, some businesses have had very close ties with those making and administering policy. ICI, for example, seconded a number of top executives to assist and advise the Thatcher Government.

Despite the fact that trade unions have played a less significant political role under the Thatcher Government, and despite the attempts to 'reform' trade union law, the trade unions as organisations remain intact. No permanent reversal of the developments prior to the election of the Conservative Government in 1979 have been achieved. Further than that, the experience of the small state/ monetarist strategy and the failure of the Social Contract to be little more than a vehicle for wage restraint has sharpened the political vision of the trade unions. The trade unions would be reluctant to concede wage restraint in future. Further, trade union mistrust of business investment intentions has been heightened. This strengthens the position of those who argue for greater state initiatives to plan and co-ordinate broad investment strategies. It may even strengthen the position of those who would call for more nationalisation. Presently, these views of the trade unions are muted by the election defeats of the Labour Party in 1983 and 1987. But should Labour be in a position to return to office a strengthened role for the state will almost certainly be part of that electoral programme.

Social dimension

The social dimension concerns the changing pattern of the relations between the state and society, either through its relationship to the economy or to classes and their organisations. During the first phase of the recession the state increased both the share of economic resources passing through its budgets and the amount of productive and financial assets under its control. The relationship between the state and private sectors of the economy was altered when the state moved towards the centre of the industrial economy through the nationalisation of British Leyland which took the state well beyond the confines of the mixed economy. Through the strategy of the Social Contract and the National Enterprise Board, the state moved into the areas of the economy that were either immediately or potentially profitable and appeared to be poised for a permanent role in the profitable sector.

This expansion of the state generated a great deal of ambiguity, as no clear rules were developed to manage the relations between the two sectors. It appeared to private capital that the state had encroached on its legitimate sphere and was in a position to challenge and displace capital whenever it chose. There is a sense in which the passage of the state beyond the confines of the mixed economy did open up uncertainty about the relationship between the state and privately owned sectors of the economy. By moving into manufacturing and profitable areas of the economy the state had acquired the potential to compete with private firms and to make their economic viability more difficult. It is in this sense that the social consequences of the state's response to the onset of the recession became important.

On this question the policies of the Thatcher Government have been quite effective. It is not that the state has been returned to a more strictly infrastructural role. That may never have been the aim. The demand that nationalised industries become more capable of self-financing meant that indirect subsidies through their pricing policies were no longer an option. On this the two major political parties were agreed. Nor was there a move to force the state to sell off all of its assets in manufacturing industry. The commitment was to sell off profitable assets, obviously unprofitable ones would be difficult to sell, and such a programme reduced but did not remove the manufacturing role of state enterprises. So, if the selling of state assets was not to return the state to an infrastructural role, its importance must lie in recreating the dominance the Thatcher Government accords to private capital. Selling profitable state assets is the promise that the private sector will not be squeezed or challenged by the expansion of the state to meet the problems of prolonged recession. Beyond that, the gesture is also part of an attempt to articulate the rules concerning the relationship between the state and privately-owned sectors of the manufacturing economy.

Thus, the strategy of the Thatcher government has been to remove the amibiguities inherent in haphazard expansion of the state in the first phase of the recession and to assert the dominance of the private sector in the economy as a whole. It has also begun generating, not on the basis of its theoretical precepts, practical rules for the co-ordination of the state and private sectors of the economy in the stage beyond the development and consolidation of the mixed economy.

In the popular political presentation of the small state/monetarist strategy much emphasis was given to freeing private enterprise from the constricting effects of state policy. It was certainly implied that the state was to play a less significant role in the conduct of the economy and that the market would be increasingly the locus of economic and social co-ordination. In this area the strategy would appear to have had mixed success. State actions are still at the heart of all debates over economic performance. Questions of what the state will do still dominate discussion. Monetarist arguments that do not postulate an end to the state's role in the printing of money have always faced a dilemma. Such arguments call for a reduced role for the state in economic management yet must depend on state management of the money supply to generate the beneficial results they desire. No amount of effort in formulating unchangeable rules for state conduct can obscure the fact that monetarist analysis wants the state to change its means of economic management rather than the role of that management itself. This difficult attitude to the state as an economic manager has been evident in the range of state initiatives undertaken by the Thatcher Government. Nothing that the Government has done yet has reduced the significance of state decision for the running and success of the economy. It is still a matter of the state's policy on the money supply, taxes, interest rates, exchange rate, industrial assistance and even on its response to unemployment which is important. Choosing not to act, as it has done on increased unemployment, has not reduced the emphasis on government action. What would be achieved if it did? The private economy and private capital would be seen to be responsible for the continued recession and uneven recovery in the British economy. This is not what is sought by government action or inaction. It is only through prolonged political argument that it is possible to deflect criticism from private capital to the trade unions and to maintain the claim that government action would only make matters worse. The market, as such, can neither articulate these positions nor make them politically credible. This can only be done by political parties and political actors. Thus, the attempt to reduce the significance of the state as a policy maker has not been affected by the small state/monetarist policy of the Thatcher Government. State action still remains the focus of political effort for both those that would reduce and those that would increase the role of the state in the present context.

The problems faced by the Thatcher Government in its attempts to reduce the size of the state are of great significance for the argument here: they provide the opportunity to probe the significance of the forces that have prompted the expansion of the state built into the post-war settlement and the political development of capitalist society itself. If the Thatcher Government had succeeded in easily reducing the size of the state then that too would have been significant and would have revealed the limits within the political development of industrial capitalism. In the context of the determined neo-liberalism of the government, its slow progress is much more potent.

Consider first the failure of the government to achieve its declared aim of reducing the share of national resources passing through the hands of the state as indicated by the ratio of state expenditure to gross domestic production. When the Labour Government lost office this ratio stood at 41 per cent; by 1982-3 it had risen by 4.5 per cent.[36] Although this figure had been slightly reduced by 1986, it has not been taken back below the level of 1979. As a strategy for rolling back the state it has been demonstrably ineffective. Part of the explanation for this failure lies in the unexpected severity of the initial downturn and the weakness of the recovery to reduce the high level of unemployment.

As Conservative defenders have argued, if sustained, high levels of growth returned then the relative size of the state would rapidly shrink. Unfortunately, that has always been the problem. Although the Government has cut the delivery of welfare services, whatever reductions have occurred have been matched by increases in spending on the police and armed forces. (Riddell provides a very convenient table showing the pattern of changes in 1982-3. The major areas of reduction have been on housing and EEC contributions, the most dramatic increases have been on defence and law and order.)[37]

This failure to reduce the size of the state is made even more important by the fact that it happened at the same time as a major sale of state assets. As is well known, the Thatcher Government has been determined to reduce the size of the public sector by selling off state-owned activities to the private sector. This is meant to be part of the effort to revitalise private, entrepreneurial capitalism in Britain. The forms of disposal have been varied, ranging from the complete sale of assets to only partial sales; from reducing the size of the state's share holding in a particular area to retaining either a minority or majority share holding. In terms of getting rid of state assets, of 'privatisation', the policy has been a success but this does little to establish the purpose or significance of this process. Consider these aspects. Sometimes shares were priced below their value so that they would be sold quickly, allowing their purchasers to realise easy profits as their market price rapidly rose. Sometimes when distributed at value, the shares proved difficult to sell and the brokers were left with considerable proportions to sell off later. The assets sold have little in common, except that they were sufficiently profitable to be sold. The government could not sell off all the activities of the state that were beyond the limits of infrastructural activity because many of these were insufficiently restructured and profitable to make them attractive to the private sector. British Leyland, which was the most significant intrusion of the state into the manufacturing sector of the economy remains, largely, in state ownership. Some of the state's infrastructure has been sold. These are attractive to private owners because they are either natural or protected monopolies able to win secure profits for their new owners. The sale of Telecom and the sale of North Sea Gas are examples. When the profitability of a firm is dependent on its monopoly status, its sale into private hands does nothing to increase the degree of competition or enterprise in the economy. The Government's response has been to set up some form of regulatory structure, some form of public supervision. (This parallels the way in which the denationalisation of the steel industry was managed.)[38] This is ironic because much of the neo-liberal critique in the United States stressed the failure of regulation to control monopolies. Instead they identify a process of 'regulatory capture' whereby the monopolies come to neutralise the effects of regulation. In Britain, such regulation is a device to legitimate this transfer of essential public services to the private sector. Its effectiveness as a form of control on monopoly is entirely secondary.

Despite these sales, the state still remains a significant presence in the manufacturing sector. So long as Leyland remains state owned, the barriers between manufacturing and infrastructure remain broadly as they were when the Thatcher Government was elected in 1979. This is significant as it reflects the problems faced by the Government in its attempts to restore the 'balance' between the public and private sectors which had been upset during the Social Contract period, and which was the focus of much business opposition to the Labour Government and the size of the public sector.

This pattern of action and the political determination of the Conservative Government poses a sharp analytical challenge. Why should it have happened like this? If the Government had only talked about 'rolling back the state' and had made no determined efforts in that direction, then there would be no analytical problem.

Failure would be the product of intention. The effort, however, means that the result needs to be explained. Consider the following set of explanations that all seek to link up the ambiguous and contradictory consequences of the policy with the severity of the economic problems confronting the British economy for the foreseeable future. Firstly, selling off state assets can be driven by an assessment of the revenue needs of the state. Revenue collection is limited by the pattern of persistent recession and uneven recovery. True, profitable state property makes a contribution to revenue, but it is always less in a given period than the value of its assets, even if these are sold below their proper value. The limitation of this 'strategy' lies in the fact that such revenue can only be raised once and used to fund one-off projects such as tax cuts. (It would be possible to use the funds generated by sales to increase state revenue by investing it in financial ventures with higher rates of return, but there is no evidence to suggest that this is what the Government intends.) Hence, the comment that this policy embraces the folly of 'selling the silver to pay the milkman' remains pertinent. It is important to consider the circumstances under which this becomes a 'rational' strategy. Prolonged recession with no prospect of sustained growth would be the only scenario to fit this assumption, and, it could indeed apply to Britain in the present period.

Secondly, the selling of state assets has the effect of making true the equation of state ownership with unprofitable enterprises. Although this may have some ideological significance, the fact that has to be made true by political action undermines its potency. Such a policy of sales certainly impoverishes the state as it denies the state access to their surplus funds and it intensifies the consequences of funding the unprofitable remnants of the public sector, even when these are essential for public provision of needed services. It certainly increases the problems for state rescues of ailing industries in an attempt to fulfil social objectives.

Thirdly, and building on the previous point, the sale of profitable state property deprives successor governments of financial and other forms of leverage. As such it could work as a barrier to renationalisation (with compensation) as the impoverished state would have problems mobilising resources for such a programme. It could work as a barrier to a more concerted effort at a state co-ordinated industrial policy and the development of more effective forms of economic planning. As such the sale of these assets could serve as a method of limiting the future use of the state to modify or supplant the workings of the market.

None of these three explanations are definitive or conclusive. There is nothing that says the outcome has any relationship to intention. It could well be that the perverse consequences of the programme express the underlying logic of the development of class state relations and state economy relations. The attempt to reduce the size of the state is difficult because it contradicts the logic of the political regime, the dynamic, developing on-going relationship between political and economic processes. It remains 'technically' possible to reduce the size of the state as Jimmy Carter did in 1979 and as was proposed by the Think-Tank report of 1982, but not within the complex of state, social, economic and political objectives. Being re-elected, fighting wars, controlling the population, maintaining national unity and all this within the context of a declining economy, one which can 'grow' but cannot provide full employment, which promotes greater inequality and poverty more easily than affluence, means that the attempt to reduce the size of the state will take a contorted form and produce contradictory and ambiguous results while failing to reverse the logic of the post-war situation. Despite cuts, sales and determined campaigns the Thatcher Government has had problems reducing the size and scope of the state and has not, as yet, succeeded in completely changing the social character of the state.

Just as the attempt to reduce the importance of state economic decisions has had uneven consequences, so too has the attempt to loosen the relationship between the state and the various classes and class organisations. To the extent that 'corporatist' institutions of the Social Contract were seen as providing the basis for expanded state action, the government has sought to remove or nullify those institutions. Here the government has been singularly successful. The campaign against quangos gained a popular momentum, and various bipartite and tripartite bodies linking the state, labour and capital have either been abandoned, destroyed or downgraded. The only one which remains basically as it was is NEDO, and it probably is important that this should be concerned with planning issues, be most significant at low levels of the economy (industry and region) and not spectacularly successful. And even NEDO has had its levels of funding cut. Over wage negotiations there can be little doubt that the Thatcher Government has ended the attempt to generate co-operatively agreed national economic policy.

What is the significance of this apparent reversal of the gradually developing close relations between labour, capital and state in the making of national economic policy? Has the Thatcher Government been successful not just in ending those arrangements created by the preceding Labour Government, but in reversing the underlying problems and forces that encouraged the emergence of these institutional arrangements? It is here that the most serious doubts can be raised about the significance and permanence of the Government's achievements. Both capital and labour remain organised. They both seek to influence national economic policy to their advantage. Parts of business have occasional doubts about the militant approach of the government and might welcome some national forum within which to argue their case. The trade unions, though weakened by the recession, still retain their ambitions to influence economic and social development and continue their close relations with the Labour Party as the best vehicle for the exercise of that influence. Both the Labour Party and various parts of the Social Democratic Party–Liberal Party combination leave such class–state negotiations over incomes and economic policy on the political agenda. Hence, though the pattern has been interrupted, it is only the continued election of Conservative governments, under the leadership of zealous neo-liberals such as Margaret Thatcher, that stops such underlying forces from generating institutional arrangements for negotiations between classes and the state.

This brings us to the possibility that the Thatcher Government does not represent a serious reversal of the development tendencies identified in the history of capitalist development since the interwar depression. Consider these matters: the size of the state has not been substantially reduced; the boundaries between the public and private economies have not been qualitatively altered; the state has not ceased to be the focus for the disputes over the best response to economic and social misfortune; the basis for closer institutional links between classes and state over the negotiation of national economic policy, and the recession has not ended.

As such the present period neither negates the historical tendency for greater class and state organisation nor the increasingly institutional dialogue between class organisations and the state. What the Thatcher Government represents is a major effort to slow the pace of that development in the midst of great economic difficulties and to remove important ambiguities that arose over the relationships of the private and state-owned parts of the economy. In this the Government has been successful. Nonetheless its efforts have not been such as to remove the potential for a further expanded or consolidated role of the state, especially if the return to secure capital accumulation is not swift. In these matters of historical development of class relations, it is the potential and the persistence of problems which is so important.

NATIONAL VARIATIONS

In considering the development and significance of neo-liberal government in Britain and the workings of the small state/monetarist strategy, emphasis has been placed on the historical context within which this strategy became pertinent. Two factors have been given greatest weight: the objective expansion of the size of the state and the ambiguous transformation of the role of the state in the first phase of the recession, and the expanded political presence of the trade unions forming the political and social underpinning for the expansion of the state. Britain is the country in which these developments had gone furthest and where the neo-liberal strategy has been advocated with greatest vehemence and implemented with the greatest militancy. Hence, the argument about the pertinence of the small state strategy is skewed by this coincidence. The same kind of strategy, at different times, became government policy in France and Germany, and was implemented with varying degrees of dedication. In neither case was the expansion of the state influence predicated on as dramatic an increase in the political presence of trade unions as it was in Britain. Thus it is necessary to consider the national variations in neo-liberal strategies in France and Germany.

France

Since 1945, both the size and the role of the state has increased. Nationalisation plus the sharebuying of state agencies and private sector firms has increased the state's economic significance. Of course, planning enhanced the role of the state and, despite the variations in state strategy including the so-called 'demise' of

French planning, the nature of the choices made by the state has had a significant impact on the pattern of economic activity.[39] Hence, the neo-liberal response to recession was constructed against this pattern of the expanding role of the state. It is not possible, however, to see this state expansion as the product of an increased political presence of the trade unions.[40] True (growing out of its war-time resistance role), the initial post-war reconstruction was based on the support of the trade union movement. But in the subsequent history of state policy, the trade unions have been spectators rather than initiators. The formal tripartite institutions of the modernisation commissions were not the source of great trade union influence, nor was the Social and Economic Council.[41] The dominance of conservative political forces minimised the significance of trade union demands, except perhaps in the aftermath of the May events in 1968. Even though near full employment increased the bargaining power of French trade unions, it is not possible to interpret the French neo-liberal experiment as a response to a changed balance in class forces, or the institutionalised political presence of the trade unions.

Even though some firms prospered from the policies adopted by the state, business was not the social base for the expansion of the state. It did not support the post-war nationalisations and its endorsement of planning was always conditional. The constant pattern of state expansion was not the result of business support or initiative. Business's ambivalent attitude to state expansion (based on the coincidence of benefits gained without active support) was reflected in the disputes within French business organisations over the most appropriate policy response to state programmes and the changing economic environment.[42] If it was not the social base for this increased level of state action, how did business respond? How has business been affected by the change in the size of the state and the scope of its actions? Or, how did business *think* it was affected by state action? The area for investment decisions, for example, was constricted by planning (even if the plan assisted private firms to modernise and compete profitably) and the scope for a paternalistic style of labour relations was undermined by the technocratic emphasis of state programmes. The degree of 'modernisation' encouraged or enforced by the French state and the attendant relative decline in the significance of small firms provided very fertile grounds for business discontent over the policies of the state.

Although large firms dominated the CPNF, and accommodation was reached with the state after May 1968, substantial segments of French business remained implacably opposed to the role played by the state. Although, as was pointed out before, such attitudes are common among business people, in France there was more of a mass base for this position. It matters little what the objective consequences of state action were. In the minds of some sections of business, the state was the source of the problems they faced. On such a perspective could be constructed the neo-liberal response to the onset of the recession. The specific character of French business and its historically conditioned sensitivities may go some way to explaining why the neo-liberal experiment was tried so much earlier in France than in Britain or other industrialised capitalist countries.

This argument opens up an important possibility. Business opinions here appear more as a permissive than as a determining factor. The state appears as a much more significant social factor, an impression strengthened by the weakness of the privately owned French financial sector.[43] From the initial nationalisation of financial institutions up till this time, the significance of the state-owned financial sector steadily increased. French business organisation was not as obviously significant as its British counterpart. The various changes in the state strategy towards the shape and character of the French economy do not appear to have happened as a response to business pressure. Rather they represented an adjustment *by* the state to the pressures and opportunities of the European and international economy.[44] Such is the explanation for the decision to promote the competitive strength of France's largest firms in the period before the full operation of the EEC. If this remained the case, then the basis for the neo-liberal experiment in France was the political judgement of significant politicians and state officials about the problems that the increase in oil prices and the onset of global recession created for the French economy and the place of the state within it. The plausibility of this proposition is strengthened by a consideration of the contradictory way in which neo-liberalism was adopted.[45] There was the emphasis on controlling the money supply, not as novel in France as in Britain since orthodox economic thought was not as influenced by Keynes as in some other countries, and an emphasis on reducing government expenditure.[46] But there was no campaign to sell off state-owned assets – indeed, the troubled steel industry was brought substantially into public ownership during these years. Further, the state did not withdraw from the task of demand management and the pursuit of social welfare goals, increasing the transfer payments made to needy families and individuals. There were attempts to make more cost effective the form of welfare provision, as in the attempt to modernise the crisis-ridden health insurance schemes.[47] So it can be seen that the neo-liberal package was not as dramatic a reversal of the post-war position as that attempted by the Thatcher Government in Britain. The less militant stance is to be explained by just those different factors that conditioned the social background to the neo-liberal strategy – the limited political presence of the trade unions and the relatively greater significance of state action in France if measured against the pattern of initiation and resistance of French business and labour organisation.

The neo-liberal strategy did not work.[48] Economically, its failure was marked by the persistence of recession and the continued weakness of the state's finances. Politically, the strategy failed to protect the government from criticism over its attitude to the economy and the steadily deteriorating employment position. Inflation continued and remained a political issue. In social terms, there was no sign that neo-liberalism brought political realism to the representatives of labour. In some areas, neo-liberalism opened the field of social criticism and sharpened the programme of the opposition. The left's policy of increasing the size of the state, and the frequency and extent of its economic initiatives, was given greater pertinence by the neo-liberal stance and its clear failure. As such, the flirtation with neo-liberalism and its apparent failure paved the way for the expansion of the state when Mitterrand beat Giscard in the 1981 Presidential election.

In 1981 Mitterrand was elected President of France and the Parti Socialiste (PS) swept to power in the general election that followed. As a result there was every opportunity to experiment with the *Projet Socialiste* and an expanded state response to the persistent recession. What set the *Projet Socialiste* apart from the programmes of other contemporary social democratic political parties was its commitment to a break with capitalism. As Kesselman remarks:

> France was unique among capitalist democracies because its two left parties ... continued to proclaim that socialist transformation necessitated the abolition of capitalism.[49]

This claim was rhetorical and based more on the need to secure a unity of left parties to win within the electoral system of the Fifth Republic.[50] The actual programme introduced did not aim at a socialist transformation of France but was another version of the expanded state response to recession and had a close affinity with the programme of the Wilson/Callaghan government. What differed was the timing: the British Labour Party came to office just as the first phase of the recession started, the PCF/PS, just as the second phase of recession intensified.[51]

The government moved to extend the size of the state through nationalisation, to intensify planning, to increase transfer payments to the poor and disadvantaged, to improve work conditions and increase paid vacations.[52] They sought to reflate the economy by stimulating demand. Unfortunately they were out of step with both the phase of the recession and the policies of the US, British and German governments. It was much as the last time such a programme had been tried (in 1936, as a response to the inter-war depression). Social opposition mounted, the franc came under pressure, there was a balance of payments crisis and there was a decline in the viability of the French domestic economy. This time the Government responded with a *plan de rigueur* which reversed its initial thrust. It now sought to manage the recession by reducing the size of the state, promoting private investment and by allowing a greater scope for market forces. Kesselman noted that

> The *plan de rigueur* adopted in 1982 departed from traditional austerity by including provisions for redundant workers, early retirement for workers in depressed industries, and social sector employment programmes . . . the lowest paid workers were excluded from the wage price freeze.[53]

Unlike the Social Contract period in Britain the expansion of the state was only loosely tied to the support of the trade union base. There was a trade union base in the CGT and the CGTF but it was not tied to the programme on the basis of trading wage restraint for an increase in its social power. In neither phases of the government's programme was the trade union movement greatly mobilised either to support the programme or to push for an increase in the influence of trade unions. The trade unions certainly held no levers to push the programme along at the time it came under challenge from pragmatists responding to the intensification of the recession.

The Mitterrand programme was not without its ambiguities. The Auroux reforms of 1982-6 made provision for the 'direct' and 'collective' consultation of workers in enterprises of greater than a specified size on issues relating to the organisation of work.[54] There was also an extension of collective bargaining with trade unions at the company level. In the past the CNPF had campaigned to stop enterprise level negotiations, preferring to work at the level of the sector or of industry as a whole.[55] Since these reforms offered a new forum for worker influence they were strongly opposed by both the CNPF and the political parties of the right fearing that they would empower workers through the trade unions or directly in the factories. Although the number of agreements reached at the enterprise level has increased steadily[56] the dire consequences feared by business have not eventuated.[57] Partly this is a product of the economic and political circumstances in which they were introduced. The social consequences of the recession and the austerity programme placed trade unions on the defensive and management has, in many instances, been able easily to dominate these new forums and to use them as part of a campaign to increase 'realism' in the work place and to campaign for greater flexibility in working arrangements.

If the component parts of the Mitterrand strategy were carefully summarised, and the austerity programme treated as a pragmatic response to the difficult political and economic circumstances in which the government had to work, then it would be easy to see this as another version of an expanded state strategy empowering workers and/or their various trade unions, posing a threat to the prerogatives of business and setting the scene for a popular neo-liberal revival. Indeed, these social changes coupled with the austerity programme (which undermined left claims about the recession and the role of the state) produced the circumstances in which a centre right coalition of Rassemblement Pour la République (RPR) and Union Pour la Démocratie Française (UDF) under Chirac were able to gain a parliamentary majority. During this period of 'cohabitation' the Chirac government sought to 'roll back the state' in true neo-liberal style by denationalising some of the firms taken over by the state. It took some time to frame the legislation which would be agreed to achieve this goal and it stopped short of a full-scale privatisation programme as in Britain. During its time in office, the Chirac government moved to liberalise the labour market, phase out exchange and price controls and to make it easier for firms to declare redundancies. Interestingly, his government did not repeal the Auroux laws.[58]

The period of the Chirac government was important for setting the framework of a political agenda. In the 1988 Presidential election campaign Mitterrand indicated that renationalising privatised firms was not his goal and he appeared to accept that the boundaries between the state and the private sector would remain roughly as they were. Mitterrand's re-election and the election of a new majority socialist government in 1988 will slow the 'liberalisation' moves proposed by the parties of the right, though it is unlikely that there will be a radical change in the policy directions away from moves to reduce the size and role of the state and to give a greater scope to the market. Despite the sharp contrasts between PS governments and the centre right coalition there was also a sense of continuity. Nonetheless, the significance of the Auroux laws and other moves to increase or protect the position of trade unions should not be minimised. In this period these moves have not worked to weaken the rights of management but they do provide a new forum in which negotiations and conflicts between business and labour will be explored. The form of the right to direct and collective consultation may also become a source of conflict in other economic and political circumstances. Despite the orthodoxy of the austerity programme, the state still owns large parts of the French economy and is an obvious and significant economic actor. Its labour reforms have granted, extended or protected rights to consultation and information sharing that are not supported by the business community. No degree of moderation on the part of Mitterrand and PS governments will alter the fact that the parties of the centre and right will frame their policies on the basis of further weakening the position of labour and further reducing the size and scope of the state. For them, the policies of the Mitterrand government have been those of an expanded state strategy and this will form the basis for a neo-liberal mobilisation and, should they gain office, a neo-liberal reform campaign.

Germany

The situation in Germany does not reflect the same forces as those identified in France and Britain. The doctrine of neo-liberalism held no surprises in the Federal Republic since, in the social-market variation, it had been the economic philosophy enshrined in the constitution and the rhetoric of the post-war Christian Democratic Government. With the downturn in the mid-1960s and the election of a coalition government dominated by the Social Democratic Party, the equations ought to have been changed. The Social Democratic Party in the Federal Republic was like all other social democratic parties, accepting the legitimacy of the existing social order, committed to limited reforms and with a strong trade union base. If events in Germany had followed the same pattern as those in Britain then the expansion of the state ought to have been linked to some expanded political presence of the trade unions and some modification of the balance between the class forces of capital and labour. Whatever happened, nothing like the Social Contract came to link the two wings of the labour movement. And yet there were some signs of a connection between the expansion of the state and the expanded political presence of the trade unions. When the recession started there was some sense of 'negotiation' between trade unions and 'their' government over wage restraint in the face of increasing recession and potential unemployment.[59] The role and size of the state did expand, even when the Government remained within the spirit of the constitutional restrictions on a government's role in the economy.[60] Although not enthusiastic about inflation out of line with the world economy, in the first phase of the recession the state did play an active part in sponsoring investment.[61] The position of the trade union movement was institutionalised through the Government's sponsorship of legislation to extend the sphere of co-determination arrangements.[62] Again, taking into account the specific sensitivities of German businesses, who were implacably opposed to any expansion of the rights of trade unions, this combination of recession, expanded role of the state and the trade unions could have formed the social base for a new period of neo-liberal policy.[63]

Developments in Germany do not support this argument in any uncomplicated way. The response by the state to the problems of continued recession was not to reject either the active role of the state nor the whole tradition of state-economic management rhetoric of the post-war period. Hence, as the recession continued there was no dramatic reversion to some social democratic version of neo-liberalism. Instead, there was a steady tightening of the areas of state action, more emphasis on cost efficiency, more concern with 'supply side' policies by boosting investment assistance/incentives and restrictions of spending on welfare provision.[64] To state it in this way gives it more coherence and force than would appear justified by the literature. It was only after the second oil price rise that more obvious elements of monetarism and neo-liberal small state policies were introduced and it would seem that it was a matter of emphasis rather than of a total policy orientation. The election of a conservative Christian Democratic led coalition government just strengthened this development.

The progress of neo-liberalism in the Federal Republic does not seem to crucially depend on the party composition of government. The initial response to recession did not undermine the assumptions of the social market economy and 'neo-liberalism' was only evident in the 'tightening' of the scope of state action. The policy stance of the SPD/FPD government in its final years was almost indistinguishable from the standard neo-liberal package and the tensions between the SPD in government and the party and the trade union movement was a reflection of this.[65] The Kohl Government has tightened the scope for state action again and been 'tougher' in expressing the logic of neo-liberal policy prescriptions and has stopped efforts by trade unions to increase their co-determination rights or their political presence. There was a significant conflict over what seemed a minor revision of the labour laws denying social security benefits to certain workers affected by strikes but effectively countering union attempts to pursue 'qualitative' demands using traditional techniques of collective bargaining.[66] Nonetheless, trade unions in Germany have not been rendered powerless by the change of government. IG Metall has been able to win campaigns to reduce working hours without financial penalty, and to negotiate significant wage increases despite relatively low rates of inflation.[67] The Kohl Government has pursued other elements of a neo-liberal strategy by selling off state holdings in various companies (such as Volkswagen) and by seeking to increase flexibility in the labour market. Nonetheless, for Germany, the passage from one coalition government to another, though accompanied by heated accusations and claims, continues the management of the social market economy with, at most, a slight change of emphasis. Undoubtedly, business prefers the coalition of the right as it slows the move to extend co-determination.

Why did events turn out like this in the Federal Republic? The simple answer would rely on some notion of the balance of class forces in that the strength of business over labour was so great that neither trade unions nor a social democratic government were able to displace the essentially pro-business policy framework of the social market economy. And yet this is by no means a complete explanation. It is true that business survived the war in a far healthier state than did the trade unions, and that conservative forces dominated the construction of the framework within which the state–economy relation would be conducted. But this is not a sufficient explanation for why those parameters remained so unaltered by the rise of full employment and the political success of a social democratic political party. Undoubtedly the success of the German economy provides an additional part of the explanation.

Increasing significance in the European and world economy and substantial improvements in the standard of living of German citizens would combine to make radical departures from the post-war orthodoxy less imperative. Even the onset of the world recession in the 1970s did not prompt such a revision as the increased importance of the German economy was reflected in the comparative ease with which it adjusted to the new circumstances. It was only the aftermath of the second oil shock and the rather sudden downturn in output and employment and an increase in inflation in the early 1980s that prompted a reaction; and that reaction when it came was in line with post-war orthodoxy – more support for business and less government spending in other areas.

As in the British and French cases, the return to neo-liberalism did not reduce with the size or the significance of the state in the economic and political system. The lesser militancy of the German trade union movement and the less radical vision of the German Social Democratic Party combined to move the state less significantly against the prerogatives of private capital than in either France and Britain. It is this as much as any other factor that explains why the neo-liberal experiment in Germany lacked the drama of the British case or the contradictory aspects of the French.

CONCLUSION

This account of the neo-liberal response to the prolonged recession and the changed framework of class and state interactions in the post-war period poses many important questions. How does the neo-liberal reversion fit into the history of the developing and changing parameters of class and state relations in the years since the interwar depression? Has neo-liberalism affected any major changes in the parameters of state–class relations, reversing the tendencies for the state to increase in size and significance and for the relations of business and labour to be altered as part of that increase? The relationship between neo-liberalism and the passage of the recession needs to be considered. In Britain and Germany, the degree of economic recovery has given credence to its claims to be able to manage a recession successfully. In France, the continuation of the recession undermined the claims of neo-liberalism and paved the way for a further dramatic increase in the size of the state and its relationship with the economy. Can it be read from this coincidence that if recession returns in Britain and Germany in the near future that this too will pave the way for a subsequent expansion/consolidation of the role of the state? What of the political and social consequences of the neo-liberal 'interlude'? In social terms, any ambiguity about the relationship between private accumulation and the state would seem to have been removed. Politically, the 'pacification' of labour would seem to be much less permanent than neo-liberals hoped and the lessons of 'economic realism' rather strictly confined to the period of acute recession. This raises the question of the overall potential pattern of class–state relations. Further, it is necessary to consider the relationship between the passage from economic depression to affluence and back to recession and the changing framework of class and state relations.

NOTES

1. The initial response by the OECD was very much a continuation of its boom-time analysis and is well expressed in the McCracken Report, *Towards Full Employment and Price Stability* (OECD, Paris, 1977). It

was not until after the 'second oil shock' that its perspective changed to place the fight against inflation first and to emphasise the need for tight 'non-accommodative' fiscal and monetary policy. This change can be seen in the *Economic Outlook*, July 1980 and the summary in *OECD Observer*, 105, July 1980. It should be noted that the OECD never became an enthusiast for monetarist orthodoxy, and often cautioned against expecting too much recovery as a result of these policies. See *OECD Observer*, 117, July 1982, and OECD, *Economic Survey: United Kingdom*, 1981-82 (OECD, Paris, 1983).
2. Thatcher (1977).
3. *Ibid.*, pp. 4-5, 6, 7, 8, 73, 77, 94-5.
4. *Ibid.*, p. 74.
5. *Ibid.*, p. 5.
6. *Ibid.*, 'The Health Society', pp. 81-6.
7. *Ibid.*, p. 12.
8. *Ibid.*, p. 12.
9. This would be consistent with the comments on the size of state expenditure that is compatible with democracy and a free society. *Ibid.*, p. 18. Note that in her foreword to the Conservative Party's Election Manifesto, Thatcher refers to the encroachment by the state having occurred in 'the last five years', and does not place it in the context of the whole trend of change since 1945. *Conservative Party Manifesto*, 11 April 1979 from *Keesing's Contemporary Archives*, 1 June 1979, p. 29633.
10. In the period between her election as Conservative Party leader and the general election in 1979, Thatcher did not often speak at length about the role of trade unions. When she did speak of them, it was in terms of the rule of law and the relationship between the trade unions and the Labour Government in the Social Contract. Thatcher (1977), pp. 35, 37. For a more extended commentary on the problems caused by the trade unions, see, Margaret Thatcher, House of Commons speech, *Hansard*, Vol. 957, 1 November, 1978, Columns 30-33.
11. *Conservative Party Manifesto*.
12. Thatcher (1977), pp. 51-9, 87-92.
13. *Ibid.*, pp. 56-8.
14. As Milton Friedman suggested in 1982.
15. OECD, *Economic Surveys: United Kingdom*, 1982-3, Section I.
16. OECD, *Economic Surveys: United Kingdom*, 1985-6, Section II.
17. OECD, *Economic Surveys: United Kingdom*, 1982-3, p. 43ff and 1985-6, p. 37.
18. CBI (1976), pp. 21-2.
19. *The Times*, August 1982.
20. CBI (1982).
21. OECD, *Economic Surveys: United Kingdom*, 1983-4, p. 35.
22. Buiter and Miller (1984), pp. 352ff.
23. OECD, *Economic Surveys: United Kingdom*, 1983-4, pp. 30-1.
24. Peter Riddell (1985), p. 112; see also, Mullard (1987), chap. 6.
25. *Ibid.*, p. 114.

26. The OECD gives the figures in *Economic Outlook* No. 39, May 1986, p. 181 for total outlays of Government as percentage of GDP as:

	United Kingdom	France	Germany
1979	42.9	45.5	47.6
1980	45.1	46.4	48.3
1981	47.8	49.2	49.1
1982	47.3	49.4	45.1
1983	47.3	48.4	52.0
1984	48.0	48.2	52.6

27. OECD, *Economic Surveys: United Kingdom*, 1987-8, pp. 36-7.
28. Central Statistics Office (CSO), *Social Trends 18*, p. 83.
29. Chancellor's Budget Speech, *Financial Times*, 16 March 1988, pp. 12-13.
30. CSO, *Social Trends 18*, p. 77 (OECD basis . . . UK Government basis, 11.5 per cent, p. 65).
31. OECD, *Economic Surveys: United Kingdom*, 1987-8, p. 18, refers to the significant success of reducing to 40 per cent of total unemployed those claiming benefit for more than a year.
32. OECD, *Economic Surveys: United Kingdom*, 1987-8, p. 17; CSO, *Social Trends 18*, for OECD calculations.
33. OECD, *Economic Surveys: United Kingdom*, 1985-6, p. 23.
34. *The Times*, August 1983.
35. Wyn Grant with Jane Sargent (1987), chaps 8 and 11; Grant (1983), pp. 163-82.
36. Riddell (1985), p. 112.
37. *Ibid.*, p. 114.
38. McEachern (1980), chaps 6 and 7.
39. For the debate on French planning, see Green (1978), pp. 60-76; Collis (1979), pp. 256-61.
40. Reynaud (1975), pp. 277-317; Ross (1982), pp. 13-93.
41. Hayward (1966).
42. Brizay (1975), chap. IV; Hayward (1975), pp. 93-151; Birnbaum (1980); Caron (1979), p. 352ff; Michalet (1974), pp. 105-25.
43. Lewis (1978) pp. 51-5.
44. Caron (1979), chap. 14; Hough (1982), pp. 51ff and chap. 5; Michalet (1974).
45. Frears (1981); Hanley, Kerr and Waites (1979), p. 47.
46. Hough (1982), pp. 135ff.
47. Cohen and Goldfinger (1975), pp. 35-41.
48. 'France - A Survey', *The Banker*, **128** (624) 1978; Hanley, Kerr and Waites (1979), pp. 57ff; Frears (1981), ch. 7; Hough (1982), pp. 136-7 and 145-6; OECD, *Economic Surveys: France*, 1979 and 1980.
49. Kesselman (1985-6), p. 233.
50. The puzzled tone of many authors dealing with the apparent contradiction between what was said and done is strange, after all these

years and all the studies of social democratic parties in office. For example see Kesselman (1985-6); Ross, Hoffman and Malzachier (1987).
51. It could be argued that though calendar time was different, in terms of the progress of the recession they occurred at the same time. For France the first oil crisis was only an interruption to growth, which then resumed more strongly than in Britain and it was only in the late 1970s and 1980s that the recession really hit France. The parallels between the policies of the Labour Government in Britain and the PS Government in France are even more marked.
52. This programme should be compared to that of the Popular Front Government of 1936 and the post-war coalition government.
53. Kesselman (1985-6), p. 235.
54. Delamotte (1988), pp. 221-41.
55. Eyraud and Tchobanian (1985), pp. 244-5.
56. 'France: Recent Trends in Collective Bargaining', *European Industrial Relations Review*, **175**, August 1988, pp. 11-13.
57. Moss (1988), p. 68.
58. *Ibid.*, pp. 68-9, 73-6.
59. Clark (1979), p. 253; Kuhl (1981), pp. 123-56; Müller-Jentsch (1981), pp. 105-22.
60. Owen-Smith (1979), pp. 160-68.
61. OECD, *Economic Surveys: Germany*, 1978, p. 9.
62. von Beyme (1978), pp. 399-415; Markovits and Allen (1980), pp. 68-86; Markovits and Allen (1984), pp. 91-188.
63. As evident in their legal challenge to the extension of co-determination, Clark (1979), p. 256.
64. OECD, *Economic Surveys: Germany*, 1979, p. 49ff; 1980, pp. 8, 12, 20, 29 and 34.
65. Pagett (1987), pp. 333-7.
66. Silvia (1988), pp. 155-74.
67. Hartman and Horstmann (1987), pp. 371-88.

CONCLUSION: CLASS STRUGGLES IN A CYCLICAL ECONOMY

The last five chapters have presented a schematic history of the development of the political regimes in the three industrialised capitalist countries of Britain, France and Germany. This account has set out a map of the way in which the relations between classes and the state (the essential elements of political regime) have been altered in the years between the inter-war depression and the recession of the 1970s and the early 1980s. The main elements in this account were: the changes in the organisation of the contending classes; in the strategic and tactical assessments made by these class organisations and their associated political parties that sought to form successive governments; the organisation of the state and its increased range of actions; and the pattern of initiative between the various classes and the state. These were all considered against a backdrop of problems in capital accumulation and the search for renewed or sustained economic growth. It is now necessary to consider what the evidence presented can be made to reveal about the character and consequence of class struggles in a society based on such a cyclical pattern of capital accumulation. It is also necessary to evaluate the significance of this expansion of the size and role of the state and the attendant alteration in the workings of the relationships between the economic and political processes of industrialised capitalism.

The pattern of change in the schematic history suggests a number of tendencies in the developing relations of classes and the state. Over time, there has been a tendency for the classes to become more consciously and comprehensively organised. On the side of capital, this can be seen in the succession of organisations seeking to represent the different sections of business in the political process and in the relative consistency of those business organisations dealing with trade unions. On the side of labour, there has been the move towards more inclusive forms of central organisation, bringing 'white' and 'blue' collar workers, professional and manual employees into common organisations. On both sides there has been the growth of bureaucracy and specialised organisation to manage the relations between the classes and their representation in the more formal arenas of the political process. Despite the substantial developments there has been no reduction in the internal division in the two classes; their unity still has to be organised on specific matters, though this is still easier for capital in its confrontations with labour. Along with these have gone some quite significant changes in the strategic and tactical perspectives of these class organisations. For organised labour this can be seen in the changing attitude to socialism, socialisation and nationalisation, with a gradual rejection of these objectives in practice, whatever formal commitments may have lingered on. In specific circumstances, where the failure of private capital was most marked, as it was in the case of Britain and France, the demand for increased state ownership re-emerged as part of a strategy to protect employment and to strengthen the position of the state in its dealings with private capital. For organised business, the developing perspectives parallel the changes in the attitudes of labour to a surprising degree, reflected in a lessening hostility to the state and all its works. This more accommodative attitude faded with the persistence of recession in the 1970s and the resurgence of neo-liberal attitudes that reactivated a traditional hostility to the state.

It was not only in the areas of class organisation and political parties that there were fairly clearly identifiable tendencies. The state also changed in its organisation, scope of action and in its strategic and tactical perspectives. Like the class organisations, the state became more organised, bureaucratised, professional and centralised. Its economic size, measured by the proportion of domestic production that passed through the various branches of the state, as well as the proportion of production generated by state activity and the very cost of administering the state itself all increased. These increases in the size of the state seem to have some symmetrical relationship to the problems experienced in capital accumulation. The range and pattern of state actions have also increased and altered over time. Leaving aside the unusual development of the state in Germany during the Nazi years, the state can be seen to have moved further into the economy and society through nationalisation, economic management and support for private business and welfare provision. Each of the successive stages in the development of capital accumulation seems to have provided a setting within which the state increased its size and the scope of its actions. Even though such an expansion may not have been consciously and deliberately sought, that was the consequence of the state seeking to assist private capital in the struggles for greater accumulation within the confines of a single geographic unit in an increasingly internationalised economy. The neo-liberal experiment represents the only deliberate attempt to move against this tendency, and its uncertain success serves better to illustrate the real economic, political and social forces behind this steady expansion in the size and scope of the state. Even when neo-liberalism has been most assiduously pursued it has not undermined the tendency towards the state becoming more organised, professional and centralised. One of the most significant achievements of the challenge of neo-liberalism has been to improve radically the efficiency and co-ordination of the state as a centralised institution. It is the significance of this extension of the state, and of the changing relationship between economic and political processes in industrialised capitalism, that most needs to be the subject of critical assessment.

ALTERNATIVE EXPLANATIONS FOR THE CHANGING RELATIONS OF CLASSES AND THE STATE

To help explore this history of changed relations between classes and the state, and the significant expansion of the state itself, it is useful to consider a variety of alternative interpretations that have achieved some kind of currency in the debates.

From liberal to monopoly to state-monopoly capitalism

A common way to interpret this history is as a passage from liberal, competitive capitalism to a system dominated by monopoly which, in turn, moves, as a result of its inherent contradictions, towards state monopoly capitalism. This is explicitly argued in Ben Fine and Lawrence Harris's *Rereading Capital*[1] where they make a systematic attempt to link the passage from one stage to another to the changing imperatives of the economic process of capital accumulation, with the 'general laws of the accumulation of capital' as the prime cause.² It is not just a mechanical scheme of transformation (even though they tend to embrace self-conscious economic determination) since a part is played by 'the class relations associated with' the process of accumulation.³ They summarise their approach thus:

> Our basic principle for periodising the capitalist mode of production then is to examine how capitalism's socialisation of production brings about distinct stages involving the restructuring of the social relations of production.⁴

Fine and Harris's account of the passage from *laissez-faire* to monopoly capitalism is illustrative of their approach to the relationship between economic developments and political consequences. On an economic level they conflate the growth of large scale firms and monopolies with the change from the extraction of absolute to relative surplus value – thus doing damage to the actual historical sequence. They then argue that technical change contains imperatives for the formal organisation of capitalist production.

> But machinery does not simply stimulate the Factory Acts. For machinofacture accelerates over manufacture the minimum capital required to produce at sufficiently high levels of productivity. This requires the accumulation of capital to be accomplished through its centralisation, the gathering of many capitals into the hands of the few. It has as its immediate effect the centralisation of labourers in even larger numbers at the point of production; it requires the breaking down of local labour markets and the creation of freedom of exchange for labour-power.⁵

The most important part comes with the account of the consequence this has for the behaviour of the working class.

> However, the transformation of economic relations is not all that is included. The development of the monopoly stage of capitalism requires that the working class struggle for the limitation of the working day prove successful. This presupposes the political representation of working-class interests and can have the additional effects of moderating class struggles.⁶

This passage reduces the struggles of the working class against the conditions of their social domination and economic exploitation to that of epiphenomena fulfilling the requirements of the modernisa-

Changing relations of classes and state 187

tion of the capitalist processes of production and reproduction. The various phases of initiative and response are jumbled here, even though all the ingredients of the process remain: the passage from assembly to machine production; the rise of larger economic units, some of which will take the form of monopolies; the response by labour to their experience of society. It is the basic approach as much as anything else that gets in the way of a better assessment of what these changes involved and the assessment of whether such changes amount to a new stage in the capitalist mode of production.

This broadly suggests how they treat the history of class–state interactions. Liberal capitalism existed sometime in the mid nineteenth century giving way to monopoly capitalism between the late nineteenth century and the Second World War (roughly coinciding with the period identified as a passage away from a liberal regime). Reconstruction after 1945 saw the gradual development of state monopoly capitalism, when the state achieved some form of economic predominance. The move to this later stage was based in the successful 'political' struggles of labour. The terms of the periodisation can be stretched only by loosening the connection between technical change and the broader regime changes.

The passage from monopoly to state monopoly capitalism is treated in much the same way as the rise of monopolies and is open to the same sort of objections:

> Monopoly capitalism is characterised as a stage then in which there develops an intensification of class struggles over economic crises. These struggles are confined within the limits compatible with the reproduction of capitalist social relations as a whole by the development of struggle for political democracy as a means to social reform. The partial 'resolution' of these contradictory tendencies that both promote and moderate class struggle under *monopoly capitalism* is to be found in the development of the economic role of the state. The state's predominance in economic reproduction is the distinguishing feature of *state monopoly capitalism* (SMC) the latest stage of the capitalist mode of production.[7]

This passage also links the rise of the new stage in the mode of production to the political struggles of labour, but it still mis-states the process in terms of the economic salience of the political changes. It again picks a key point, the predominance of the state in economic reproduction – which could certainly mark a new stage in the relations between the economic and political processes of industrialised capitalism – and interprets the far less dramatic changes which have actually occurred in those exaggerated terms.

Fine and Harris do not sufficiently consider the significance of the changes they identify. Do these changes alter the defining class relations of the capitalist mode of production? Hardly; labour still remains defined on the basis of its separation from the means of production and the commodity form of its ability to work. Capital remains defined on the basis of its possession and control of the means of production. So the changes exist at a different level from that of the characteristic features of the capitalist mode of production: at the level of the organisational forms of labour and capital's response to the experience of capitalist production and their relations to each other. In other words, these are changes in the history of capitalist society: changes in the way in which classes respond to the historical experience of the reality of capitalist social relations. That history can be periodised even if the mode of production can not.

What is the crucial difference between *laissez-faire* and monopoly capitalism? It is to be found in the ablity of monopoly firms to offset the more immediate workings of market relations. Although Fine and Harris link the rise of monopoly to changes in technology, the organisation of production, the character of the extraction of surplus value and a change in the organisation and objectives of the labour movement, the central point of reference is the centralisation of capital and the rise of monopoly. The political changes and the change in the role of the state are matters of a lesser order of significance. This ordering of the elements involved in the change is suspect. What defines the *laissez-faire* situation, or the core relations of the liberal competitive order, is the role of the state and its relationship to the market. In the passage away from the liberal order, it is not the rise of monopolies but the changed set of relations between the state and the market which is decisive. The quantity and extent of competition neither causes nor 'requires' the alteration in the size and role of state actions. It is the real forces of capital and labour both seeking ways of avoiding or minimising the impact of market relations that creates the social circumstances in which the economic failure of a largely autonomous market becomes the setting for a changed role of the state and its relationship with the market, expressed as a reworking of the means

Changing relations of classes and state

of balancing class rule and accumulation, of linking classes and state and of co-ordinating the political and economic processes of industrialised capitalism. Similar criticisms could be made of their account of the passage from monopoly to state monopoly capitalism. This time it is necessary to notice the changed role of the state, but they date the change as happening too early, they exaggerate the extent of the increased presence of the state in the economy and they miss the significant extent to which the changed relations between classes and the state give a new bias to the conflicts between the classes and the debate over the role of the state. In a sense their chronology and periodisation is both skewed and compressed and fails to pick up the tensions that grow from the particular form of reorganisation that happened after the Second World War nor the equally significant new forms of conflict generated in the management of renewed recession in the 1970s.

The version of liberal, monopoly, state-monopoly capitalism given by Fine and Harris is superior to many other variants because it finds room for the active response of the working class and its politics. Its central emphasis still lies with the forms of capitalist reproduction and not the tensions between rule and accumulations and between the political and economic processes of capitalist societies. The dynamic of the regime's development does not just derive from the form of capitalist accumulation or reproduction but from the active history of class-based organisations in conflict and a changing role for the state in the context of capital accumulation which is, from time to time, full of problems and uncertainties.

Fordism and neo-fordism

Another approach, of growing influence, also concerned with the relationship between economic developments and forms of periodisation is that of the 'regulation school'.[8] A group of French authors working with and around Aglietta developed a conception of 'regulation', of the regularity of reproduction of epochs of capitalist development.[9] For them, the focus is on how forms of production (regimes of accumulation or reproduction) and forms of consumption are combined to produce a stable environment within which reproduction (both economic and social) can occur. Alain Lipietz, a practitioner of this approach, describes it in these terms:

> The term *mode of regulation* refers to the ensemblement of institutional forms, networks and explicit or implicit norms which assure compatibility within a regime of accumulation, in keeping with the actual pattern of social relations, and beyond (or even through) the contradictory, conflictual nature of relations among economic agents and social groups.[10]

It was the search for such combinations of forms of production and the economic and social requirements for stable reproduction that made it possible to identify a period of mass production/mass consumption as 'fordism' and the present period as an attempt to find a new stable regime, a pursuit of 'neo-fordism'. Different authors using this approach produce different periodisations and different accounts of the rise and fall of such stable combinations but common emphasis is on the mode of consumption to secure conditions of stable reproduction.[11] The reference to fordism is a 'metaphor'. It does not refer to the reality of what Ford did to secure his fortune through the mass production of cars but to the image of a high wage–high profit economy which he sought to promote.[12] As Hirsch describes the key features of the 'fordist' phase:

> This phase is marked by an intensified mode of capital accumulation and a change to the production of relative surplus value. It is based on Taylorized mass production of durable consumer products (e.g. Henry Ford's assembly-line automobile production); relatively high wages; the emergence of a sharp polarization between skilled and deskilled, 'Taylorized' labor; expanded state intervention including a high degree of administrative regulation of the reproduction of labour (social security, health, education). Fordism thus denotes a secular 'long wave' of expanded capitalist accumulation by which the reproduction of labor becomes a central sphere of the valorization of capital. A consequence of this is a sharp, thorough capitalization of the whole society (commodity-form of social relations, individualization, and social disintegration). Politically, this includes the emergence of social reformism, Keynesianism and mass regulative bureaucracies. Fordism, therefore, refers to more than a form of material production and reproduction (as Taylorism does). It is a historically distinct form of capitalist social formation with its own economic, political and ideological characteristics.[13]

In this way the term 'fordism' was associated with the long boom and a rising standard of living. A crisis of fordism occurred in the late 1960s and 1970s as its basic assumptions started to unravel and the present era is characterised by the search for a new effective combination, such as that identified by Mike Davis for America of 'over consumption of high consumption–low wages',[14] or by Joachim Hirsch as an inability of the political system to incorporate dissenting 'interests'.[15]

This characterisation and periodisation is both impressionistic and vague and hence can be shaped to fit the changes that I have mapped in the preceding chapters. In this way it would become: the interwar period as a problem for a regime of 'extensive accumulation', replaced after 1945 by an intensive regime, by fordism with its period of uncertainty before the recession seeking a new regime with, as yet unstable resolutions. The key features of the period of post-war reconstruction can easily be presented in terms of a fit between the social and economic requirements to sustain expanded, mass consumption and, indeed, for a considerable time the combination seemed stable. It certainly began to weaken in the late 1960s and as yet a new, stable 'mode of regulation' has not been established.

The regulation approach concentrates on changes in the organisation of production and the organisation of consumption and the state is only marginally significant. It concentrates on the need for modes of regulation to secure stable reproduction though it tends to over-emphasise the mode of consumption as a way of securing stability and economic reproduction. It is largely in this context that the state enters the account. The expansion of the state, increased state welfare provision and state economic management to secure full employment are treated as ways of securing reproduction through securing a particular mode of consumption. This obscures a recognition of the significance of the changed size and role of the state as also altering the relations between classes and between the economic and political processes of capitalist society. The reordering of the relationship, in fact, provides the social basis for the construction of new 'modes of consumption' and new ways of securing social cohesion. The regulation approach interprets this as the foundation for secured capital accumulation and economic and social reproduction rather than the significant reordering of state–class relations in the political regime. It seems likely that the regulation approach will gather many adherents because of its seemingly impressive attempt to link what happens in production with consumption and social reproduction but in the end, fordism/neo-fordism is a metaphor which fails to explore the significant changes in the role of the state.

Organised/disorganised capitalism

Another alternative account of the processes shaping this history can be found summed up in the contrast between organised and disorganised capitalism. This view is most distinctly found in Scott Lash and John Urry's *The End of Organized Capitalism*.[16] They soundly criticise the liberal, monopoly, state-monopoly capitalism periodisation and substitute a liberal-competitive, organised, disorganised capitalism scenario.[17] In their analysis they stress the importance of the particular way in which each country comes through these phases, the importance of distinctive national configurations and histories. Lash and Urry chart changes in the organisation of capital (including the rise of monopolies and cartels via a consideration of 'concentration' in ownership and production) and changes in the organisation of labour, via an index of changes in the density of union membership and the introduction of state welfare provision. On this basis they identify a passage to 'organised' capitalism. For them, organised capitalism was built, in different countries at different times, from the last years of the nineteenth century and was consolidated in the inter-war years and dominated the period of post-war reconstruction. Some form of 'corporatist' relations can go along with the organised phase, though they treat capital–state relations as far more decisive than tripartite negotiations incorporating labour.[18] The disorganisation phase covers the period from tension appearing in the mid-1960s up until the present, as capitalist production is reorganised, breaking up the local/regional/residential concentrations of the organised phase. Lash and Urry would like to argue that their approach is not a 'disorganisation of labour' thesis and yet it is. They do not show that capital has become disorganised. They do not pretend that there has to be a significant de-concentration of capital ownership and control.[19] Their indicator for the disorganisation of capital is the decline in the number of large industrial plants and the rise of dispersed, smaller plants integrating wider production processes. Here the emphasis on disorganisation is largely one-sided. It is labour which is disorganised by the changed forms of production; it is labour whose ability for collective action is weakened by the 'disorganisation' of regions and residential location.

The argument about events in Britain, France and Germany is directly relevant to this book. It is significant to note that Britain and Germany stand out as having been influenced by strong organisations of labour in either the making of organised capitalism (Britain in the inter-war years and post-war reconstruction), or in slowing the rate of disorganisation (Germany). France, in both organisation and disorganisation has been strongly conditioned by the actions of the state with a far less significant political role for trade unions. But, does the account actually work?

Like accounts that focus on the passage from pluralism to corporatism and those dealing with the passage from liberal to monopoly to state monopoly capitalism, the organised/disorganised thesis fails in its treatment of the state. This weakens its account of the rise of organised relations between classes and the state and in its identification of 'disorganisation' as the key to understanding the present situation. Organisation is not the key to understanding either of these processes. It is true that organisation has been an important part of the institutionalised history of capitalist societies. It is also true that this has something to do with increased concentration of capital, at least for the development of more effective forms of business organisation. But to focus on organisation/disorganisation is to miss the point. What has changed, prompting at times and responding at others to organisation, has been the expanded and changing role of the state. The passage from one phase to another is not some accidental, coincidental, contingent process. It is made by people responding to the situations in which they find themselves, of classes, class organisations and the state in conflict. The rise of what they describe as a 'disorganisation' is part of a strategy by capital, parts of capital, and parts of the state, as a response to the problems of international competition, technological change *and* organised and effective trade unions. To understand how these different societies have changed over time, the emphasis needs to be placed on class–state relations in the context of conflicts between classes and the passage of the economy through periods of growth and contraction.

Pluralism/corporatism

Numerous works were produced in the 1970s and early 1980s identifying a shift from pluralism to corporatism as a meaningful way to account for the changes in the institutional history of capitalist societies. Some, such as that of Keith Middlemass's, *The Politics of Industrial Society*,[20] bear a passing resemblance to the periodisation of Lash and Urry. Middlemass finds 'corporatism' flourishing in the interwar period and declining in the mid-60s. Others, like Harrison, in *Pluralism and Corporatism*, see an evolutionary process from one structure of political power and influence to another; away from a competitive, diffuse structure of power to one of a few selected groups in close co-operation with the state.[21] This approach has been weakened by the confident assurance of neo-liberal governments and the triumph of strongly anti-labour conservative parties which often sought to weaken forms of political negotiations that gave legitimacy to labour, though plenty of efforts remain to find the continuing 'corporatist' thread preserved in neo-liberal policies. Another strand has moved from a concern with tripartite structures, of labour, capital and the state, to a concern with how the state shapes the processes of representation that are effective in a given society.[22] Both these concerns are relevant to a consideration of the developments mapped in the preceding chapters.

There are some very strong points in the midst of this pluralist/corporatist account. Proper attention is paid to the importance of the political process, the state and the attempts to influence policy outcomes. There is a proper concern with the increasing importance of the state in the process of representation, in the selection of 'representatives', of those who have a political presence and voice in the political system and to the increasing importance of 'organised' representation. But at the centre of this account are two areas of weakness. The first concerns the dynamics of class interaction. In so much of the corporatist literature the sense of class, of the dynamics of class interactions, of the sequence of struggles that generate new organisations, new ways of struggling, is missing, misrepresented or under-emphasised. Politics is frequently treated as sufficient unto itself. The second weakness concerns an interesting contrast to the approaches previously considered: the emphasis here is too much on politics and the state and not enough on class relations and on the economy. This frequently led the corporatists to mistake the importance of the developments in the 1970s and so both these 'corporatist' institutions and their interpretation were undermined by determined neo-liberalism. On the whole, they could not handle the politics of managing the recession when it went beyond a reliance on securing the institutional co-operation of labour. Undoubtedly tripartite structures will continually be recreated in the institutional history of capitalism but to focus on just these political, organisational forms is to miss the dynamics which underlies both their creation and their passing.

Neo-liberalism

Strictly speaking, neo-liberalism does not generate a periodisation of the developing relations between classes and the state despite the fact that it has an interpretation of them. The neo-liberal approach forms a sharp contrast with the approaches considered so far. The preceding accounts have all, in distinctive ways, tried to come to terms with the expansion of the state and the changed relations between classes and the state. This is not true of the neo-liberal approach. For neo-liberalism there is a past which it is hoped will be the future. There was in some country at some time, an unfettered market with a state strictly confined to limited rule-setting and certainly non-interventionist action. Since that time there has been a decline with increased state action weakening the workings of market mechanisms. Why this should have happened can, in neo-liberal terms, be debated. Too much democracy, not enough awe for the fundamentals of market economics, too many weak people seeking security and certainty and unwilling to enjoy the excitement of unrestricted competition, these could all produce ways of moving away from the market and an increasing reliance on an expanding state. It is not a question of 'periods' of developing state–class relations, it is an unending succession of deviation from the principles of a free-market economy. Its account of the history of developing class–state relations is rather like another version of the fall.

Neo-liberalism's interpretation promotes a vision of the future and a hope for action. People must be persuaded to give up their reliance on the state, they must abandon their past habits of seeking to avoid the uncertainties of the market by turning to the state. Like the utopian socialists of old, they must seek converts in positions of power and influence to make their doctrine into policy and to reverse the trends evident for so long. For much of the post-war boom they were like prophets crying in the wilderness but, with the renewed recession they have been, to a degree, successful. Governments have been elected who have been committed to the faith and they have acted on the age-old precepts. But for the pure neo-liberals, these converts have not been determined enough. Monetary policy has not been used in the way that it should and cuts in government spending have not been great enough, tax cuts have not reversed historical trends towards the state collecting and redistributing greater levels of revenue. Only the return of growth has softened their criticisms of the politicians who have tried to implement their creed and return the state to the limits of the once glorious and free market past.

Whatever its policy prescriptions, neo-liberalism does not give an effective or systematic account of the forces that have shaped the development of class–state relations, or the dynamics that have underlain the steady expansion of the state. It works from assumptions about the economic and social efficacy of market arrangements and has no effective categories for dealing with the real histories of people, either as owners and controllers of business or as workers, responding to the conditions in which they find themselves. The rational choices of these people are not the rational choices of the theory. They often seek state action as a solution to the problems they face and live with the consequences of their choices.

In these five alternative approaches a number of common points are identified, such as the importance of what happened in the relations of classes and state after the Second World War. There are also extensive points of contrast and differing emphasis. They do not tell the same story or identify in different terms the same periodisation. It is not possible, by some simple reformulation, to reconcile the differences between them and to find a unified interpretation to embrace them all. A key feature picked up in their variety concerns the ways in which political and economic relations are changed by the forces underlying the expanded and changed role of the state, and this needs to be probed further. Another feature that needs a more explicit examination is the logic of a history of conflicts and interactions that produce a steady expansion in the size and role of the state. This too will be considered in its turn.

THE CHANGING RELATIONSHIP BETWEEN POLITICS AND ECONOMICS

In the introductory discussion of the different approaches to the history of the changing relations between classes and the state, the two main forms of conventional wisdom on the relationship between the political and economic processes of industrialised capitalism were considered. There the complementing orthodoxies of the dominance of economics or the dominance of politics were rejected in favour of a more detailed consideration of the ways in which the relationships had changed over the period since the interwar depression. Having presented that account of the gradual modification of the workings of the relationship, it is now necessary to return to that original and basic question: what is the significance of the changes wrought in the relationship between economics and politics in the historical development of industrialised capitalism?

The problem can be usefully considered by tracing the pattern of effectiveness of political decisions on the economy, especially in the post-war years, since one of the clearest objectives of state policy since the war has been to influence economic developments. In part, the essence of the post-war settlement and the rise of Keynesian management techniques was to modify substantially the impact that the market (the central expression of the autonomy of the economy) would have on the patterns of growth, development and standards of living within these societies. If we consider the long-term impact of government policy in its broadest intentions and effects, then it can be seen that the period of post-war prosperity was of limited duration, that it gave way to periods of slow growth and then a major and as yet unfinished, recession. Does this suggest that, although politics is formally 'in command' in the sense that the policies of the state are more or less consistently obeyed, the major rhythms of economic expansion and contraction are beyond its control? It has been possible to lengthen the period of expansion, delay the onset of recession, modify the consequences of depression so that it appears as a recession, but not to remove nor to manage the passage of the economy from growth to recession and back again. Does this mean that economics, in some very broad sense, largely synonymous with capital accumulation, is not dominated by political decisions but has a very real 'relative autonomy' and shapes the environment within which political decisions are made even more decisively than political decisions shape the environment for economic developments? If the accumulation process is, in this sense, dominant, what then of the relative autonomy of politics? Is this nothing more than a disguised way of saying the relative impotence of politics?

To answer these questions it is necessary to rethink the terms in which the dominance of economics and politics are assessed. The schematic account of the history of industrialised capitalism since the inter-war depression reveals the extent to which the working relationship between politics and economics has been altered such that the conception of very distinct spheres of society needs to be re-evaluated. It is not that the sphere of political relations has expanded and that of the economy has contracted but rather that very specific ways of combining political and economic processes have come to replace a situation (the character of which is greatly exaggerated in the literature) in which economics and politics were largely separate parts of a single social whole. Although some enthusiasts saw the post-war settlement as ending the primacy of economics and giving 'power' to democratically elected governments to determine economic consequences, what in reality had occurred was a modification of the way in which the market worked. The measures of governmental influence did not extend far into market transactions themselves and only went a small way beyond the influence-by-purchase which had been possible in most industrialised capitalist countries in the inter-war years and before.

The gradual increase in the size of the state, its revenue requirements, the extent of its support for private industry in the pursuit of a more rationally structured and more efficiently working economy does not alter the relative importance of political and economic processes, although it does add greater complexity to the arena within which private capitalists make their investment and production decisions. It is only when the state moves from infrastructure (which can include finance, once it is state owned and not operated as a source of private appropriation of a surplus generated elsewhere in the economy) into the direct manufacture and circulation of commodities, or begins to make arrangements that direct investment, rather than simply encouraging it by promises of greater or more secure profits than would otherwise be the case, that the relationship between economic and political processes are substantially changed. Such a development only just started in the prolonged recession of the 1970s and 1980s. When it did happen, it was not as a deliberate challenge to the autonomy of the market, the dominance of economics nor the prerogatives of private capital. Rather, it was a pragmatic response to the failure of private capital, in the context of the onset of a major recession.

It is necessary to consider the extent to which the growth of the state and its attendant expansion of the scope of politics, altering the workings of the relations between the economic and the political processes, constitute a challenge to the economic, political or social position of private capital. Certainly parts of business treat the expansion of the state in such a way. Equally, a generation of Marxist arguments has contended that the expansion of the state is no threat to capital; rather the expansion of the state, even if opposed by business, is in fact in capital's own best interests. Such a view implies not just the functional efficacy of state expansion but also the impossibility of any state expansion which is not undertaken to destroy private capital, contradicting or threatening the class interests of capital. As I suggested in the analysis of the contrasting state responses to the recession, intention is not the most appropriate guide to the significance or consequences of state action.

In this broader framework it is possible to make further observations about the causes and significance of expanded state action and assess its potential for weakening the position of private capital. So far it can be said that the expansion of the state to the point at which it begins to move from infrastructure and into the heartland of capitalist production has rarely been the result of conscious policies enacted with the goal of overthrowing capitalism, destroying the economic, political and social power of private capital and raising the working class to a position of a dominant class. The expansion was a deliberate response to the failure of private capital to generate full employment and/or secure or improve standards of living. It was on that basis that the role of the state established in the post-war settlement has expanded ever since. During the era of neo-liberal experimentation the state expanded despite the intentions and desires of the government and private business. It is this which suggests that there are some underlying forces which link the size of the state inevitably to the struggles between classes over the conditions which will allow for sustained capital accumulation.

This is not the only explanation. Within a more or less cyclical economy, which is what the industrialised capitalist economy would seem to be, there is a degree of inevitability about the periodic failure of private capital to both invest profitably and secure employment and rising standards of living. Once the crucial divide is passed, after which business failure often has political significance, then the regular failure of private business provides the setting within which *both sections of capital and labour* will seek political solutions to their economic and market problems. This is a potent force encouraging, though not impelling in any authoritative or determinist manner, the sustained expansion of the size and the role of the state. The combination of market failure and this political sensibility in the class organisations of labour and capital suggests that the state will, in the context of recurrent problems in capital accumulation, continue to expand. Nothing is implied about the extent, character or timing of that expansion. National variation, failed initiatives and international ramifications will all affect the rate at which the state expands and its role is transformed. If this underlying pattern of economic failure and political solutions is present, then it is reasonable to suppose that private capital will be involved in a continual battle to ensure that the expansion of the state does not undermine the economic position of capital, nor weaken its dominance as a social and political force. The period of neo-liberal experimentation represents just the first of such attempts to protect private capital from the economic and social implications of the unsystematic expansion of the state. Only if business has manageed to work a major change in the imperatives behind the expansion of state programmes will this be the last such aggravated period of tension between private capital and the state.

Though a degree of antagonism between private capital and the state is implied in the above remarks, it should not be taken to mean that the steady expansion of the role of the state will lead to some unintentional transformation of the economic and social order on behalf of the subordinated class of labour. It is true that labour struggles have played an important part in encouraging the expansion of the state, either through the demand for protection from the consequences of the market or through programmes generated for managing the revival of industrialised capitalism in particular countries. But even where these programmes have been argued for on behalf of the subordinate class, they have never been implemented as part of a conscious class strategy to destroy the position of private capitalism and to transform the social order. Indeed, it has been the combination of struggles within capital in the context of such class-less conscious struggles by labour, with a state concerned to preserve its own position, which have formed the basis for both the fact and character of the state expansion that has occurred. Despite the possibility of an alliance between a self-interested state and organised labour to displace private capital, this is not likely to happen. The reality of the position of private capital in the accumulation process and the shared experience of the state and private capital as the employers of labour suggests that any changes that occur will be such that, from the position of the subordinate class, they will not escape from the logic of the existing social order. Thus it would seem that the expected unconscious, contingent expansion of the role of the state, even though it may create some problems for private capital, is most unlikely to displace the prevailing alliance between private capital and the state. In that sense, social democracy that sponsors the expansion of the state in the hope that it will lead steadily and peacefully to the socialist transformation of capitalism will have its expectations confounded by a larger state and no transformation of the social order.

CLASS STRUGGLES IN A CYCLICAL ECONOMY

The above discussion of the changing character of the relationship between the economic and political processes in the historical development of industrialised capitalism contains important implications for an assessment of the significance of the class struggles that have occurred in this cyclical pattern of capital accumulation. Throughout the passage from inter-war depression, to post-war settlement, to the long boom, its weakening and the return to recession, it has been classes, their organisations and political parties, and the expanding state which have struggled over the most appropriate political responses to changing economic circumstances.

The first point to be made is that, yes, these are forms of class organisations and the struggles between them are forms of class struggles. The most common objection to this view works on the basis of asserting the absence of 'class consciousness' of those that make up the organisations, their programmes, or the class constituencies from which they seek support. This is most often said of the class organisations of labour, yet by extension the same case could be made about the class organisations of capital. There are both 'left' and 'right' varieties of this basic position. Rejections of the class character of these organisations are based on assumptions about what class consciousness *ought* to be like. When reality is judged by these standards of pure reason it is, unsurprisingly, found wanting. If we drop the assumption about what class consciousness ought to be like, and work with a number of far less restrictive assumptions, it is possible to make some quite telling observations on the history of class struggle and why industrialised capitalism is faced with the social and political troubles that it is. The only assumptions that need to be made are these. Classes exist, not on the basis of any shared consciousness, but on the basis of their positions in the processes of production, circulation and exchange, positions which are dependent on shared positions in terms of the ownership and control of the means of production. On the basis of that existence, those that make up classes experience the economic, political and social relations of that class society, form various understandings of that reality and then act and respond to it, seeking to alter it, and at the same time learning from their interactions with the other classes and institutions. It is these 'understandings' that are the form of class consciousness that develops and it is these class organisations that are created. Sometimes some of these class organisations *may* come to understand that society is based on class relations, that one class dominates another and for capital this relationship needs to be preserved and for labour this relationship needs to be ended. But, whether these forms of consciousness become dominant is not the inevitable outcome of the inner-workings of the system, rather it is the product of massive struggles within and between classes, struggles in which the actions of the state are important. There is another sense in which these organisations are class organisations and their consciousness is a form of class consciousness: their programmes and actions are class relevant and have class consequences or effects. In this they feed into the process by which problems are generated and appear to classes and similarly have an impact on the way in which classes seek to respond to the circumstances in which they exist.

With these assumptions, classes and class struggles are not related to Marx's assumptions about the way in which they could develop to produce a socialist transformation. Rather, classes are treated as the fact of a capitalist society, and then considered for the attitudes, learned responses and strategies that arise in the course of the struggles within classes, between classes and again between classes and the state. What is being sought is the logic of the interactions between classes constituted in this way, with forms of consciousness that, on the whole, respond to the circumstances of class without seeking the destruction of the social domination of capital. There is a process of class learning that leads to the formation of classes as organisations and the development of broad strategies to secure goals that are defined differently as the struggles go on and the societies within which they live are changed without being decisively transformed. Such a view undervalues the experience of labour during the construction of capitalism and the struggles in which it was then involved. Forms of socialism that rejected the new system and the class domination of capital did develop and were of significance within the worker's movement for a considerable time. Marxism was perhaps the most highly developed form of this socialist rejection. Nonetheless, it is possible to consider the character of labour struggles without explicit reference to this perspective since, for much of the time it had either been emasculated by the orthodoxy of the Comintern and its successor bodies or marginalised by the successful creation of social democracy as the leading force in the trade unions and in the political parties based on them.

It is not difficult to illustrate just how this 'learning' process affected the strategic perspectives of a developing labour movement. Consider, as an example, the British labour movement from the middle of the inter-war depression to the present day in terms of the arguments presented in the schematic history of the development of the political regime in Britain. In this account no attempt is made to treat the complexity of the rich internal divisions in the party – other very good studies already exist for that purpose. Instead, emphasis is placed on the developing assessments of the nature of their class society and the strategic and tactical responses to it evident in the official programmes of the Party. Although this both exaggerates and distorts the extent of the changes in the Party, the reality is not so different that the account is made worthless. The strategic assessment made in 1945 was based on the experience of the inter-war depression and a judgement about the nature of the situation and what was possible within it. Even though some of the Party saw the enemy as private capital, the terms in which this was understood generated a very distinctive response. The system was seen as not working, generating depression, unemployment and war and the main cause of these problems was private ownership of the means of production which enabled a group of privileged citizens to ignore the wishes of a democratically elected government. But not all private owners acted in this way. The only sections that needed to be controlled were those that had failed the nation (i.e. those implicated in the economic and political problems caused the labour movement in the inter-war years) or controlled the 'commanding heights' of the economy. Only these had to be nationalised.

Such a strategy was successful in the sense that it could be, and was, implemented and that economic growth, if not flourishing, put the worst features of the depression a long way behind. The sucess of the strategy encouraged a revision of the Party's strategic approach, rejecting further public ownership (with the exception of the denationalised steel industry) as unnecessary and anachronistic. A greater capacity for economic planning (conscious ways of linking the public and private sectors of the economy together) may need to be developed but the real concern would be in the realm of distributing the surplus produced in the combined public and private sectors.

Even after it became obvious that the long boom was over, that the British economy was lagging behind its international rivals, very little changed in strategic terms, except the attempt to generate a more comprehensive state initiative over the discovery and application of the new technologies.The longer the problems of low growth persisted, the more inadequate became this account of the realities of British society and the continued potency of class relations. The election defeat in 1970, the neo-liberal rhetoric of the

Class struggles in a cyclical economy 205

new Prime Minister and his government's class-sensitive actions over trade unions and incomes policy encouraged a reassessment of both the analysis and the priorities of the Party. The nationalised 'commanding heights' turned out to be less significant than that; their 'occupation' had not altered much about the operations of the capitalist system and indeed, the workers who worked in them found it difficult to distinguish between them and private enterprises. Once rationalisation and technological change began to erode job security it became less and less clear what the advantages were in working for a government-owned enterprise. This 'failure' of the initial wave of nationalisation did have some impact on the Party and encouraged it to expand the range of ways that it would seek to influence the development of the system through winning elections and expanding the role of the state. The assessment may not have been as coherent or as consistent as it could be, yet it did mark a change in the direction of official policy. The state would still nationalise those industries that failed the nation by being of doubtful viability while employing large numbers of people – hence the nationalisation of Leyland and the ship building and repair industry. In addition there would be an emphasis on workers' co-operatives, a response to the failure of nationalisation to change the work environment of state owned enterprises, and on greater worker/trade union participation in the management of publicly and privately owned firms. The state would make a greater planning initiative through moves to identify, encourage and support investment in lucrative new technologies with direct and indirect forms of state participation in the firms concerned.

This new strategy more or less worked, its relevance being heightened by the onset of the new recession. But the implications of the success of the strategy and the social ambiguities opened up by the programme in the context of an overwhelming electoral defeat, engendered great tensions within the Party, resulting in a number of people abandoning both the new and old forms of the social democratic party to form a new party, using the name Social Democratic Party but lacking its defining features. Those left in the Labour Party again reassessed their lessons and generated a new version of the arguments from the 1970s, promising an expanded, more active state, further nationalisation and more authoritative forms of state planning.

This pattern in the British Labour Party is quite instructive. The

Party did not want to develop a sustained class critique of capitalism. It has not, however, been able to avoid the implications of its own success and failure and as a result devised more and more ways of increasing the role of the state and acting, perhaps inadvertently at times, against the interests of private capital, especially as these are understood by private business. It is not that the Party has become more class conscious (some within the Party have, but they have been the subject of massive political campaigns to ensure their marginalisation), but rather it has become more system conscious and has encouraged the expansion of the state as a response to this recognition. More on the implications of this assessment below.

A similar kind of account (but not the same account for, although the end point is roughly comparable, the national variation in the history of labour movements is pronounced) could be generated for the labour movement in France and Germany and their associated political parties. The turning points and issues are different, as are the circumstances of their implementation and they both show the same kind of development, a strategic conception modified by experience to generate a new perspective encouraging the expansion of the state, as understood within the confines of their national history. The German Social Democratic Party is perhaps the most interesting as it was the first of the political parties of the workers' movement to abandon an explicitly socialist past in favour of the social democratic revision. Its Weimar history, especially its refusal to endorse a plan to reduce unemployment through deficit spending and public works was a curious interlude in the struggle over relations with 'its' trade union movements. In the aftermath of the Second World War, although it remained social democratic in practice, the rhetoric of the past was still enshrined in the Party's programme. It was only in 1959 at the Bad Godesberg conference that the Party programme removed the traditionalist and apparently Marxist terminology. The new 'reformed' version accepted the realities of the German economic recovery and the prevailing arrangement of public and private sectors in that recovery. When the Party came to office, it still acted to increase the role of the state and to promote forms of class–state cooperation in the Concerted Action programme and its management of the early phase of the recession showed the same commitment to the constitutional provisions of the social-market economy

Class struggles in a cyclical economy 207

and an expanded role for the state in promoting capital accumulation. Much like the British Labour Party, but without the same militant conclusions, the limited ability of the SDP Governments to solve the problems of recession and make some reforms encouraged an extensive internal debate over the most appropriate role for the Party, again encouraging (relatively) an expanded role for the state.

The even more complicated history of the developing character of the trade union movement in France and the perspective of its associated political parties shows a suitably complicated version of the same kind of reflection on the character of society on the basis of its ability to influence the patterns of post-war development. Again, the expansion of the state in the post-war settlement was the major point of reference and the rise of the Socialist Party and the decline of the Communist Party, with the debate over the expansion of the state sector as a crucial one, reflected this reassessment.

In considering the character and extent of this 'learning' process, it can be seen that, in many ways, the labour movement and its political expression became more realistic in their assessment of the character of capitalist society and the consequences of political action within it. For example, the rather comforting simplification involved in the belief that state action, state ownership or welfare reforms would change the character and consequences of the system has either been dropped or substantially modified. The reappearance of recession has taught lessons about the efficacy of state economic management, but the lessons have been ambiguous with contradictory implications for political action. On the basis of the post-war history it is equally possible to advocate greater or lesser efforts to transform society. One set of learners may read the message as encouraging less state action, since previous actions did not permanently achieve their desired objectives. Hence, for them, no more expansion of the state, rather strive to manage the present balance between state and private sectors. Others may learn a different strategy from this history. Piecemeal state expansion does not displace private capital, nor does it prevent the harmful social consequences of private capital failure and the return of economic conditions full of difficulties for both working people and social democratic government. In these circumstances, the appropriate response is not to hold the existing boundaries between state and private sectors, but to completely rework them in such a way that the state is so placed within the accumulation process that private business failures can not interfere with politically defined goals or the welfare of the bulk of the population. In practice, the tensions between these two positions, accommodationist and rejectionist, have been characteristic of the labour movement, reflecting on its experience between the last recession and this one.

As with the education of labour, so with the education of capital. Business organisations show a similar, not even inverse, learning from the experience of the passage between depression and recession. As has already been documented, the dominant sectors, although reluctantly and without the majority support of the business community as a whole, altered their position on relations with the state and with the spheres of state action. It is not so much that business came to support the steady expansion of the state on the basis of a change in principles. Rather, given the problems faced by business, it was willing to accept the state as a legitimate economic and social actor whilst struggling to make sure it neither harmed business as a whole, nor conferred advantages on one section of business before others. Hence the struggle for neutral state programmes, so evident in the Federal Republic and underlying the demands of the less fervently ideological Confederation of British Industry. This pursuit of the neutral impact of state programmes had different consequences. In Germany, perhaps, it was successful; more so than in either France, where the state's planning initiatives were always discriminatory, or in Britain, where governments of all kinds sought to promote regional development and to protect endangered industries.

The fragility of the accommodation between state and private capital was revealed as business responded to the continued recession by reverting to neo-liberal arguments to challenge the continual extension of the state. The strength of (and the basis for) the accommodation was revealed by the rapidity with which businesses, hit hard by the recession and neo-liberalism, called for changes in government policy to help them through the troubled times.

A similar pattern of assessment of the post-war settlement can be seen in the various Conservative Parties. Take the British Conservatives as an example. Churchill's 1945 election campaign was as close a return to liberalism as was possible. After Labour's success, the Party easily reached an accommodation with the expanded role of the state and the running of the 'mixed' economy. As growth faded and Labour governed, a neo-liberal reaction tried to emerge. Briefly it came to the fore under Heath but it only gained ascendancy with the election of the Thatcher government in 1979. It is quite clear that since then a division exists within the Conservative Party over the correctness of the neo-liberal stance of the leadership. Again, similar patterns can be found in the French conservative forces which had a surprisingly close relationship with the state under de Gaulle and before Giscard's neo-liberal experiment, and in the German Christian Democrats, though, as is to be expected, the degree of accommodation with state action was less overt in Germany than in either Britain or France.

If it is possible to show the ways in which capital and labour have learnt from the struggles between them and from the growing role of the state, is it possible to make a parallel argument about the state itself? It is much more difficult to construct a case about the strategies generated by the state as a self-contained social entity since the most vocal centre of the state is the government made up of politicians. By a process of subtracting what is done from what was promised, it may be possible to deduce a state presence in the making of policy that is the contribution of the more permanent part of the state's institutional ensemble. But for the present purpose this is unnecessary. Though the state expands less than the rhetoric of those who would see it expand and contracts less than those who would see it shrink, whatever the pattern of state action and growth it is possible to make two comments. Firstly, the state has not expanded on the basis of its own needs and vision of the future but has depended upon the demands and supports of other classes and groups affected by the problems of capital accumulation. Secondly, the extent to which it has sought expansion, this has been in terms of generating policies responding to the problems of capital accumulation within the context of preserving a situation of social (and, up until the point at which private capital is displaced by state action, hence, class) rule. This lack of state self-consciousness parallels the lack of class self-consciousness, and provides a three-sided pattern of interaction governing social development (and the role of the state), none of which acts other than on the basis of learnt responses to the historical experience of the system and with all the key actors seeking changes within rather than against the system itself. This provides a framework within which can be assessed the character and significance of the class struggles that have occurred in (almost) cyclical passage from depression to affluence, to uncertain growth, to recession and, now, to uncertain recovery.

Let us consider the growth of the state from the perspective of the contending classes. For capital, the expansion of the state appears as a product of the existence, and power, of labour, the self-action of the state, and as the accumulated perverse consequences of the demands of some sections of business for state action to protect or enhance their profitability. To the degree that businesses have continually sought to modify the impact or the workings of the market mechanism, the expansion of the state is the unexpected and unwelcome expression of their own political actions and expectations. From the perspective of labour, the creation of a larger, more active, more significant state is even more closely tied to their efforts to avoid or modify the workings of the market. And yet what has been achieved has not done much to solve the problemse of labour as a class. The state as an employer is not all that different from private capital, especially during times of economic hardship. Even welfare gains are eroded at the time when they are needed most. In terms of social power, the expansion of the state has achieved least of what was sought, the power of working people to control the impact of economic decisions on their lives. The growth of the state has not increased the social and political power of the class of labour: it has given the state a greater independent economic and political presence. Here, the expansion of the state, and the way in which it has increased the significance of politics at the expense of the economy, appears to labour as a distorted form of its own social and political challenge. A greater importance has been won for the political process, as against economics, but it has not been a political process subject to the dominance of working people, except in the most formalistic sense. Working people remain subject to those who employ them, either the state or private capital, and their range of social influence is neither greater not more significant with one or the other.

This, of course, gives rise to a major objection to the growth of the state – that it cannot improve human welfare but only harm it, and that private capitalism guarantees greater human freedom than the state dominated alternative. For this reason, capital and labour, employed, unemployed or whatever, all have mutual interests in ensuring the domination of private capitalism and a system based on the dominance of market relations. Certainly, this argument does have some presence within the labour movement. Indeed, the most realistic strands of reformism have this as their foundation. But for labour, the propositions are neither self-evidently true nor false. The main premise would seem to be that labour, under capitalism, can choose not to struggle against capital, and not to invoke its electoral strength to motivate politicians to act to accommodate its demands. This is not the case. Not to struggle is to lose, even within the system. To struggle is not a choice but an imperative that arises directly out of the experience of market relations, and is an essential part of the market relations between labour and capital, as classes. That this enhances the power of the state while not liberating labour is a perverse result but it is not as bad for labour as it is for private capital, for whom it is not so bad as is often proclaimed.

The modifications to the workings of the market that have been won by labour and which are expressed in the growth of the state and the increased significance of politics are not completely harmful to labour. The state provision of welfare, even if niggardly supplied, is better than having only the direct sale of labour-power as the source of income and standard of living. State intervention in the economy is 'better' than unrestrained, cyclical market failure for, although the cycles are not removed, their impact is lessened. Hence, in the absence of a choice over the struggle against capital, there is no basis for judging the position of labour within a system more dominated by the state as worse than in one dominated by private capital. In some senses, as the history of class struggle since the last depression reveals, the situation is better. A state which acts in a system still dependent on formal processes of representation, on the consent and acquiescene of the governed, is more likely to be subject to some influence (however limited and obscure in its impact) than a state that has grown as a result of an unrestrained alliance with private capital (e.g. France during the Second Republic) or where the state has seized the social initiative largely on its own behalf (e.g. Nazi Germany). These arguments aside, to the extent that the state wins greater political influence over economic decisions it does not, by these actions, extend the freedom of labour, except to the extent that such freedom is expressed within and through loyalty to the state.

Considering the growth of the state through the perspectives of the demands and actions of the two basic classes suggests a pattern in which the growth of the state is both based on and reinforces 'mutual spoilation' of the contending classes in that neither is able to achieve, through the expansion of the state, the social goals sought and that each is locked into a situation where the struggles and the mutual spoilation must continue. This implies, and the implication is supported by recent experience of the neo-liberal experiment, that it is not in the direct economic imperatives of capitalism as a mode of production or as a system of accumulation that the tendency for the expansion of the state lies. Nonetheless, the cyclical problems of capital accumulation provide very great encouragement to those processes that do generate the tendency for the steady (but not immediately predictable) increase in the size and significance of the state. The state expands on the basis of the actual struggles between classes as they have historically been organised, with the forms of consciousness (and political strategies) that they have acquired in the process of historical development, responding to the economic, political and social problems generated by the evolution of capitalism as a determinate form of class society. It is the logic of this historically given form of class struggles that implies the tendency for the state to steadily expand over time and through the upturns and downturns in capital accumulation.

NOTES

1. Fine and Harris (1979).
2. *Ibid.*, p. 106.
3. *Ibid.*, p. 108.
4. *Ibid.*, p. 112.
5. *Ibid.*, p. 116.
6. *Ibid.*, p. 118.
7. *Ibid.*, p. 121.
8. There is a lot written using variations on this 'regulation' approach. De Vroey (1984); and Bonefield (1987) give personal summaries of the field as well as brief critiques.
9. See particularly Aglietta (1979, 1982); Lipietz (1982).
10. Lipietz (1983), p. xvi.
11. See especially Aglietta (1979).
12. For a sharp critique of the loose use of the concept of 'fordism' see Foster (1988).

Notes 213

13. Hirsch (1983).
14. Davis (1984).
15. Hirsch (1983), pp. 80–7.
16. Lash and Urry (1987).
17. Their periodisation is summarised in table form, *Ibid.*, p. 16.
18. See their discussion of France in chaps 3, 5 and 8, and the general discussion of neo-corporatism in chap. 8.
19. See chap. 7, which largely deals with the consequences of capitalist development for political processes and the status of national autonomy rather than the proposition that capital has, in some significant sense moved into a phase of disorganisation. At best they could claim that the form of the organisation and co-ordination of capitalist production and exchanges has been altered.
20. Middlemass (1979).
21. Harrison (1980).
22. For an example of this approach applied, see Keeler (1985), pp. 229–49.

BIBLIOGRAPHY

Abendroth, W. (1972), *A Short History of the European Working Class*, London: New Left Books.
Aglietta, M. (1979), *A Theory of Capitalist Regulation: The U.S. experience*, trans. David Fernbach, London: New Left Books. First published as *Régulation et Crises du Capitalisme* (1976), Paris: Calmann-Levy.
Aglietta, M. (1982), 'Phases of U.S. capitalist expansion', *New Left Review*, **136**.
Ardagh, J. (1977), *The New France: A society in transition 1945–1977*, 3rd edn, Harmondsworth: Penguin Books.
Armstrong, P., Glyn, A. and Harrison J. (1984), *Capitalism Since World War II: The making and breakup of the great boom*, London: Fontana.
Arndt, H-J. (1966), *West Germany: Politics of non-planning*, Syracuse: Syracuse University Press.
Ashford, D.E. (1982), *Policy and Politics in France: Living with uncertainty*, Philadelphia: Temple University Press.
Attlee, C. (1937), *The Labour Party in Perspective*, London: Victor Gollancz.
Barry, E.E. (1965), *Nationalisation in British Politics: The historical background*, London: Jonathan Cape.
Bauchet, P. (1964), *Economic Planning: The French experience*, London: Heinemann.
Baum, W.C. (1958), *The French Economy and the State*, Princeton, New Jersey: Princeton University Press.
Behrens, R. (1980), *The Conservative Party from Heath to Thatcher: policies and politics 1974–1979*, Farnborough: Saxon House.
Berger, J.P. (1975), *A Seventh Man: A book of images and words about the experience of migrant workers in Europe*, Harmondsworth: Penguin Books.
Berger, S., Hirschman, A. and Maier, C. (eds) (1981), *Organizing Interests in Western Europe: Pluralism, corporatism, and the transformation of politics*, Cambridge: Cambridge University Press.
Beyme, K. von (1978), 'The Changing Relations Between Trade Unions and the Social Democratic Party in West Germany', *Government and Opposition*, **14** (4).
Birnbaum, P. (1980), 'The State in Contemporary France', in R. Scase (ed.), *The State in Western Europe*, London: Croom Helm.

Blank, S. (1973), *Industry and Government in Britain: The federation of British industries in politics, 1945-65*, Westmead and Lexington: Saxon House/Lexington Books.
Block, F. (1977), 'The Ruling Class Does Not Rule: Notes on the Marxist theory of the state', *Socialist Revolution*, 33.
Block, F. (1980), 'Beyond Relative Autonomy: State managers as historical subjects', *Socialist Register*.
Bonefield, W. (1987), 'Reformation of State Theory', *Capital and Class*, 53.
Bonnaud, J.-J. (1975), 'Planning and Industry in France', in J. Hayward and M. Watson (eds), *Planning, Politics and Public Policy*, Cambridge: Cambridge University Press.
Born, K.E. (1972), 'Government action against the great depression', in Herman Van Der Wee (ed.), *The Great Depression Revisited: Essays on the nineteen thirties*, The Hague: Martinus Nijhoff.
Bornstein, S. and Gourevitch, P. (1984), 'Unions in a Declining Economy: The case of the British T.U.C.', in Gourevitch, Martin and Ross *et al.*, *Unions and Economic Crisis: Britain, West Germany and Sweden*, London: Allen & Unwin.
Boyle, A. (1967), *Montague Norman: A biography*, London: Cassell.
Brady, R. (1933), *The Rationalisation Movement in German Industry: A study in the evolution of economic planning*, Berkeley: University of California Press.
Brady, R.A. (1937), *The Spirit and Structure of German Fascism*, London: Victor Gollancz.
Brady, R.A. (1943), *Business as a System of Power*, New York: Columbia University Press.
Brady, R.A. (1950), *Crisis in Britain: Plans and achievements of the Labour government*, Berkeley and London: University of California Press.
Braunthal, G. (1965), *The Federation of German Industry in Politics*, Ithaca: Cornell University Press.
Braunthal, G. (1976), 'Codetermination in West Germany', in James B. Christoph and Bernard E. Brown (eds), *Cases in Comparative Politics*, Boston: Little Brown.
Braunthal, G. (1978), *Socialist Labor and Politics in Weimar Germany: The general federation of German trade unions*, Hamden, Connecticut: Anchor Books.
Braunthal, G. (1983), *The West German Social Democrats, 1969-1982: Profile of a Party in Power*, Boulder, Colorado: Westview Press.
Briggs, A. (1969), *The Age of Improvement*, London: Longman.
Brittan, S. (1975), 'The Economic Contradictions of Democracy', *British Journal of Political Science*, 5 (2).
Brizay, B. (1975), *Le Patronat: Histoire, structure, stratégie du CNPF*, Paris: Éditions du Seuil.
Brown B.E. (1974), *Protest in Paris: Anatomy of a revolt*, Morristown, NJ: General Learning Press.
Brown, G. (1972), *In My Way: The political memoirs of Lord George-Brown*, Harmondsworth: Penguin Books.

Brown, M.B. (1972), *From Labourism to Socialism: The political economy of Labour in the 1970s*, Nottingham: Spokesman Books.
Budd, A. (1978), *The Politics of Planning*, London: Fontana.
Buiter, W.H. and Miller, M.H. (1984), 'Changing the Rules: economic consequences of the Thatcher regime', *Brookings Papers on Economic Activity, No. 2*, 1983, Brookings Institution, Washington D.C.
Bunel, J. and Saglio, J. (1984), 'Employers associations in France', in J.P. Windmuller and A. Gladstone (eds), *Employers Associations and Industrial Relations: A comparative study*, Oxford: Clarendon Press.
Bunn, R.F. (1984), 'Employers associations in the Federal Republic of Germany', in J.P. Windmuller and A. Gladstone (eds), *Employers Associations and Industrial Relations: A comparative study*, Oxford: Clarendon Press.
Burn, D. (1940), *The Economic History of Steel Making, 1867-1939*, Cambridge: Cambridge University Press.
Caron, F. (1979), *An Economic History of Modern France*, trans. Barbara Bray, London: Methuen & Co.
Carré, J-J., Dubois, P. and Malinvaud, E. (1975), *French Economic Growth*, Stanford: Stanford University Press; trans. John P. Hatfield. Originally in French, *La Croissance Française: Un essai d'analyse économique causale de l'après'-geurre*, Paris: Editions du Seuil.
Castles, S. and Kosack, G. (1972) 'The function of labour immigration in Western Europe capitalism', *New Left Review*, 73, May-June.
Castles, S. and Kosack, G. (1973), *Immigrant Workers and Class Structure in Western Europe*, London: Oxford University Press.
Castles, S. with Booth, H. and Wallace, T. (1984), *Here For Good: Western Europe's new ethnic minorities*, London: Pluto Press.
Chalmers, D.A. (1964), *Social Democratic Party of Germany*, New Haven: Yale University Press.
Cipolla, C.M. (ed.) (1980), *The Fontana Economic History of Europe*, London: Fontana.
Clark, J. (1979), 'Concerted Action in the Federal Republic of Germany', *British Journal of Industrial Relations*, 17 (2).
Clay, Sir Henry (1957), *Lord Norman*, London: Macmillan.
Cliff, T. (1975), *The Crisis: Social contract and socialism*, London: Pluto Press.
Coates, D. (1975), *The Labour Party and the Struggle for Socialism*, Cambridge: Cambridge University Press.
Coates, D. (1980), *Labour in Power? A study of the labour government 1974-1979*, London: Longman.
Cobler, S. (1978), *Law, Order and Politics in West Germany*, Harmondsworth: Penguin Books.
Cohen, S.S. (1977), *Modern Capitalist Planning: The French Model*, Berkeley: University of California Press (1977 updated edition).
Cohen, S.S. and Goldfinger, C. (1975), *From Permacrisis to Real Crisis in French Social Security: An essay on the limits to normal politics*, Berkeley: Institute of Urban and Regional Development, University of California, working paper 250.

Cohn-Bendit, G. and D. (1969), *Obsolete Communism: The left wing alternative*, Harmondsworth: Penguin Books.

Collis, C.M. (1979), 'The Demise of French Planning? - A Comment', *West European Politics*, **2** (2).

Confederation of British Industry (1976), *The Road to Recovery*.

Confederation of British Industry (1977), *Britain Means Business 1977*.

Confederation of British Industry (1980), *Trade Unions in a Changing World: The challenge for management: a discussion document*.

Confederation of British Industry (1981), *The Will to Win: Summary*.

Confederation of British Industry (1982), *Annual Conference Report*.

Corden, W.M. and Fels, G. (eds) (1976), *Public Assistance to Industry: Protection and Subsidies in Britain and Germany*, London: Macmillan for the Trade Policy Research Centre.

Crosland, C.R.A. (1956), *The Future of Socialism*, London: Jonathan Cape.

Crouch, C. (1979), 'The State, Capital and Liberal Democracy' in Colin Crouch (ed.), *State and Economy in Contemporary Capitalism*, London: Croom Helm.

Crouch, C. (1980), 'Varieties of Trade Union Weakness: Organised labour and capital formation in Britain, Federal Germany and Sweden', *West European Politics*, **3** (1).

Crouch, C. (1982), *The Politics of Industrial Relations*, London: Fontana.

Crouch, C. and Pizzorno, A. (1978), *The Resurgence of Class Conflict in Europe*, London: Macmillan.

Cullingford, E.C.M. (1976), *Trade Unions in West Germany*, London: Wilton House Publications.

Dalton, H. (1935), *Practical Socialism for Britain*, London: Routledge and Sons.

Davis, M. (1984), 'The political economy of late-imperial America', *New Left Review*, **143**.

Delamotte, Y. (1988), 'Workers' participation and personnel policies in France', *International Labour Review*, **127** (2).

Denton, G., Forsyth, M. and Maclennan, M. (1968), *Economic Planning and Policies in Britain, France and Germany*, London: George Allen and Unwin for PEP.

De Vroey, M. (1984), 'A regulation approach interpretation of contemporary crisis', *Capital and Class*, **23**.

Dorfman, G.A. (1979), *Government versus Trade Unionism in British Politics Since 1968*, London: Macmillan.

Dyson, K.H.F. (1981), 'The politics of economic management in West Germany', *West European Politics*, **4** (2).

Dyson, K. and Wilks, S. (eds) (1983), *Industrial Crisis: A comparative study of the state and industry*, Oxford: Martin Robertson.

Ehrmann, H.W. (1947), *French Labor: From popular front to liberation*, New York: Oxford University Press.

Ehrmann, H.W. (1957), *Organized Business in France*, Princeton: Princeton University Press.

Bibliography

Einaudi, M., Byé, M. and Rossi, E. (1955), *Nationalization in France and Italy*, New York: Cornell University Press.
Erhard, L. (1960), *Prosperity through Competition*, 3rd edn, London: Thames & Hudson.
Esser, J. and Fach, W., with Dyson, K. (1983), 'Social Market and Modernization Policy: West Germany' in Kenneth Dyson and Stephen Wilks (eds), *Industrial Crisis: A comparative study of the state and industry*, Oxford: Martin Robertson.
Eyraud, F. and Tchobanian, R. (1985), 'The Auroux Reforms and company level industrial relations in France', *British Industrial Relations*, **23** (2).
Feldman, G.D. (1970), 'German Business Between War and Revolution: The origins of the Stinnes-Legien agreement', in Gerhard A. Ritter (ed.), *Entstehung und Wandel der Modernen Gesellschaft: Festschrift für Hans Rosenberg zum 65. Geburtstag*, Berlin: Grugher and Co.
Fels, G. (1976), 'Overall Assistance to German Industry', in W.M. Corden and G. Fels (eds), *Public Assistance to Industry: Protection and Subsidies in Britain and Germany*, London: Macmillan for the Trade Policy Research Centre.
Fine, B. and Harris, L. (1979), *Rereading Capital*, London: Macmillan.
Flamant, M. and Singer-Kerel, J. (1970), *Modern Economic Crises*, translated from the French by Pat Wardroper, London: Barrie and Jenkins; originally part of *Que Sais-je?* published 1968, Presses Universitaires de France, revised and 'augmented'.
Flora, P. and Heidenheimer, A. (eds) (1981), *The Development of the Welfare State in Europe and America*, New Brunswick: Transaction Books.
Fohlen, C. (1980), 'France 1920–1970', in Carlo M. Cipolla (ed.), *The Fontana Economic History of Europe*, London: Fontana, vol. 6.
Foot, P. (1968), *The Politics of Harold Wilson*, Harmondsworth: Penguin Books.
Foster, J. (1974), *Class Struggle and the Industrial Revolution: Early industrial capitalism in three English towns*, London: Weidenfeld and Nicolson.
Foster, J.B. (1988), 'The fetish of Fordism', *Monthly Review*, **39** (10).
Frears, J.R. (1981), *France in the Giscard Presidency*, London: George Allen and Unwin.
Freymond, J. (1974), *Le IIIe Reich et la Réorganisation Économique de l'Europe, 1940–1942: Origines et projets*, Leiden: A.W. Sitthoff.
Friedman, M. (1965) *Capitalism and Freedom*, Chicago: Chicago University Press.
Geyer, M. (1984), 'The State in National Socialist Germany', in Charles Bright and Susan Harding (eds), *Statemaking and Social Movements: Essays in history and theory*, Ann Arbor: University of Michigan Press.
Geyer, M. (1986), 'The Nazi State: Machine or morass', *History Today*, **36**.
Glyn, A. and Sutcliffe, B. (1972), *British Capitalism, Workers and the Profit Squeeze*, Harmondsworth: Penguin Books.
Gold, D.A., Lo, C.Y.H. and Wright, E.O. (1975), 'Recent Developments in

Marxist Theories of the Capitalist State', *Monthly Review*, **27** (5) and (6).
Gough, I. (1972), 'Productive and Unproductive Labour', *New Left Review*, **76**.
Gough, I. (1979, reprinted 1982), *The Political Economy of the Welfare State*, London: Macmillan.
Gould, B., Mills, J. and Stewart, S. (1981), *Monetarism or Prosperity?* London: Macmillan.
Gourevitch, P.A. (1984), 'Breaking with Orthodoxy: The politics of economic policy responses to the Depression of the 1930's, *International Organization*, **38** (1).
Gourevitch, P., Martin, A. and Ross, G. *et al.* (1984), *Unions and Economic Crisis: Britain, West Germany and Sweden*, London: Allen and Unwin.
Grant, W. (1983), 'The business lobby: Political attitudes and strategies', *West European Politics* **6** (4).
Grant, W. and Marsh, D. (1975), 'The Politics of the CBI: 1974 and after', *Government and Opposition*, **10** (1).
Grant, W. and Marsh, D. (1977), *The Confederation of British Industry*, London: Hodder and Stoughton.
Grant, W. with Sargent, J. (1987), *Business and Politics in Britain*, London: Macmillan.
Grebing, H. (1969), *The History of the German Labour Movement: A survey*, published in German in 1966; this text abridged by Mary Saran and translated by Edith Körner, London: Oswald Wolff.
Green, D. (1978), 'The 7th French Plan – The Demise of French Planning?', *West European Politics*, **1** (1).
Green, D. (1979), 'Individualism versus Collectivism: Economic choices in France', in Vincent Wright (ed.), *Conflict and Consensus in France*, London: Frank Cass.
Green, D. (1983), 'Strategic Management and the State: France', in K. Dyson and S. Wilks (eds), *Industrial Crisis: A comparative study of the state and industry*, Oxford: Martin Robertson.
Green, D. (1984), 'Industrial policy and policy making, 1974–82', in Vincent Wright (ed.), *Continuity and Change in France*, London: Allen & Unwin.
Grosser, A. (1974), *Germany in Our Time: A political history of the postwar years*, Harmondsworth: Penguin Books.
Grunberger, R. (1971), *A Social History of the Third Reich*, London: Weidenfeld and Nicolson.
Hallett, G. (1973), *The Social Economy of West Germany*, London: Macmillan.
Hanley, D.L., Kerr, A.P. and Waites, N.H. (1979), *Contemporary France: Politics and society since 1945*, London: Routledge & Kegan Paul.
Hardach, K. (1980), *The Political Economy of Germany in the Twentieth Century*, Berkeley: University of California Press; originally published in German in 1976.

Hardach, K. (1980), 'Germany 1914-1970' in C.M. Cipolla (ed.), *The Fontana Economic History of Europe*, London: Fontana, vol. 6.

Harris, N. (1973), *Competition and the Corporate Society: British Conservatives, the state and industry 1945-1964*, London: Methuen and Co.

Harris, R. and Seldon A. (1977), *Not From Benevolence . . . 20 Years of Economic Dissent*, London: Institute of Economic Affairs.

Harrison, R. (1980), *Pluralism and Corporatism: The political evolution of modern democracies*, London: Allen and Unwin.

Hartman, H. and Horstmann, J. (1987), 'A trade union information strategy: the case of the German Metal Workers Union', *British Journal of Industrial Relations*, 25 (3).

Hayek, F.A. (ed.) (1935), *Collectivist Economic Planning: Critical studies on the possibilities of socialism*, London: Routledge & Kegan Paul.

Hayward, J. (1975), 'Employer Associations and the state in France and Britain', in Stephen J. Warnecke and Ezra N. Suleiman (eds), *Industrial Policy in Western Europe*, New York: Praeger.

Hayward, J. (1979), 'The Dissentient France: The counter political culture', in Vincent Wright (ed.), *Conflict and Consensus in France*, London: Frank Cass.

Hayward, J. (1984), 'From planning the French economy to planning the French state: the theory and practice of priority action programmes', in V. Wright (ed.), *Continuity and Change in France*, London: Allen and Unwin.

Hayward, J. and Watson, M. (eds) (1975), *Planning, Politics and Public Policy: The British, French and Italian experience*, Cambridge: Cambridge University Press.

Hayward, J.E.S. (1966), *Private Interests and Public Policy: The experience of the French economic and social council*, London: Longman.

Henderson, W.O. (1958), *The State and the Industrial Revolution in Prussia, 1740-1870*, Liverpool: Liverpool University Press.

Hirsch, J. (1980), 'Developments in the Political System of West Germany since 1945', in R. Scase (ed.), *The State in Western Europe*, London: Croom Helm.

Hirsch, J. (1983), 'The Fordist Security State and New Social Movements', *Kapitalistate* 10 and 11.

Hodgson, G. (1984), *The Democratic Economy: A new look at planning, markets and power*, Harmondsworth: Penguin Books.

Hodson, H. A. (1938), *Slump and Recovery, 1929-1937: A survey of world affairs*, London: Oxford University Press.

Holland, S. (1972), 'State entrepreneurship and state intervention', in S. Holland (ed.), *The State as Entrepreneur: New dimensions for public, enterprise: The IRI state shareholding formula*, London: Weidenfeld & Nicolson.

Holland, S. (1975), *The Socialist Challenge*, London: Quartet Books.

Bibliography 221

Holloway, J. and Picciotto, S. (1978), *State and Capital: A Marxist debate*, London: Edward Arnold.
Hough, J. R. (1982), *The French Economy*, London: Croom Helm.
Hughes, J. (1973), 'Nationalisation and the private sector', in J. Urry and J. Wakeford (eds), *Power in Britain*, London: Heinemann Educational.
Hurstfield, J. (1953), *The Control of Raw Materials*, London: HMSO and Longman.
Jay, D. (1938), *The Socialist Case*, London: Faber & Faber.
Jessop, B. (1977), 'Recent Theories of the Capitalist State', *Cambridge Journal of Economics*, **1** (4).
Jessop, B. (1978), 'Capitalism and Democracy: The best possible political shell', in G. Littlejohn, B. Smart, J. Wakeford, N. Yuval-Davis (eds), *Power and the State*, London: Croom Helm.
Jessop, B. (1979), 'Corporatism, parliamentarism and social democracy', in P. C. Schmitter and G. Lehmbruch (eds), *Trends Towards Corporatist Intermediation*, Beverly Hills and London: Sage.
Jessop, B. (1980), 'The transformation of the state in post-war Britain', in R. Scase (ed.), *The State in Western Europe*, London: Croom Helm.
Jessop, B. (1982), *The Capitalist State: Marxist theories and methods*, Oxford: Martin Robertson.
Johnson, C. (1980), 'The Problem of Reformism and Marx's Theory of Fetishism', *New Left Review*, **119**.
Jones, A. (1973), *The New Inflation: The politics of prices and incomes*, London: Deutsch.
Joy, N. V. (1950), 'Fair Compensation under the British Labour Government', *Political Science Quarterly*, **65** (4).
Kalecki, M. (1938), 'The lessons of the Blum experiment', *Economic Journal*, **1**.
Kalecki, M. (1971), *Selected Essays On the Dynamics of the Capitalist Economy, 1933-1970*, Cambridge: Cambridge University Press.
Keeler, J. T. S. (1985), 'Situating France on the Pluralism-Corporatism Continuum: A critique of and alternative to the Wilson perspective', *Comparative Politics*, **17** (2).
Kemp, T. (1972), *The French Economy 1913-39: The history of a decline*, London: Longman.
Kesselman, M. (1985-6), 'Lyrical illusions or a socialism of governance: Wither French socialism?', *Socialist Register*.
Kindleberger, C. P. (1964), *Economic Growth in France and Britain, 1851-1950*, Cambridge, Mass.: Harvard University Press.
Kindleberger, C. P. (1967), *Europe's Postwar Growth and the Role of Labour Supply*, Oxford: Oxford University Press.
Kindleberger, C. P., (1973), *The World in Depression, 1929-1939*, London: Allen Lane.
Kipping, Sir Norman (1972), *Summing Up*, London: Hutchinson.
Kolinsky, M. and Paterson, W. E. (eds) (1976), *Social and Political Movements in Western Europe*, London: Croom Helm.
Kuhl, J. (1981), 'Labour markets and industrial relations in the recession in Germany, 1973-1978', in Ezio Tarantelli and Gerhard Wilke (eds), *The*

Management of Industrial Conflict in the Recession of the 1970s: Britain, Germany and Italy, Badia Fiesolana, Firenze: European University Institute.
Kuisel, R. F. (1981), *Capitalism and the State in Modern France: Renovation and economic management in the twentieth century,* Cambridge: Cambridge University Press.
Küster, G. H. (1974), 'Germany', in R. Vernon (ed.), *Big Business and the State: Changing relations in Western Europe,* Cambridge, Mass.: Harvard University Press.
Laclau, E. (1975), 'The specificity of the political: The Poulantzas-Miliband debate', *Economy and Society,* **4** (1).
Lash, S. and Urry, J. (1987), *The End of Organized Capitalism,* Cambridge: Polity Press.
Lefranc, G. (1965), *Histoire Du Front Populaire: 1934-1938,* Paris: Payot.
Lewis, V. (1978), 'Nationalisation – a serious threat?', *The Banker,* **128** (624).
Lieberman, S. (1977), *The Growth of European Mixed Economies, 1945-1970: A concise study of the economic evolution of six countries,* Cambridge, Mass.: Schenkman.
Lindblom, C. E. (1977), *Politics and Markets: The world's political-economic systems,* New York: Basic Books.
Lipietz, A. (1982), 'Towards global Fordism?', *New Left Review,* **134**.
Lipietz, A. (1983), *The Enchanted World: Inflation, credit and the world crisis,* London: Verso, trans. Ian Patterson.
Lorwin, V. R. (1966), *The French Labor Movement,* Cambridge, Mass.: Harvard University Press.
Luxemburg, R. (1970), 'Reform or revolution', in Waters, M-A. (ed.), *Rosa Luxemburg Speaks,* New York: Pathfinder Press.
McArthur, J. H. and Scott, B. R. (1969), *Industrial Planning in France,* Boston: Graduate School of Business Administration, Harvard University.
Macdonald, D. F. (1976), *The State and the Trade Unions,* 2nd edn (1st edn 1960), London: Macmillan.
McEachern, D. (1980), *A Class Against Itself: Power and the nationalisation of the British steel industry,* Cambridge: Cambridge University Press.
MacPherson, C. B. (1964), *Possessive Individualism,* Cambridge: Cambridge University Press.
MacPherson, C. B. (1978), *The Strange Life and Times of Liberal Democracy,* Nottingham: Spokesman Books.
Manchester, W. R. (1969), *The Arms of Krupp, 1587-1968,* London: Michael Joseph.
Markovits, A. S. and Allen, C. S. (1980), 'Power and Dissent: The trade unions in the Federal Republic of Germany re-examined', in Jack Hayward (ed.), *West European Politics* **3** (1).
Markovits, A. S. and Allen, C. (1984), 'Trade unions and the economic crisis: The West German case', in Peter Gourevitch, Andrew Martin,

Bibliography 223

George Ross et al., Unions and Economic Crisis: Britain, West Germany and Sweden, London: Allen & Unwin.
Marx, K. (1970), 'Wage Labour and Capital (1847-9)', in *Karl Marx and Frederik Engels: Selected works*, Moscow: Progress Publishers.
Mason, T. (1981), 'The workers' opposition in Nazi Germany', *History Workshop*, 11.
Mattick, P. (1971), *Marx and Keynes: The limits of the mixed economy*, London: Merlin Press.
Maunder, P. (ed.) (1979), *Government Intervention in the Developed Economy*, London: Croom Helm.
Merritt, R. L. (1976), 'American influences in the occupation of Germany', *Annals, American Academy of Political and Social Science*, 428.
Michalet, C.-A. (1974), 'France' in R. Vernon (ed.), *Big Business and the State*, Cambridge, Mass.: Harvard University Press.
Middlemass, K. (1979), *The Politics of Industrial Society: The experience of the British system since 1911*, London: Andre Deutsch.
Miliband, R. (1970), 'The capitalist state: Reply to Nicos Poulantzas', *New Left Review*, 59.
Miliband, R. (1973a), *The State in Capitalist Society*, London: Quartet Books. Originally published in 1969.
Miliband, R. (1973b), *Parliamentary Socialism*, 2nd edn, London: Merlin Press.
Miliband, R. (1979), *Marxism and Politics*, Oxford: Oxford University Press.
Miliband, R. (1982), *Capitalist Democracy in Britain*, Oxford: Oxford University Press.
Miliband, R. (1983), 'State power and class interests', *New Left Review*, 138.
Milne-Bailey, W. (ed.) (1929), *Trade Union Documents*, London: G. Bell and Sons.
Milward, A. S. (1970), *The New Order and the French Economy*, Oxford: Oxford University Press.
Milward, A. S. (1976), 'Fascism and the Economy', in W. Laqueur (ed.), *Fascism: A readers' guide, Analyses, Interpretation and Bibliography*, Berkeley: University of California Press.
Minnerup, G. (1976), 'West Germany Since the War', *New Left Review*, 99.
Moran, M. (1977), *Politics of Industrial Relations: The origins and death of the 1971 Industrial Relations Act*, London: Macmillan.
Morrison, H. (1933), *Socialism and Transport: The organisation of socialised industries with particular reference to the London Passenger Transport Bill*, London: Constable.
Moss, B. H. (1988), 'After the Auroux laws: Employers, industrial relations and the right in France', *West European Politics* 11 (1).
Mullard, M. (1987), *The Politics of Public Expenditure*, London: Croom Helm.
Müller-Jentsch, W. (1981), 'Industrial Relations in the Federal Republic of Germany During the 1970s', in E. Tarantelli and G. Wilke (eds), *The Management of Industrial Conflict in the Recession of the 1970s:*

224 Bibliography

Britain, Germany and Italy, Badia Fiesolana, Firenze: European University Institute.
Neuhman, F. (1942), *Behemoth: The Structure and Practice of National Socialism,* London: Victor Gollancz.
O'Connor, J. (1973), *The Fiscal Crisis of the State,* New York: St. Martins Press.
Offe, C. (1974), 'Structural Problems of the Capitalist State: Class rule and the political system. On the selectiveness of political institutions', *German Political Studies,* 1.
Offe, C. and Ronge, V. (1975), 'Theses on the theory of the state', *New German Critiques,* 6.
Owen-Smith, E. (1979), 'Government intervention in the economy of the Federal Republic of Germany', in P. Maunder (ed.), *Government Intervention in the Developed Economy,* London: Croom Helm.
Pagett, S. (1987), 'The West German Social Democrats in opposition, 1982–86', *West European Politics,* 10 (3).
Pahl, R. E. and Winkler, J. T. (1974), 'The coming corporatism', *New Society,* 30 (627).
Paine, S. (1974), *Exporting Workers: The Turkish case,* Cambridge: Cambridge University Press.
Panitch, L. (1976), *Social Democracy and Industrial Militancy: the Labour party, the trade unions and incomes policy, 1945–1974,* Cambridge: Cambridge University Press.
Panitch, L. (1979), 'The development of corporatism in liberal democracies', in P. C. Schmitter and G. Lembruch (eds), *Trends Towards Corporatist Intermediation,* Beverly Hills: Sage.
Panitch, L. (1980), 'Recent theorisation of corporatism: Reflections on a growth industry', *British Journal of Sociology,* 31 (3).
Panitch, L. (1981), 'Trade unions and the capitalist state', *New Left Review,* 125.
Paterson, W. (1976), 'Social Democracy – The West German example', in M. Kolinsky and W. E. Paterson (eds), *Social and Political Movements in Western Europe,* London: Croom Helm.
Pickles, D. M. (1938), *The French Political Scene,* London: Thomas Nelson and Sons.
Piven, F. F. and Cloward, R. A. (1972), *Regulating The Poor: The functions of public welfare,* London: Tavistock.
Posner, C. (ed.) (1970), *Reflections on the Revolution in France: 1968,* Harmondsworth: Penguin Books.
Poulantzas, N. (1969), 'The problem of the capitalist state', *New Left Review,* 58.
Poulantzas, N. (1973, 1968), *Political Power and Social Class,* London: New Left Books, originally published as *Pouvoir politique et classes sociales,* Maspero.
Poulantzas, N. (1975, 1974), *Classes in Contemporary Capitalism,* London: New Left Books, first published as *Les Classes Sociales dans le Capitalisme Aujourd'hui,* Paris: Éditions du Seuil.

Poulantzas, N. (1977), 'The new petty bourgeoisie' in Alan Hunt (ed.), *Class and Class Structure*, London: Lawrence and Wishart.
Poulantzas, N. (1978), *State, Power, Socialism*, London: New Left Books, first published as *L'Etat, Le Pouvoir, le Socialisme*, Presses Universitaires de France.
Pritt, D. N. (1941), *The Fall of the French Republic*, London: Frederick Muller Ltd.
Pryke, R. (1971), *Public Enterprise in Practice: The British experience of nationalisation over two decades*, London: McGibbon and Kee.
Reynaud, J.-D. (1975), 'France: Elitist society inhibits articulated bargaining', in S. Barkin (ed.), *Working Militancy and Its Consequences, 1965-75; New Directions in Western Industrial Relations*, New York: Praeger Publishers.
Richardson, J. J. (1971), 'The Administration of Denationalisation: The case of road haulage', *Public Administration*, **49** (4).
Riddell, P. (1985), *The Thatcher Government*, Oxford: Martin Robertson.
Robbins, L. (1934), *The Great Depression*, London: Macmillan.
Robson, W. A. (1950), 'The governing board of the public corporation', *Political Quarterly*, **21** (2).
Robson, W. A. (1960), *Nationalized Industry and Public Ownership*, London: Allen and Unwin.
Rogow, A. A., (with the assistance of P. Shore) (1955), *The Labour Government and British Industry 1945-1957*, Oxford: Basil Blackwell.
Roll, E. (1939), 'Germany', in H. A. Marquand *et al.*, *Organized Labour in Four Continents*, London: Longmans Green.
Rosenberg, A. (1965), *Democracy and Socialism: A contribution to the political history of the last 150 years*, Boston: Beacon Press.
Ross, G. (1982), 'The Perils of Politics: French unions and the crisis of the 1970's', in P. Lange, G. Ross and M. Vannicelli, *Unions, Change and Crisis: French and Italian Union Strategy and the Political Economy, 1945-1980*, London: Allen and Unwin.
Ross, G., Hoffman, S. and Malzachier, S. (1987), *The Mitterrand Experiment: Continuity and change in modern France*, Cambridge: Polity Press.
Ross, G. W. (1965), *The Nationalisation of Steel: One step forward two steps back?*, London: Macgibbon and Kee.
Roth, A. (1972), *Heath and the Heathmen*, London: Routledge and Kegan Paul.
Salter, S. (1983), 'Structures of consensus and coercion: Workers' morale and the maintenance of work discipline, 1939-1945', in David Welch (ed.), *Nazi Propaganda: The power and the limitations*, London: Croom Helm.
Sayers, R. S. (1976), *The Bank of England 1891-1944*, vols 1 and 2 and Appendixes, Cambridge: Cambridge University Press.
Scase, R. (ed.) (1980), *The State in Western Europe*, London: Croom Helm.
Schmitter, P. C. (1979), 'Still the century of corporatism?', in Phillipe C.

Schmitter and Gerhard Lehmbruch (eds), *Trends Towards Corporatist Intermediation,* London: Sage.

Schmitter, P. C. (1981), 'Interest intermediation and regime governability in contemporary Western Europe and North America', in Suzanne Berger (ed.), *Organizing Interests in Western Europe,* Cambridge: Cambridge University Press.

Schmitter, P. C. and Lehmbruch, G. (eds) (1979), *Trends Towards Corporatist Intermediation:* Contemporary political sociology, vol. 1, Beverly Hills and London: Sage.

Schneker, E. (1963), 'Nationalisation and denationalisation of motor carriers in Great Britain', *Land Economics,* **39** (3).

Schott, K. (1982), 'The rise of Keynesian economics: Britain 1940–1969', *Economy and Society,* **11** (3).

Schweitzer, A. (1964), *Big Business in the Third Reich,* Bloomington: Indiana University Press.

Seldon, A. (ed.) (1979), *The Taming of Government,* London: Institute of Economic Affairs.

Servan-Shreiber, J.-J. (1968), *The American Challenge,* Harmondsworth: Penguin Books.

Sheahan, J. (1963), *Promotion and Control of Industry in Postwar France,* Cambridge, Massachusetts: Harvard University Press.

Shonfield, A. (1965), *Modern Capitalism: The changing balance of public and private power,* London: Oxford University Press.

Shonfield, Sir Andrew (1980), 'The VIIIe Plan: Assumptions and constraints', *Revue Économique,* **31** (5).

Shuchman, A. (1957), *Codetermination: Labor's middle way in Germany,* Washington: Public Affairs Press.

Silvia, S. S. (1988), 'The West German labour law controversy: A struggle for the factory of the future', *Comparative Politics,* **20** (2).

Skocpol, T. (1979), *States and Social Revolutions: A comparative analysis of France, Russia and China,* London: Cambridge University Press.

Skocpol, T. (1980), 'Political responses to capitalist crisis: Neo-Marxist theories of the state and the case of the new deal', *Politics and Society,* **10** (2).

Smith, G. (1979), *Democracy in Western Germany: Parties and politics in the Federal Republic,* London: Heinemann.

Smith, W. R. (1981), 'Paradoxes of plural unionism: CGT-CFDT relations in France', *West European Politics,* **4** (1).

Soskice, D. and Ulman, L. (1983), *Unionism, Economic Stabilisation and Incomes Policy,* Washington: Brookings.

Spiegelberg, R. (1973), *The City: Power without accountability,* London: Quartet Books.

Stevenson, J. and Cook, C. (1977), *The Slump: society and politics during the Depression,* London: Cape.

Stolper, G. with Hauser, K. and Borchardt, K. (1967), *The German Economy: 1870 to the Present,* London: Weidenfeld and Nicolson. Translated by Toni Stolper.

Taylor, A. J. (1978), *Laissez-faire and State Intervention in Nineteenth-Century Britain*, London: Macmillan.
Thatcher, M. (1977), *Let Our Children Grow Tall: Selected Speeches 1975-1977*, London: Centre for Policy Studies.
Therborn, G. (1977), 'The rule of capital, and the rise of democracy', *New Left Review*, 103.
Thompson, E. P. (1972), *The Making of the English Working Class*, Harmondsworth: Penguin Books.
Thomson, A. W. J. (1981), 'Industrial relations in Britain during the period of the recession, 1974-1978', in Ezio Tarantelli and Gerhard Wilke (eds), *The Management of Industrial Conflict in the Recession of the 1970s: Britain, Germany and Italy*, Badia Fiesolana, Firenze: European University Institute.
Tivey, H. (ed.) (1925), *The Book of the Labour Party: Its history, growth, policy and leaders*, in three volumes, London: Caxton.
Tivey, L. (1973), *Nationalisation in British Industry*, revised edition, London: Jonathan Cape.
Tomlinson, J. (1981), 'Why was there never a "Keynesian Revolution" in economic policy?', *Economy and Society*, **10** (1).
Townsend, P. (1979), *Poverty in the United Kingdom: A survey of household resources and standards of living*, London: Allen Lane.
Turner, G. (1969), *Business in Britain*, London: Eyre and Spottiswoode.
Turner, H. A. (1985), *German Big Business and the Rise of Hitler*, New York: Oxford University Press.
Turner, J. (1984), 'The politics of "organised business" in the First World War', in J. Turner (ed.), *Businessmen and Politics: Studies of business activity in British politics, 1900-1945*, London: Heinemann.
Urry, J. (1981), *The Anatomy of Capitalist Societies: The economy, civil society and the state*, London: Macmillan.
Van Der Wee, H. (1972), *The Great Depression Revisited: Essays on the economics of the thirties*, The Hague: Martinus Nijhoff.
Veblen, T. (1964, 1915), *Imperial Germany and the Industrial Revolution*, New York: Viking Press, reprinted 39th edn, originally published 1915.
Vernon, R. (ed.) (1974), *Big Business and the State: Changing relations in Western Europe*, Cambridge, Mass.: Harvard University Press.
Wallich, H. C. (1955), *Mainsprings of the German Revival*, New Haven: Yale University Press.
Warde, A. (1982), *Consensus and Beyond: The development of Labour party strategy since the Second World War*, Manchester: Manchester University Press.
Wilkinson, E. (1939), *The Town That Was Murdered: The life story of Jarrow*, London: Left Book Club.
Williams, P. M. (1972), *Crisis and Compromise: Politics in the Fourth Republic*, London: Longman.
Wilson, H. (1974), *The Labour Government: 1964-1970*, Harmondsworth: Penguin Books, first published 1971.
Woolston, M. Y. (1968, 1941), *The Structure of the Nazi Economy*, New York: Russell and Russell.

Wright, E. O. (1976), 'Class boundaries in advanced capitalist societies', *New Left Review*, **98**.
Wright, V. (1978), *Government and Politics of France*, London: Hutchinson.
Wright, V. (ed.) (1979), *Conflict and Consensus in France*, London: Frank Cass (special issue of West European Politics, vol. 1, no. 3).
Wrigley, C. (1976), *David Lloyd George and the British Labour Movement: Peace and war*, New York: Harvester Press, Hassock and Barnes and Noble.
Yaffe, D. S. (1973), 'The Marxian theory of crisis, capital and the state', *Economy and Society*, **2** (2).
Youngson, A. J. (1980), 'Great Britain 1920–1970', in Carlo M. Cipolla (ed.), *The Fontana Economic History of Europe*, vol. 6, pt. 1, London: Fontana.

INDEX

agency, 4ff
Aglietta, M., 189-92
Atlee Government, 74-6, 81-2, 95
Auroux laws, 174-5

Bank of England, 60, 74-5
banks, 59, 74-5, 76-7, 117, 120, 133, 151-2, 156
Barre, R., 136, 145
Benn, T., 124
Bernstein, E., 6
Block, F., 21-2
Brady, R., 81
British political parties
  Conservative Party, 87, 98, 101ff, 134-5, 145-50, 159, 208-9
  Labour Party, 60, 86-7, 95, 121ff, 203-6
  Social Democratic Party, 205
Brown, M. B., 105, 120
business organisation
  in Britain 60, 85-6, 101ff, 121, 124-5, 134-5, 148-50, 151-2, 153, 155ff, 160-1, 168
  in France, 61-2, 86, 128, 136, 170-1, 174
  in general, 32, 48, 54-5, 57, 68-9, 88ff, 117ff, 141, 183ff, 208-9
  in Germany, 62ff, 86, 109ff, 130, 137-8
business/trade cycle, 47-8, 54-5, 58-9

capital accumulation, 2, 3, 10-11, 16, 27, 32, 184, 186, 190ff, 199, 209
  see also economic growth
capitalism, organised/disorganised, 55, 192-3
cartels, 48, 49, 50-1, 58-9, 60
Chirac Government, 174-5
Christian Democrats, 85

class consciousness, 7-9, 28, 202ff, 206, 209ff
class organisation, 5ff, 22, 24, 31ff, 38, 47-9, 55ff, 88ff, 183, 202ff
class struggle, 7, 15, 25, 54, 183, 186, 193, 194, 201-12
classes
  capital, 13ff, 22, 47ff, 88, 151-2, 193, 208ff
  and class rule, 3, 9, 16ff, 27-8, 46, 53
  definition, 13-16, 188, 202, 203
  interests, 7, 17ff, 22, 27, 28, 29, 31ff, 35ff, 42, 43, 47
  labour, 13ff, 47ff, 87ff, 152-4, 186ff, 203ff
  petty-bourgeoisie, 14
  professionals, 15
  and state, 9, 10-11, 17-30, 31ff, 73, 84-8, 183-213 *passim*
co-determination, 85, 98, 109, 137ff, 176-7
Concerted Action, 109ff, 136, 206-7
corporatism, 3, 34-41, 61, 103, 109, 139-41, 167, 192, 194-5
Crosland, A., 95
Crouch, C., 130

Dalton, H., 74
Davis, M., 191
depression, 59, 115
  Britain, 60
  France, 60-1
  Germany, 62-5

economic growth, 18ff, 39-40, 45-6, 94ff, 100-11, 115, 122-31, 158, 204ff
EEC, 106, 171
employment, 184, 191, 199

229

Index

false consciousness, 8-9
Fine and Harris, 65-6, 84, 185-9
Fordism/neo-fordism, 189-92
free trade, 50, 60
full employment, 39, 94, 97, 100, 102, 111, 116, 118, 119

general strike, 60, 74
German Social Democratic Party, 95ff, 108ff
Giscard Presidency, 126-7, 135-6, 145, 171-2
Glyn and Sutcliffe, 105, 131
gold standard, 60, 74
Gourevitch, P., 66-9
Green, D., 126
Grenelle Agreement, 107-8

Hardach, K., 64
Harris, L., 65-6, 84, 185-9
Healey, D., 145
Heath Government, 104-5, 132
Hirsch, J., 190-1
Hodgson, G., 84

ideology, 49
incomes policy, 38, 102-3, 105, 110ff, 119ff, 131-9, 140
Industrial Relations Act (1973), 104, 120
inflation, 102, 116, 117, 119, 121, 125-6, 132, 135ff, 141, 146, 151-2, 154ff
International Monetary Fund, 133
investment, 47, 75, 101-2, 111, 117, 120-1, 122-31, 149, 155, 176-7, 198

Jay, D., 74
Jessop, R., 9, 26-7

Kalecki, M., 38
Kesselman, M., 172-3
Keynesian economics, 1, 82, 95, 99, 109, 116, 122, 171, 197
Kohl Government, 177-8
Kuisel, R. F., 62

laissez-faire, 49, 50-1, 134, 186, 188
Lash and Urry, 192-3
liberal capitalism, 45-72 *passim*, 187ff, 192

liberal democracy, 25-6, 46-7, 49ff, 53ff, 211-12
Lipietz, A., 189-90
Luxemburg, R., 6

market, 1, 15, 46, 48, 62-3, 78-81, 83ff, 90, 96, 188, 196, 197-8, 210-12
Marx, K., 41-2, 54, 203
marxists, 2, 17-18, 22ff, 53, 95
Matignon Agreement, 61, 108
Mattick, P., 116
May-June 1968, 29, 107ff, 171
Miliband, R., 4, 18ff, 29, 84
Mitterrand Presidency, 97, 172-5
mixed economy, 1, 75ff, 82, 86-8, 90-1, 98, 118, 134, 146-7, 161ff, 198, 209
monetarism, 116
monopoly capitalism, 65-6, 187ff, 192

nationalisation, 73, 74-8, 83, 95ff, 103, 111, 120, 123ff, 162, 169, 184, 204ff
NEB, 123ff, 139, 161
NEDO, 38, 102, 167
Nazi Germany, 62-5, 77, 85, 184
neo-liberalism, 1, 77, 78, 80-1, 86, 90, 99, 109, 116, 134, 136, 145, 146-50, 153, 170ff, 177-8, 179, 185, 195-6, 199, 200, 204, 208-9
Norman, M., 74

Offe, C., 19-20
oil crisis, 104, 115, 125-6, 128, 141, 145

Panitch, L., 37-40
PCF, 97, 127, 173, 207
planning, 39, 73, 76, 78-82, 99, 102-3, 105-8, 120, 122-31, 170, 204
pluralism, 35, 37, 194
political franchise, 51-54, 55, 211
Popular Front, 60-1, 85
Poulantzas, N., 4, 18ff, 29
privatisation, 157, 162, 164-5, 166-7, 175
profit, 16, 47, 49, 85, 101, 110, 118, 119, 129-31, 131-9
protection, 50, 60
PS, 61, 97, 127, 172-3, 175, 207

regulation approach, 191ff

Index 231

Schmidt Government, 137
Schmitter, P., 35-7
Scokpol, T., 19, 23-4
SFIO, 97
Shonfield, A., 126
Social Contract, 102, 123-5, 132-5, 139-40, 147-8, 153, 159, 161
social democracy, 6ff
social market economy, 12, 77ff, 97, 176ff, 206-7
SPD, 95-6, 108-10, 129, 137-8, 176-7, 206-7
state
  authoritarian/dictatorship, 53ff, 62-5
  autonomous, 17-18, 30
  debate, 2-3, 9, 20, 22-3, 24-5, 26-7, 31-4
  and economy, 30, 50-2, 60, 129, 197ff
  increased role, 2-3, 32-3, 55-65, 76, 90-1, 115ff, 120ff, 124, 129-131, 136, 146-7, 150-1, 161-9, 184-5, 189, 197-201, 207ff, 209-12
  political form, 49ff, 52-4, 62-5, 89-90, 183-213 passim
  range of actions, 31ff, 75ff, 111, 115ff, 188ff
  reduced role, 57-8, 76ff, 145, 147, 149, 150-1, 157, 161-9, 207ff, 209-12
  relative autonomy, 17-18, 21ff, 198
  and social order, 30, 80, 118-19, 146, 189-92, 209-12
state-monopoly capitalism, 65-6

Thatcher Government, 154-69
Thatcher, M., 146-50
trade unions
  in Britain, 102-4, 120-1, 131-5, 153, 159-61, 168
  in France, 85, 97, 108, 127, 135ff, 170, 173
  in general 32-3, 39, 48, 51, 55ff, 60ff, 69, 84ff, 89, 95ff, 103-4, 117, 119, 131ff, 141, 147-8, 183ff, 192-3
  in Germany, 62ff, 85, 109ff, 129ff, 137-9, 176-7

unemployment, 117, 119, 141, 153, 155, 158-9, 204
Urry, J., 9, 24-6, 84, 192-3

Vichy Regime, 61-2, 76

wages, 16, 101, 102, 110-11, 116, 130, 131-9, 146, 153
Wallich, H., 77-8, 81
Weber, M., 21ff,
Weimar Republic, 50, 62, 85
welfare, 73, 82-4, 134, 135, 146, 157
Wilson Government, 102-5
Wilson-Callaghan Government, 123-5, 132-5
World War I, 55ff
World War II, 55, 60, 73

Yaffe, D., 84, 116